FAITH OF

MAINSTREAM *SPORT*

FAITH OF OUR FATHERS

FOOTBALL AS A RELIGION

ALAN EDGE

MAINSTREAM
PUBLISHING

EDINBURGH AND LONDON

First published in 1997 by Two Heads Publishing

This edition 1999 published by
MAINSTREAM PUBLISHING COMPANY (EDINBURGH) LTD
7 Albany Street
Edinburgh EH1 3UG

Reprinted 2000

ISBN 1 84018 201 6

A catalogue record for this book is available from the British Library

Printed and bound in Finland by WSOY

Contents

To the memory of all victims of Heysel and Hillsborough and for all those, past and present, who have inspired me, helped me and tolerated me.

Also, for Albie who hounded me.

The Preface

We were in Menorca in July '83. That particular morning – it was a Monday, I think – began no differently to any other. Up at around 9.00 am, we strolled from our apartment along the white sandy beach in the direction of the little seaside village of Santo 'Mickey' Tomas. Sticking to what had by then become our daily ritual, we headed towards the row of shops, about ten minutes distant, which housed a little open–air cafe. There, amidst the endless haunting refrains of Julio Iglesias, the ex–Stockport County goalie, awaited our customary breakfast of toast, jam, coffee and jugs of luscious hot milk. The heavens, just in case you're interested, were a rich blend of Everton royal and City sky. Below, the Mediterranean shimmered, remarkably like the grass at the Nou Camp Stadium, only aqua–marine blue. All in all, I suppose you could say that everything was perfect, idyllic even. Well, apart from the prospect of Julio's matchless treatment of 'All Things Bright and Beautiful' and it being the close season, that is.

Actually, as enticing or not as all this may sound, I feel I really ought to mention at this point that when I was recounting this story to my wife, her recollection of events was rather different to mine. According to her reckoning, that particular year we were, in fact, ensconced in a caravan in Prestatyn and on the fateful morning in question it was raining as usual and I never got up till lunchtime and had too bad a hangover even to contemplate eating anything. Now it may be that she has a point in all this. The way I see it, though, wherever we were the gist is still the same, so for what it's worth, we may as well stick with Menorca.

Anyway, soon we arrived at the first shop in the row, one of those chaotic mini supermarket affairs which sell literally everything under the sun or rain that you might wish to buy. It was then that it happened. Suddenly, as we idled past all the eye-catching displays, I glimpsed something whose sheer awfulness ranks alongside even the outrageous kipper ties and pointy collars worn by Paddy Crerand and Bob McNab on the ITV World Cup panel in 1974. It really was that bad. And bear in mind I speak as someone who has seen Carlton Palmer suck a lemon at half-time.

Scarcely affording me the opportunity even to draw breath, let alone to begin to orchestrate any worthwhile defensive strategy, it dealt me a crushing blow, striking low and vicious, somewhere between crotch and navel, as if I'd been hit by one of Stuart Pearce's free kicks, only harder. Within seconds, my disbelieving gaze settled on the hideous, yet irresistible sight in front of me. There, all horrible and motionless, across the shop's front counter, lay the crumpled remains of the previous day's *Daily Mirror* newspaper with a back page headline of brutal, unpalatable scorn:

'LIVERPOOL SNUBBED: CHARLIE NICHOLAS SIGNS FOR GUNNERS!'

Now cynics may well laugh, but at that precise moment the headline meant the end of the world. Okay, so maybe not quite the end of life as we know it but, as far as I was concerned, it came pretty close. Others around me, by contrast, appeared not quite so bothered. Patently none of them were football fans. Had they been, their reaction would surely have mirrored their own allegiance and degree of fanaticism.

Arsenal fans would, no doubt, have been absolutely ecstatic for their surprise bonus, fellow Liverpool fans utterly desolate for their loss, Everton and Man United fans delighted for the same reason, Tottenham fans sickened by Arsenal's gain and so on, in varying degrees, through other football and sports fans with merely a cursory interest right down to non–sports fans, who would likely have not known Charlie Nicholas from Charlie Drake and, indeed, may even have failed to notice the headline at all, in spite of its earth–shattering ramifications.

I should add that in my own case, I was reacting before I had actually ever seen Charlie Nicholas kick a ball, and certainly prior to the startling *News of the World* allegations concerning his fortnightly hair–washing sessions with Venezuelan sperm whale oil. This I am sure may help explain things a bit for all those discerning fans who would otherwise find my over-the-top response to Charlie's opting for the Gunners a trifle puzzling. The thing was, at the time, neither Charlie, let alone his Torrey Canyon polluted bonce, had been seriously viewed outside of Glasgow and with the newspapers' portrayal of him as the next Scottish Superstar, the guy was, believe it or not, genuinely considered a prize catch for the Reds and others. Understandably, with me being a fanatical member of the Liverpudlian tribe of fandom, the effect of Charlie's snub was truly a devastating blow and my world really did collapse as I'm sure now even those not cursed with fanaticism, as well as those since exposed to all Charlie's shortcomings both on the pitch and in the barbers, can well imagine. Without any doubt, it was Black Monday in Menorca for me and, rather embarrassingly, the spectacle which ensued was not an edifying one.

As the extent of the headline's implications hit home, I reeled outside, stricken by Charlie's treacherous underhand betrayal of his moral obligation to sign for us. I felt queasy and palpitations, the like of which I had not experienced since the time when Bill Shankly actually threatened us with the mortifying prospect of bringing Ian Ure to Anfield to play left–back, shook my entire body and, as anyone else who has ever reacted in such a way will confirm, palpitations induced by thoughts of Ian Ure playing in any position are possibly as bad as such things can get.

Fearing the worst, my wife and friends rushed to my aid. My children, understandably, slid away in shame. Soon my quivering nausea had succumbed to a paralysing numbness. I froze like Chris Waddle taking a penalty, unable to move a limb, fearing for a fleeting moment that I had contracted tetanus, only for my wife, who thankfully had once done a first aid course with the Everton Red Cross, to reassure me comfortingly that you didn't get tetanus from shock. I began rambling incoherently.

"Why boring boring Arsenal, for God's sake?

Hasn't the man got any taste (nor manners, nor decency, for that matter)?

Has someone bribed him with the promise of those hideous North Bank harlots?" – (actually, even in my shell–shocked state, I was pretty sure this wasn't the case, since they would have acted as a deterrent, as those of us who have witnessed them would testify, though it has to be said, Charlie was not exactly Robert Redford, so I supposed it was a possibility.)

Is there a God, and if so, why didn't he make him sign for us?"

Such frantic and muddled attempts to rationalise the situation, whilst obviously understandable in the circumstances, were patently fruitless and of scant help to me which, sadly, I have to say, always seems to be the case wherever I am concerned. I suppose the bottom line is that there are only ever really two types in these situations. The first are those who cope – the cool, calm, unflappable Rudyard Kipling 'If' types such as your Hansens, Gullits and Beckenbauers. The second are the crazed, irrational sorts who first flounder and then proceed to flap around like demented Galatasary supporters responding to the referee turning down a dubious throw-in appeal. Needless to say, I'm pretty clear about what I am and have to admit I've never brought the ball effortlessly out of defence in my life.

Conforming to type, I started to shout and gesticulate wildly in a desperate attempt to exorcise my bitter disappointment. Unfortunately, this crude approach proved as futile as Jimmy Greaves trying to tackle back, and seemed, likewise, to do more harm than good, succeeding merely in disconcerting some fellow holiday makers standing nearby, who all glared at me scathingly as if I should be certified or, at the very least, sliced in half with the sharp edge of one of Kenny Dalglish's verbal volleys. Undaunted I continued my tirade.

"You stupid bastard, Nicholas! You ignorant, two–faced, low–down, lousy, good for nothing, double– crossing, long–haired piece of Scottish dog crap! We didn't want you any way!".

But of course, we did.

And it hurt.

And it was all to no avail, for no matter how much I pointed and flapped about or swore and cursed, or ranted and raved at him or the counter or the newspaper or even the poor Spanish proprietor, it could not dispel my feelings of despair nor my numbness, nor, indeed, get Charlie to change his mind. Besides, he couldn't hear me anyway. He was by now, I suspected, in Majorca or Colwyn Bay, most probably decked out in all his new Arsenal gear lying on a beach devouring the latest Alexander Solzenitzen epic or a copy of 'Tit–Bits' amidst, no doubt, rather contrasting peace and serenity. Or was that Steve Coppell, the one who could read?

My wife and friends attempted, once more, to comfort me. It was, however, no use, for I had soon passed far beyond the point at which reason prevails and by the time they had become alive to the full extent of what was happening, I had already left this world and tamely entered the Charlie George twilight zone of Zombie expressions. I suppose I should add in mitigation, this is not, in any way, shape or form, intended as any slur on the aesthetic properties of the North Bank hero. On the contrary, for many of the most beautiful people ever to come out of Haiti were Zombies. It is just that most Haitian 'undead' did happen also to have that faraway vacant sort of look so reminiscent of Charlie at his most pensive, making the comparison perhaps not quite so odious as first appears and lending it more than a touch of validity. Certainly, at the very least, it will serve to give fellow fans some idea of the wretched state I was by then in.

The background to the crisis I was experiencing was straightforward enough. It had begun when I had read of Charlie's desire to move South from Celtic, most likely to us, whilst I had been waiting anxiously for our holiday flight departure at Liverpool Airport. "Another Dalglish", I had instantly thought, (as I said earlier, this was before we'd all seen him play, remember). Our hard-earned and long awaited holiday had, at that precise moment, assumed an even rosier perspective than scarcely seconds earlier. Goal-scoring visions of Charlie and Kenny in sublime harmony flashed through my mind. Suddenly, life and everything about it seemed utterly perfect, so much so that within a matter of seconds, even the flight I had been so dreading had begun to assume the innocuous proportions of a Brian Hall aerial challenge.

Before long, I was ambling cheerfully aboard the plane, laden with every newspaper carrying news of Charlie's imminent transfer, ready to read and re–read them over and over again. I scoured every line of every report. Every word, every phrase, every intimation titillated my intense desire for Charlie to don the red shirt.

As the days passed, we had become hot favourites to get him. Each day of the holiday, the likelihood of his signing for us had grown ever more certain, ever more real; our desire to land him ever stronger. We had him in our grasp. He was bound to follow Kenny, or so the newspapers had assured us. Each passing hour I had yearned for his arrival ever more ardently, sating myself with the unfolding news reports of his imminent capture. The waiting and anticipation may have ached slightly, rather like those nagging little pains you get after eating a dodgy pie at the match, but my fantasies of his future exploits for us were, nonetheless, as blissful as could be.

Then, starkly, without any warning, our blossoming holiday romance was over. Charlie – the treacherous mollusc – had broken it off; he had slipped the net and would go on to score goals (or not, as the case may be) in a different red shirt altogether, leaving me a desolate empty shell. The smart arse scribes, meanwhile, had got it all wrong once again, just like they had ten years earlier when Sunderland had beaten Leeds at Wembley. To them, the change of clubs meant nothing; they were simply words. To me, however, it was a life–threatening disaster. Their pathetic miscalculations had effectively destroyed my holiday and put my life on a temporary hold. The lovely Menorcan sky had at once assumed a distinctly grey Old Trafford complexion. Only a December home fixture against Wimbledon or Sheffield United could possibly have been worse. Everything lay in ruins.

Later, it was to dawn on me that my whole zest for the holiday had, in fact, become focused on my expectations and excitement at the prospect of Charlie Nicholas signing for us. I could just as easily have been sat at home in my favourite armchair on a dull, rainy day, poring over the same news snippets while fantasising about his signing. Now my feelings of despondency would prevail until such time as either Jimmy Hill retired from Match of the Day or we had won our first game of the forthcoming season and I was able to substitute one facet of my fanaticism for another.

Eventually, my stupor began to lift slightly and, with assistance, I was able to manage a ponderous Martin Keown-like stagger to the cafe. As we sat down for breakfast my wife sighed a familiar resigned expression of despair. I, meanwhile, was too far gone to empathise – after all, it wasn't her who'd just been sold Charlie Nicholas's finest ever dummy; it wasn't her whose dreams had just been shattered. No matter how many Arsenal hearts Charlie would eventually go on to break with his empty promises on the pitch; no matter how many hairdressers his lanky locks would drive to despair, that particular morning, it was Liverpudlians who had been sold up the Mersey and it was me whose world had just fallen apart.

I think, at this point, it's as well for me to be frank and give a more complete picture of the way I now am. The thing is, my lapses into such sorry states as the Menorcan affair, rather like Coventry City's annual relegation struggles, are by no means isolated occurrences.

At times, even the slightest little thing can trigger me off; a photograph of Mick Pejic in an old Football League Review; a snatched sighting of the captain of the 1961 Peterborough United Fourth Division Championship side in an ancient football annual; Jan Molby abusing his Elvis Presley diet plan even now in Copenhagen (I worry about him, you see). Why, even the briefest of sightings of a young kid on the street in a Man United kit (especially Eric Cantona's old black number seven shirt), has sometimes been enough to make me leap from my car, like some manic Jesuit missionary redeeming a lost pagan soul, to confront one of these sad creatures for not supporting their local team. (The daft thing is, when I do, the little glory hunters look at me as if I'm the oddball – as if I've got the problem; the cheek of it – the little bastards – they'll get their come-uppance one of these days. There again, if they keep chopping and changing to support whoever's the most successful side, maybe they won't.)

I suppose, when you really look close, the most alarming aspect of it all is I'm actually getting worse and not even a run of success seems to be enough to stem the flow or satisfy me. It appears the older I get, the more I seem to notice and be aware of and the more frequent and prolonged are the resulting outbursts. It's almost as if I've evolved my own special set of antennae specifically to tune into anything which might upset me; like I'm on some endless emotional rollercoaster, lurching from one uproar to another.

Mercifully, however, (and I say that not just for my own sake), it's not all bad; there is a bright side to all the wretched torment, balancing things out and making life overall just about tolerable . I'll tell you the best moment. It's as if it were yesterday. I'm sure everyone has got similar ones.

It was August 1977, a week or so before the start of the new season which prior to then was shaping up to be a touch anti–climactic since it was to be minus Kevin Keegan, who had left for Hamburg following our European Cup victory at the end of the previous season. That morning, we had been all set to leave the house for a picnic in Formby Pinewoods when a radio newsflash announced some startling news – it was the totally unexpected signing of Kenny Dalglish. Needless to say, the elation I felt took my breath away. I was ecstatic and couldn't help myself. I became involuntarily manic for what must have been minutes on end. First I unleashed a piercing primeval scream, followed by a giant Duncan Fergusonesque leap in the air. Then I was off, running up the stairs, along the landing, back down again, out into the backyard, another scream and leap in the air, then dancing round the back-kitchen with Albie, our black and white mongrel, who was, if anything, dafter than me and, by then, just as delirious having frantically chased me all over the house with his huge long tongue tripping the floor . And he was an Evertonian and didn't even know who Kenny Dalglish was.

When I calmed down, a silly grin and blissful serenity replaced my elation and we went off on our picnic. And what a picnic it was; a picnic to end all picnics; fit even for teddy bears. Never has Spam tasted better. It was as if with that one newsflash, all the traumas and upsets which were always queuing up to besiege me had suddenly become worthwhile; as if a magic wand had been waved to make everything perfect; and so it was. Then again, to put things in perspective it's not every day you sign Kenny Dalglish.

So there you have it. All in all, you have to say, it's pretty pathetic, isn't it? That, however, is the way things are; the depth to which things have sunk. Sad as it may seem, such are the lives that fanatics like me lead;

lives as delicately balanced as one of Ron Atkinson's old post–match press conferences, teetering always on a crazy, irrational knife-edge of extreme joy or gloom where everything is governed by a steaming passion for a size five round leather case ball, the fortunes of our team and, in big brown Ron's case, the weather in Malaga and the availability of a sunbed. Our fanaticism is forever there stalking us, lying in wait, ready to pounce, at the slightest opportunity, like Gerd Muller in the six yard box, inducing our mania and consuming us completely. It's what we are and what we will forever be. More intriguingly, in many cases such as my own, it is what we have always been ever since we were knee high to Tony Cottee. Whether we like it or not, we are football's cannon fodder; the captive bedrock of the game.

If all this is true, then what in God's name has fashioned us in this way? What influences could possibly have created such blind devotion to a football club, spawning all the lunacy and obsessiveness? I mean not even for one minute could anyone like us be termed 'normal' in any accepted sense of the word; 'mental' would seem a more fitting description.

I'm attempting to provide an insight into some of the reasons behind all the madness; why people like me turn into knee–jerking football crazy lunatics; how my own childhood in the footballing hotbed of Fifties and Sixties Liverpool and the prevailing influences of family, community, school and religion combined to produce my obsession with football and Liverpool FC. It is a story that could apply equally to fans from any of the other great footballing hotbeds; from Tyneside, Teesside and Wearside to Clydeside, Aireside and Ribbleside, from Manchester, East Ham and Stoke-on-Trent to the mucky environs of Spaghetti Junction, Welsh Wales and the River Liffey. All are places where the culture of a working class urban childhood, force fed impregnation and cradle to grave indoctrination is part of growing up; where football is a primary, at times *the* primary life-force, supplanting religion in the lives of many.

Whilst this is a personal story, I am sure that most fans will be able to relate readily to the contents in some form or another, since, whichever club we support, whatever the team of our dreams, we all share the same essence and spirit of fandom. Although each fan has a different tale to tell, their own personal odyssey to make and sad obsession to contend with, essentially we all have three basic things in common: one, we're all powerless to do anything about it, two, we'd all kill for a nice tasty meat pie, and three, we all belong to the same broad church of incurable idiocy, which probably explains why we like the pies so much, or maybe it's the other way round. Whatever, anyway, let's face it, if we're honest with ourselves, we're all as mad, in our own little way, as Mark Dennis or that loony Brazilian TV commentator, aren't we? Most of those I know are any way.

In recent times, our church has undergone quite traumatic changes; clearly its congregation no longer simply a mass rally of working class males each Saturday afternoon or Wednesday night, but rather a melting pot of all types, classes and both sexes, though still significantly with the ordinary bloke at its heart. The blight of hooliganism, Bradford, Heysel, and later, Hillsborough, have shaken our church to its foundations, with Heysel especially causing those too disillusioned with the tragic consequences of its thuggery and brutality, particularly some loyal Liverpudlians, to lapse, never to return, their dignity and principles intact. Bradford and Hillsborough were, of course, different matters entirely; with Hillsborough's sole connection with hooliganism being the killing fences erected to control the terrace thug.

With tragic irony, those same dreadful events also appear, in hindsight, to have provided a watershed which, in the years since, seems to have helped restore at least some perspective and sanity in the wake of horror, enabling true fans to recover some of the too long absent self–respect we have always craved as disciples of what is still, after all, the game of the people.

Perhaps it was the enormity of the tragedies which was largely responsible for this, invoking a broad consensus of will and realisation amongst fans and authorities alike that it was finally time to attempt a return to better times by eradicating the cancer of the thug which had pervaded us since the very first skinheads infiltrated our ranks in the late sixties, thereafter permanently distorting our image and overshadowing and misrepresenting the vast majority of us, true fans and fanatics alike (I remember when I worked in Manchester in the early eighties, on various occasions, fruitlessly trying to relate this distortion to a work colleague, who would not contemplate taking his young, football-daft sons to a game, since he really believed the majority of fans were yobs. He resorted, instead, to taking them to Rugby League games, somewhat against my persistent persuasive efforts and their will. Yet who could blame him, given the distorted perception he had been left with).

Of course, there will always be thugs knocking around and it may well be that the welcome return during the first part of the Nineties to the sanity of more hospitable football grounds is not a permanent one. Certainly there are those who feel the 'football' thug is simply for the moment under cover and may well crawl out from beneath the stones they're currently hiding under to besmirch the game once again.

Whatever the long term outcome, the position in all this of the true fan – the overwhelming majority – deserves acknowledgement, for it is the true fan who has suffered more than most at the hands of the thug and the reality is that no-one holds these vermin in more contempt or is more desirous of their total eradication from the game than the genuine supporters, a point which is invariably overlooked in the usual pontifications about the problem.

As for fandom itself, it's now perceived in a completely different way, and has now acquired a voice to celebrate the inherent culture it has always, in fact, had. Our passions, our agonies and our ecstasies are now warmly acknowledged and embraced in print and the media. After all these years, our celebration of the glorious thud of leather on the meat of Dixie Dean's forehead has taken its place alongside the infinitely more copious literary indulgences about 'leather on willow' – albeit more SMACK! GOAL! than HOWZAT!. For better or for worse we have come of age. Obsessions once closeted are now unleashed with abandon on an unsuspecting audience, as an inexhaustible goal mine is tapped. For the first time ever, fandom has become a desirable commodity beyond the working class domain, where it has long been, for many, a vital part of everyday existence. So much so that flaunting one's fandom has now acquired a cultish propriety, rendering it the fashion throughout huge chunks of the middle classes where being a football supporter has become an eminently sociable and acceptable preoccupation.

All this was not the case as recently as ten years ago, and certainly not in the late Sixties and early Seventies when I came into contact with middle class people for the first time as a young working class scally. Then, fandom amongst that (to me) strange fraternity was seen as socially unacceptable and denigrated; something they simply were not into and did not talk about, all of which, at the time, was hard for me, coming from such a football besotted background, to understand. The transformation since has been stark but perhaps not too surprising; footballers have their purple patches and it so happens that, for those so inclined, we, now, are also having ours.

There is no doubt that not all of the dramatic changes to football are desirable. On the one hand, the demise of hooliganism at big games is clearly a massive plus, undoubtedly much indebted to the post-Taylor introduction of all-seater stadia, in themselves, intrinsically far removed from British football's traditional cloth-cap and cattle truck image.

Conversely, the consequential pricing-out and possible permanent alienation of many of the game's less affluent bedrock fans may, if allowed to continue, come back to haunt the game in future years. Indeed, though top-flight football can currently be said to be booming, it is as well to reflect that for every twinkling starlet feasting on football's recently acquired millions, there are thousands of genuine fans, who can no longer afford to contribute to those very wages as they were once only all too willing to do. Football as an entertainment and business concern may well, for the forseeable future, continue to prove commercially viable and prosper, but the game should not forget where it came from nor those who made it what it is. Who knows whether its newly found friends and admirers will turn out to be so loyal as their forebearers?

Curiously, though, even where traditional loyalties are concerned, things are no longer quite so cut and dried as they once seemed to be and there are, as ever, ironies at work. Closer scrutiny of this area of fandom, reveals a great deal of the so-called loyalty to be little more than myth and, with notable exceptions, is certainly not reflected in those attending matches over an appreciable time-span. The simple truth is that even when restricted to the convenient yardstick of attending matches at home as opposed to away – rain or shine, success or barren patch, year in and year out – the aptly-termed 'loyal diehard fan' has become in recent times – say, post-sixties – very much a rare species; a hardy reliable breed, certainly to be admired and applauded but, in relative terms, actually rather thin on the ground.

The reality is that, for some time, supporters as a genre have been quite fickle, their attendance loyalties often fleeting, rarely continuous, often dependant upon trends or the quest for glory of one sort or another and often subject to the whims of family duties and, of late, the counter attractions of cosier more middle class pursuits and leisure activities. One needed only to have visited St. James Park for a bleak mid-winter second division fixture prior to the Kevin Keegan renaissance for proof of this. Taking nothing away from the Geordie fans who must count amongst the most loyal around, it could hardly be said that standing room was then exactly at a premium nor the crush barriers what you would term invisible. Meanwhile, nearer home, I could quite readily rattle off the names of at least thirty Liverpudlians, all one-time regulars, who have barely attended a single match a season over a period of many years, even when it was eminently affordable. Yet, both the 'Johnny-come-lately' or reformed Geordies and the lapsed Liverpudlians consider themselves, quite rightly, still to be fans and

17

even the lapsed ones remain hugely passionate about their team via the media, pubs, clubs and workplaces.

Clearly then, being a fan goes far beyond the bounds of simply regular or even spasmodic match attendance; fandom is not just limited to literally following your team. There are evidently deeper bonds at work; stronger unseen ties, linking fan to club and club, in turn, to the local community. Nowadays, for the big clubs, these links extend much further afield – many ordinary Norwegians' attachment to Liverpool, for instance, is no longer simply the term 'lob-scouse'. Given such circumstances, it may be that professional football can, indeed, afford to abuse its traditional clientele, once with sub-human facilities and now with inflated prices, yet still survive intact. It would seem that, quite apart from its recent seduction of hitherto untapped lucrative markets, its traditional one will always remain well and truly captive. Maybe, whatever transformations fandom and football loyalties undergo and whatever their respective merits or otherwise, the ethos of true fandom – that sense of oneness, identity and identification with our own club – our very own team – will always remain constant and, maybe, whatever its background or roots, it can never really change. For the true fan, practising or not, perhaps it is a tie that cannot be severed; a commitment for life from which there is no release clause. If all this is the case, and there does seem to be a great deal of evidence to suggest that it is, then it really does make fandom a truly fascinating, perhaps even unique, concept.

Our fandom is the lengthiest emotional commitment we make. Except in tragic circumstances we outlive our parents, and our spouses and children arrive when our life is maybe a third through. Fandom is most definitely an affair of the heart. I, in common with all fans, actually feel a deep and strong emotional love for my 'club'. I love it unflinchingly and always will. Yet, despite the undoubted sincerity and depth of such feelings, a quick analysis of what is meant by the term 'club' shows such love to be clearly irrational.

With the demolition of the beloved Kop, Anfield now has nothing left of the original structure I first knew as a boy. (Actually, this is not strictly true, since the wall and timber capping at the front of the main stand and some of the original main stand seats are still there, but I think you'll know what I mean). The sacred turf is renewed virtually annually; the Club's oldest players have only been there ten years (and none of them have ever known me personally). Granted, on the staff side, Peter Robinson and Tom Saunders have each been there two hundred and fifty years but while I like and respect them, I certainly feel no great emotional bond with them in particular (and again, I don't know them personally). So then there is just the name of the club and, surely, there can be no rationality in feelings of deep love for just a name, especially when those feelings cannot be reciprocated by the object of their devotion.

So where does all this leave us? And for that matter, where does it leave fans of Leyton Orient, whose name keeps changing or Wimbledon, who haven't got a ground, or Huddersfield, Middlesbrough, Derby, Bolton, Sunderland, Millwall and Chester City, who have got a brand new one, or Charlton, who have only just got theirs back? With an intangible spirit perhaps? An abstract concept? A twisted mind? (Certainly in the case of Wimbledon fans. How else could they have so regularly stomached football's equivalent of the anti–Christ). Maybe Faith of our Fathers will provide some insight. There again, on the other hand more likely, maybe such things are beyond explanation, and rightly so.

There are still those, of course, who consider football fanaticism to be nothing more than simply a couple of hours' deranged lunacy on a Saturday afternoon. Clearly, they've never been near a football hotbed during the cricket season. Who knows, maybe they've never even been to church. Perhaps not even for a Christening.

Baptism

As is the case with most places apart, perhaps, from those tranquil outlying reaches of Bob Wilson's brain and Chipping Norton, there are many misconceptions about Liverpool and its people which have their origins in misrepresentation or distortion; myth or exaggeration. By way of contrast, one thing you can say with absolute certainty is that in the Liverpool of my childhood almost all of the inhabitants of the city were either Liverpudlian or Evertonian; Anfield or Goodison; Red or Blue. You did not choose.

It chose you.

Over one hundred years earlier, in 1845, around the same time as Jimmy Hill was making his professional debut for Fulham, the legendary Karl Marx had delivered his sobering judgement on nineteenth century life with his philosophical proclamation that "Religion is the opium of the masses". Sadly, Karl never survived quite long enough to drop in on my home city. Had he done so, he might well have been obliged to re-appraise his famous declaration, for, in late-fifties Liverpool, strongly religious city that it was, football transcended religion and played a far greater part in the ordinary person's every day life than anything else. Opium, as far as I am aware, played no part in those days. Liverpool was a two-colour city. Red or Blue, emotionally bonded to the people's hearts, inextricably woven into the city's fabric and ever-present in nearly every conversation, seemed to be the overriding preoccupation of everyone around, although, if the truth be known, heartfelt concern over the price of a pint also figured quite highly too.

As Bert Finney, a regular at both the Anfield Paddock and the Arkles Pub for the past sixty years so succinctly put it, "the thing was in those days we liked our pint alright, and we went to Church, too. But above all we were all football mad and everyone was either Red or Blue, one or the other. There was no in between; no question of any other colour. It was Red or Blue across the board. Basically, if you weren't a Red, you were a Blue and if you weren't a Blue, you were a Red. It was as simple as that; there were no exceptions; none whatsoever. Unless, of course, you followed Tranmere in which case you were a Blue and White, I think, or Southport or Chester or New Brighton – I can't remember what colour they were – or you never followed anyone at all which made you colourless, I suppose. Anyway that's what it was like, from what I can remember. Mine's a brown mixed, by the way."

As it happens, poor Bert wasn't the only one to be so confused by such colour blindness nor was Liverpool the only place so affected by such delirium over football. Most other provincial cities and towns and also parts of the capital itself, were, at the time, as equally football daft and beer conscious as Liverpool. For who loves their football more than a Jock or a Geordie or a lad from the Rhymney Valley and who turns out in greater numbers than the Mancs or the Brummies or the people of Barcelona and Milan when there's a big match on or there's a happy hour extension. Not many, it has to be said.

Regrettably, since the Number 1A bus went only as far as the Pier Head, I never got the chance to see for myself any of these exotic places, nor to witness first hand their love affairs with football though, to be fair, I do seem to recall that once in a while we did manage the odd charabanc trip to Morecambe illuminations from where, on a clear night, you could just about make out the top of Blackpool's floodlights, which may not sound all that much but meant an awful lot to me since it was the nearest I ever came to meeting Sir Stanley Matthews.

When we were kids Stanley Matthews was *the* name in football – as much a British institution as Buckingham Palace, fish 'n chips and Alma Cogan. In every game we played we all wanted to be him. He was everyone's idol, every inch the perfect footballer and the perfect gent, from the little white cuffs of his tangerine shirt to the spiky tip of his orange coloured 'Mohican' haircut. He was so good he even had a trick named after him – 'The Matthews feint'. It was like a forerunner of the 'Cruyff funny turn' and, just like Johan's, performed in an orange coloured shirt. All the football annuals used to describe it – "with your ball between your legs, you lean your body over one way, feinting as if you're going that way, then with the outside of the opposite foot flick your ball the opposite way to which you've feinted and spring back with your whole body to follow your ball past your bemused opponent". Easy.

In fairness it wasn't quite as difficult to understand or to follow as it might seem from that description because they also used to have a photograph for each distinct phase of the manoeuvre. We used to practice it all the time, often bemusing ourselves in the process. In fact, everyone used to practice it. We even suspected our infants teacher, Miss Formby, of once trying it in the classroom, only she never had a ball and her face just turned a sickly green colour and she ended up laying prostrate on the floorboards. She said later it was because she'd gone too long without food, which taught us never to try the feint on an empty stomach. At the time, we all thought she'd been trying to emulate that famous old black and white film clip of the 1953 'Matthews Final' against Bolton where the great man slips as he centres the ball for Bill Perry to score the winner and if she was then she made a good job of it because she went down just like old Stanley did.

The daft thing was that little piece of the '53 Final was the only glimpse of old Stanley we'd seen at that time. In fact, when I come to think of it, it's the only clip of him I've ever seen. Who knows, maybe the reality is that the 1953 Final was the only game he ever actually played. You never know. Weirder things than that have happened; a lot weirder. I know my father used to say he always used to cry off from games at Anfield or Goodison because he didn't like the crowds skitting his baggy shorts and 'Mohican' haircut, so who's to say he didn't do that everywhere? It's possible, you know.

Actually, the more you go into this, the spookier it gets – it's like the X-Files. I mean, let's face it, the clip where he centres it to Bill Perry is not exactly George Best class is it? In fact, I'd say it's not even Clyde Best. Let's be honest, if you'd allegedly played top flight football for nigh on seventy-five years like Sir Stanley, you'd think there would surely be a better snippet than one where you fall on your arse trying to centre the ball. And another thing, why, when he did eventually retire, did he go and live in Malta? I mean, name me one other footballer who went to live there. Not Tom Finney that's for sure, he stayed in Preston, which takes some doing, I can tell you. And John Charles even came back from Italy to open a pasta factory in Merthyr Tydfil. In fact, the only one I can think of was Gracie Fields and I'm not sure whether she ever played in the First Division. Besides, I think it was Capri she went to, in any case. And yet, despite the mystique which persists in some quarters, not least in Merthyr Tydfil, the fact still remains you simply don't become known as 'the wizard of dribble' by magic. It just doesn't happen for no reason. Such acclaim has to be earned. And we mustn't forget, either, that Jimmy Armfield once termed Sir Stanley 'the greatest and most fearless winger the world has ever seen' and we all know that Jimmy has never told so much as a little white lie in his entire life. The man's a lay preacher for God's sake, so anything he says must be true. All in all then, a strange business, riddled with contradictions and inconsistencies, and, at the end of the day, perhaps one best left to the experts to unravel.

Anyway, returning to the subject matter in question and regardless of geographical location or proximity to the enigmatic Sir Stanley, in those days ordination into one's particular home town club's creed was not a singular event; nor was it sparked by one. There was no actual time nor place enabling the birth of such fandom to be pinpointed; no catalytic trip to Anfield or Goodison, Old Trafford or Maine Road, Ibrox or Parkhead, St James Park or Roker Park, the Nou Camp or Bernebau, Sainsbury's or Leo's or other such shrines, inspiring us all to declare "I say, old boy, this is definitely the place for me – I think I'll come here from now on"; no precise moment when we suddenly saw the light or had the call. The plain fact is all of us were fans from before we can remember. Quite simply, the random selection of a team to follow, however attractive that team may have been, was never on the agenda. It was in the genes, at very least in the blood.

In Liverpool, as in other towns and cities, the Clubs have always been an intrinsic part of our lives. Essentially, we evolved as Reds, Blues, Whites, Greens or whichever, the brainwashed product of a process of natural selection having, in most instances, only one other alternative, which was the team in the rival colour shirt. It was all done for us and lay outside of our control, leaving us as innocent bystanders, without a say in our own destiny, all of which I suppose, make the constant proclamations about us all living in a post-war, libertarian, Nazi and Stalinist-free democracy sound a bit rich. Not that us Liverpudlians are about to complain at the way things have turned out, what with countless League titles and other major honours but what about all those fans born in Rochdale, Darlington or Workington or other such places? What chance did those poor sods stand, for Kenny's sake, with not even a Third Division North Fair Play Trophy to their name? What wouldn't they have given for some good sound decent democratic infusion. Why, with a little freedom of choice and imagination and enough money for the bus fares, they could even have supported Real Madrid or AC Milan or Ajax. But there you are, it just wasn't meant to be. They were saddled for life with Spotland Road, not to mention Cyril Smith and Lisa Stansfield, and that was that. Still a bit sad though, it must be said.

Ironically, in these more recent enlightened times, the exercising of a child's democratic rights is much more to the fore (some would argue too much so – not least my Auntie Winnie who was a fervent believer in children being seen but not heard) and this, together with more than a tadge of prompting by the media and the carrion of the business world, has seen to it that the pendulum has swung round far too far the other way, with the result that local initiation is in danger of being obliterated altogether; so much so that almost every corner of every street in the entire nation – and, more recently post-Eric, every car boot sale from Penzance to Penrith – has found itself plagued by countless millions of those hideous red, white, black, blue, green, yellow, orange, pink, brown, grey or speckled polka dot striped Eric Cantona Man United shirts. Places, where neither Mancunian nor French are spoken, are bedevilled with the things with the result that the poor little local clubs no longer get the remotest look in and, for all of us non-United fans, even those most leisurely pursuits of taking our annual holiday or even a simple High Street stroll have become little more than a nightmare gauntlet run past hundreds of mini multi-coloured Erics or Ryans.

Tommy Courtney, another long time Anfield and Arkles regular recalls a typical United shirt count one sunny afternoon on a recent chara trip to Blackpool. "We left Yatesey's at about one o'clock. It was crackin' the flags. By the time we'd reached the Gynn which is about twenty minutes walk along the Prom we'd spotted about a hundred and fifty United shirts. Yeah, a hundred and fifty of the buggers. All separate, too. We couldn't believe it. We felt sick, especially in that heat. And the worst of it was, every shirt was a different colour. I'm tellin' yer if we hadn't got to the Gynn when we did, we'd 'ave all turned into statues of Nobby Stiles – an' I'm tellin' yer, I used ter 'ate 'im. I'll 'ave a pint of mixed if that's OK."

Thank God no such nightmares could ever have happened in the old days. It just wouldn't have been possible. For a kick-off, we never went on High Street strolls and our parents couldn't afford the holidays or the kits; nor by then had Eric Cantona's ma and pa met, so there was no sign of gruesome little Eric arriving on the scene. Okay, so maybe we're leaving ourselves wide open to the sceptics in all this. I mean, after all, a Liverpool fan siding with the little clubs, and even more incredible, the sun actually shining in Blackpool are hardly events which smack of conviction, let alone believability. Don't forget though, when I became a fan in the late Fifties, Liverpool lay in the Second Division with Everton only mid-table in the First, and neither of them represented attractive propositions, particularly the Reds. Also, they have just recently discovered a gap in the ozone layer over the Fylde coast. So, all in all, there is a tiny shaft of credibility to be found in all this.

Actually, now I come to think of it, even in my time, there were exceptions to the rule. I remember a lad called Teddy Kennedy (no relation, I hasten to add, to Alan, Ray, Mark nor John Fitzgerald) who lived round the corner from us and who had supported Man United ever since his aunty had bought him that dreadful 'Manchester United Calypso' record by Edmundo Ross or whoever which just goes to show, I suppose that yes, Man United hype was going strong even then, long before Eric Cantona's first public fart had the media boys drooling. Anyway to finish off, he was tone deaf was Teddy, and, apart from that, clearly had no football taste either.

As my own initiation into the Red Faith began to gather the irresistible momentum of a surging wave of Doncaster Rovers attacking play the same brainwashing processes were, I suspect, happening throughout all the other hotbeds to most other children, particularly those with similar working class backgrounds to myself. In most instances, the principal driving forces were undoubtedly hereditary instinct and family influences, with son (and often daughter) following in the footsteps of the most persuasive or most ardent parent to graduate as a fully blown Red, Blue, Sky Blue Pink or whatever.

At times, other things would also have a say in the proceedings. For instance, in Liverpool, geographical quirks could hold quite considerable sway for while generally there was a fifty/fifty split of Red and Blue across the city, in the areas around each ground there was inevitably a preponderance of fans of the one colour. The same was also true of the actual district of Everton, particularly around the West Derby Road area, which was naturally predominantly blue, together with the outlying rhyming suburb of Netherton, where the poor deluded inhabitants grew up thinking they actually had some connection with Everton. This is why as many as 90% of them became Blues, which I suppose, as far as the remaining 10% is concerned, lends support to the old adage that you can't fool all of the people all of the time – even Nethertonians.

I must say, though, one aspect of all this geographical initiation thing has always puzzled me – the London scene. I mean everywhere else is pretty straightforward – Liverpool – the Reds and Blues; Manchester – City and United; Glasgow – Rangers and Celtic; The North East – Newcastle and Sunderland; the Potteries – Stoke and Port Vale; Sheffield – Wednesday and United; Bristol – City and Rovers; West Yorkshire – Leeds and Bradford; Nottingham – Forest and County; even Birmingham with City and Villa, (for effectively West Brom and Walsall, Wolves and Coventry are all separate entities). But London – it's just a hotchpotch. There's Spurs, Arsenal, Palace, West Ham,

Chelsea, Fulham, QPR, Millwall, Charlton, Brentford, Wimbledon and Leyton Orient for starters and I'm sure I've missed some out. So how the hell does the geographical thing work there. I think I can just about grasp the West Ham and Millwall bit but after that it's a complete lottery – there's no pattern to it. No wonder everyone's so mixed up down there. I'll tell you, it doesn't surprise me that some of the clubs there are contemplating moving to Dublin and that's something you'd never get up North, unless, of course, it was some sort of works outing or something like that.

Even up here things were not always quite so clearly signposted and many obstacles were often required to be surmounted before the ultimate goal could be realised, as aunties, uncles, cousins, friends, neighbours, teachers or even, at times, parents or brothers or sisters, or occasionally outsiders of the rival persuasion all lay in wait, hell-bent on changing the course of natural selection by coaxing prospective young fans away from their inborn creed, with all the guile and subterfuge of the wily old giraffe himself as he used to lope in to prise away young Anglo-Saxon starlets to stock his Irish team.

In such a way, many families found themselves in the midst of major domestic crises – split down the middle like an English defence against Diego Maradona, as offspring swore the opposite allegiance and parents of whichever persuasion were left to reflect despairingly on where they had gone wrong, knowing in their wretched, heart-broken distress that their own flesh and blood, their own seed, were destined never to tread the same path nor ever to share the same sense of spiritual communion as themselves . . .

"What are we gonna do, girl? It's just so 'ard ter take in, isn't it?"

"Mmm, look, I know it's bad, love, but let's not make it bigger than it is, eh. Worse things than this 'appen at sea, yer know. I mean, 'e could belong to . . . er . . . "

"Yer what! Worse things than this, yer say. Worse than this? Me only son an Evertonian. A lousy Blue. An' you say worse than this. Well let me tell yer. Nothin' can be worse than 'im bein' a Blue. Nothin'! I can't believe it . . . it's like . . . like 'e's no longer mine . . . "

"Oh Christ, I can't stand this. Oh God, there is somethin' worse, love . . . much worse . . . it's . . . er . . . I've been meanin' to tell yer fer years now . . . ever since . . . but . . . "

"What is it, girl? Go 'ead, what is it yer wanna tell us?"

"Oh God . . . it's our Kenny . . . 'e's not . . . 'e isn't . . . Oh God . . . 'e isn't yours . . . "

"Isn't my what?"

"Oh God, don't yer see . . . 'e's not . . . 'e's not your son"

"What! Yer mean . . . "

"Yeah . . . Yes! Yes! . . . Oh God, I wish. Oh God . . . Remember Billy Wilk . . . "

" . . . BILLY WILKINS!! THAT EVERTONIAN BASTARD!! JESUS CHRIST! Yer tryin' ter tell me 'e's the father of our little Kenny . . . Our Kenny . . . Billy Wilkins . . . "

"I'm so sorry, love . . . so sorry . . . forgive me . . . please . . . I'm so, so sorry. Oh God. Please, PLEASE, please . . . I'm so sorry . . . "

" Sorry. Yer sorry. What d'yer mean, yer sorry. Sorry fer what? Stop cryin' an' come 'ere an' gissa hug, yer daft bugger. For a while there, I was really worried. Thought I'd really let the Reds down. Just shows yer, though, doesn't it . . . things always turn out fer the best. Anyroad, think I'll just whip out fer a few jars ter celebrate. See yer later, girl."

Sadly in Liverpool, not everyone was always quite so accommodating as little Kenny's liberal-minded 'dad' in resolving their footballing identity crises. At times, similar catastrophes could drive some poor souls to the brink and the Liverpool Echo often carried harrowing accounts of how groups of these pathetic, distraught creatures were to be found prowling the banks of the city's river at night, like shell-shocked victims of a Graham Taylor Route One aerial bombardment, pondering their plight and coming to terms with their failings as they contemplated the terrible choice between the unimaginable torment of life on earth with a son or daughter of the opposite denomination, and the immediate release but ensuing eternal damnation to be wrought from drowning in the icy, black waters of the river. Truly the ultimate Catch 22 situation but one which I suppose does, at least, serve to provide a clear indication and a disturbing indictment of the way in which fanaticism can go horribly wrong. It has to be said though, in all fairness to those concerned, the prospect of either option was pretty grim and must have presented a dilemma as nightmarish in its own way as that faced by a sportswriter having to choose between Brian Kilcline and Mickey Droy for Footballer of the Year.

Thankfully, it was a choice never faced by the vast majority of such mixed families, (nor sportswriters, much, I'm sure, to their relief), since most would never let things get quite so dramatic, and would sensibly settle for practicable compromises such as painting the front of their houses Red and the rear Blue or vice versa or buying neutral mauve coloured curtains and lampshades or, even, as at the time of the Liverpool/Everton Wembley finals of the late eighties, spray painting their cars two tone Red and Blue just for the trip to London.

It all just goes to show that a give and take approach to life is always the best way, unless you happen to be Saddam Hussain or – higher up the despot league – a Tommy Smith or a Dave Mackay, in which case, of course, you basically get to do whatever the hell you want, no matter where it was you were Christened or by whom.

If only it were the case that life could always be that simple.

Indoctrination

To the undoubted relief of my dear parents, Edna and Bert, neither of whom, rather like the 1992 British Olympic Swimming Squad, had any great affinity with water, particularly of the icy black variety (nor, in my father's instance, with house painting or buying mauve lampshades), I followed the orthodox hereditary route, developing, like them, a distinctly Red hue.

In contrast, my extended family, most of whom lived within a hundred yards radius of our house – we tended to overdo the close family thing a bit – did not display quite such exclusive Redness. Certainly we were predominantly Red – Uncles Dick, Denny, Eric, Billy, Tony and Dave, Aunties Molly, Kay, Josie, Winnie, Mary, Barbara and Joyce, and cousins Graham, Peter, Eric, David, Stephen, Keith, John, Rosemary, Sheila, Elizabeth, Ken, Paul, Julie and Janice, together with our insurance man Sam, a close friend of my father, whom, I fondly recall, first enlightened us to the budding talents of a certain Sir Roger Hunt, then emerging in Liverpool's reserves. However, we also had a smaller but even more fiercely partisan Blue faction consisting of my Uncles Jack, Joe and Eddie, Aunties Matilda (Kitty), Agnes and Joan and cousins Pam, Stephen, David, Lyn, Kevin, Geraldine, Anthony, Robert and Michael together with another close friend of the family, Ebba Murphy.

The thing is, those listed amounted to virtually my whole family at the time. The only ones excluded were my Aunty Audrey and Uncle Ronnie and their children Mark, Ian and Lisa, who went on to follow a different religion, becoming Jehovah's Witnesses which, I suppose, is the equivalent in footballing terms of supporting Albion Rovers – fanatical devotion but low average gates and without the faintest glimmer of glory in this life. Indeed, apart from such odd exceptions as these, it seems following one of the local football clubs was a nigh-on obligatory function of living in a hotbed.

A good many of those I have mentioned, as far as I am aware, were never to set foot in Anfield or Goodison in their entire lives – in some instances because they could never make it past the local pub with the odd few never even venturing beyond the table football machine in the bar – but this was absolutely irrelevant. Whether they went or not, every man Jack or woman Kitty was still either Red or Blue and fully and totally committed. No sitting on the fence nor swaying on the cross-bar as far as any of them were concerned. They were Red or Blue – end of story. The colour ran through them like it does through a stick of Blackpool rock.

The pattern of life never changed. The one-upmanship and rivalry was intense; the tasteless jokes, particularly about the Second Division Reds and topical things like Billy Wright's Shredded Wheat haircut, were always at the ready (apologies to the Beverly Sisters and the late great man himself but you've got to be blunt about such things – I mean apart from Ralph Coates, Arthur Scargill and Wee Willie Harris when he played inside out for the Showbiz XI has there ever been a dafter one?). The leg-pulling and mickey-taking was unrelenting. Every issue of every argument was as passionately contested as a Glamorous Managers Competition between Jack Charlton, Jimmy Frizzell and Barry Fry but always, it seemed, in good spirit and humour; always with tongue poised ever so closely to the inside lining of the cheek; never, to my observation, with any bitterness nor ill feeling.

Maybe, in hindsight, this was because being in different Divisions, we never had to play each other apart from Liverpool Senior Cup ties, so nobody ever actually lost a match to the other, but, then again, when, in later years, we did have proper 'Derby' matches, often with a great deal at stake, things were still the same, so perhaps we all were merely good-natured souls who simply liked each other, in a manner, I suppose, not a million miles away from all that light-hearted Old Firm rivalry up there on the Clyde, except without the bazookers and hand grenades.

At family gatherings, conversations would immediately centre around Red or Blue issues of the day, or any other day for that matter. Often the dialogue would transcend normal football chat and assume a sort of religious significance – you know the kind of thing – was Billy Liddell really the Archbishop of Liverpool?, how often did Tony Kay go to Confession?, was Alex Young really born in a manger?, was Tommy Leishman actually born at all, or had he simply evolved miraculously from the floor clippings in a barber's shop in Dunfermline? – all those sort of deep, philosophical questions. So intense was the fervour that, at times, it would be almost as if we had all been transformed into fanatical followers of Buddha and sent to the sacred banks of the Ganges to pursue some spiritual calling from up on high, though in our case, everything was Evertonian or Liverpudlian, Blue or Red and we remained stuck firmly by the waters of the royal blue Mersey (what am I saying?).

At times, the pre-occupation with football verged on the ridiculous. Almost as inevitable as Joe Mercer mispronouncing Johan Cruyff's surname, the first question to greet a stranger arriving at anyone's door would be to enquire whether they were Liverpudlian or Evertonian and extract their views on the latest football gossip. This would often be even prior to it being established who they were and for what they had come and the crazy thing was that a frantic footballing debate, perhaps lasting as long as an hour or so, might ensue before the purpose of the stranger's visit was established, at which point, it might be found they had, in fact, knocked at the wrong house . . .

" . . . anyroad, sorry ter keep yer chattin' fer so long, pal . . . now, a second-hand Singer sewing machine, yer say . . . now, let me think . . . mmm . . . yeah, I think it's probably the Jones's in number 34 that yer want . . . I'm sure thee said thee were gettin' shut o' one the other day . . . anyroad, been nice talkin' to yer . . . see yer next time yer passin' . . . tarafernow . . . mind out fer the dog in number 32 . . . vicious get, 'e is . . . bit like Tony Kay, heh, heh . . . "

It was a barmy state of affairs but whatever the duration of these football sojourns, nobody seemed to mind, since all were obsessed with the concept, though pity help any poor soul who was in a hurry and had never before been to Liverpool and didn't like football or leading questions.

Somewhat inexplicably, it often seemed that feelings were most strongly evident amongst those who did not actually attend the matches, something which, for those outside of such a footballing culture understandably presents a particularly difficult paradox to attempt to grasp, since it seems a reasonable assumption to make that anyone with any such fervent passion would pursue that passion with active vigour. This, however, was not necessarily the case with football in Liverpool, and presumably, the other hotbeds too, where non-attendance at the matches seemed, if anything at times, to accentuate the ardour and fervour of those who did not go, (albeit leaving them exposed in arguments to charges of being "fair-weather fans", "part-time supporters" or even worse). To sceptical outsiders, such a concept smacks of absurdity and beggars belief in a manner reminiscent of that mythical occasion at Elland Road in the late eighties when the entire Arsenal defence was rumoured to have failed to appeal for a blatant offside. To those swept up in it, however, the intense passion they felt was simply the way things were – a major part of their lives.

Incidentally, it's only right, I suppose, to point out in connection with the Leeds-Arsenal offside that the Arsenal defence that day did not include their most committed defender, the hugely popular David O'Leary who at that moment in time was flat on his back in a London operating theatre undergoing vital stretch surgery to his right arm. At the precise moment the offside occurred, David, great pro that he was had thrust up his arm in typical Gooner fashion. The surgeon is said to be still pursuing his claim against the Arsenal club for the loss of his right eye.

Meanwhile back in Liverpool, away from the litigation, the bottom line of this involvement and passion was all pretty straightforward and went something like this: Liverpool or Everton Football Club, as the case may be – or their equivalent in the other hotbeds – were the greatest football team in the world and that, quite simply, was the way it would always be. Championships, FA Cup wins, League position, current form, players' shortcomings and such like never came into it. Who cared about such incidental triflings anyway? When you supported the greatest team in the world, whether it be from the pub, or the bingo hall, or the armchair, then even relegation into Division Two of the Lancashire Combination would have been a complete irrelevance. So what if maybe it was all naive innocence or irrational inclinations, or, more pertinently, a form of blind faith. Whatever it was, it didn't matter. What did matter was the whole thing was intoxicating and sucked us all in with its convenient, undemanding simplicity and its comforting reassurances that this was as complicated and challenging as life would ever be. None of it may exactly have been what you would term 'sophisticated' but if you liked your butties oozing with sauce, your biscuits dripping with tea and your football wall-to-wall then, without any doubt, a hotbed such as ours was the place to be.

Hard though it is to admit, it would be misleading of me to give the impression that everyone with whom I ever came into contact spent the whole time preoccupied with or talking about football for that, quite honestly, wouldn't be true. I distinctly remember on one occasion for example my Aunty Kay discussing an entire knitting pattern for a chunky red sleeveless cardigan with my mother without any reference whatsoever to Liverpool or Everton. I also recall many times my father and Uncle Tony heatedly debating the relative merits of those other Reds and Blues down in Westminster.

My father, always backed to the hilt by my mother without even the merest hint of any tact or diplomacy, would be firmly embedded in the red corner, a loyal disciple of Harold Wilson and an arch opponent of anyone who remotely sniffed of 'I'm alright Jack. Meanwhile, Uncle Tony, a bubbling extroverted Ted Heath fan, though later like most other 'human beings' including Ted himself a big Maggie hater, possessed a firm conviction that you got out of life what you put into it, that charity should begin at home and that the greatest Tory of all – Audie Murphy – was God. Politically, they were hardly what you would call a matching pair. Thankfully, their rivalry never extended to the other infinitely more important arena where 'balls' is also the operative word and so most nights they were usually able to find some common ground and end up the best of buddies, which, let's be honest, is what it's all about isn't it. After all, if what I've heard is true, even dear old Harold and Ted were known to share the odd shandy or two from time to time, even if theirs weren't quite from out of the same glass.

The point is, whatever else may have been on the agenda, football was always just under the surface, ready to pop up at any moment and command centre stage not least in the guise of the innumerable analogies invariably present whatever the topic. Whether it was the weather – 'crackin' day for footy, this' – or having babies – 'they're tryin' for a footy team' – or food – 'he eats enough to feed Blackburn Rovers' – or drink – 'I see Ted Sagar's got the Blue Anchor' – or extra-marital affairs – 'he's playing away from home' or even my Aunties Joan and Audrey and Barbara addressing me – 'you're past the post, you, Sunny Jim', somehow there always seemed to be some football connection and never was the pre-occupation more pronounced than with the stay-at-home fanatics who seemed to abound.

Typical of this breed were Aunt Kitty, short and squat with pointed nose, permanently clad in a blue Vera Duckworth nylon overall, forever piercing the atmosphere with her Emlyn Hughes-like shrieks of laughter, and Uncle Jack, her husband, a small rotund man, almost completely bald, with a huge, beaming smile. Both seemed to be stuck at around fifty years of age and both were, without fail, passionately vociferous in their condemnation of all things Red and their adulation of all things Blue (and I must here stress the word 'vociferous' when I speak of Aunty Kitty).

Quite how and why the pair of them generated such fierce dedication and loyalty to the Blue cause when Uncle Jack had not been to a game since Dixie Dean broke the League scoring record in 1928 and Aunty Kitty had never been in her life, remains a mystery.

I mean, it was not as if they had no other interests to pursue, for

Aunty Kitty absolutely lived for her tombola while Uncle Jack used to race pigeons and even in his later years, despite all his ailments, could have comfortably outpaced Willy Young with a bed settee strapped to his back. Neither, too, could it have been money problems which prevented them from going, since Aunty Kitty was extremely lucky on the horses and spent more time in the bookies than Lou Daktari during the Flat Season while Uncle Jack was an active supporter of every hostelry in the district and, give or take the odd gallon or two, drank enough ale to have comfortably made it into Arsenal's back four.

Maybe, then, it was something altogether deeper, something hidden behind their cheerful exterior. Possibly, all of their outward intoxicating enthusiasm for, and devotion to, the Blues was simply a sort of subliminal substitute for the children their marriage had never yielded, or even the cats or dogs they never had. And yet, there again, on further reflection, this is most probably not the case either since theirs was, by no means, an uncommon trait amongst other members of my family, with countless offspring and pets, as well as friends and neighbours of similar ilk. Besides, I seem to recall they did, in any case, have a pet of their own – a noisy, royal blue budgerigar, on whom they doted, called "Dixie", whose shrill squawking rivalled anything Aunty Kitty's larynx could ever produce and who could actually head a football better than Tony Hateley, even when the Liverpool centre-forward was in his prime. So this tends to dispel any notions of the substitute theory, whilst at the same time, without wishing to ruffle any feathers, clearly casts major doubts on the wisdom of Bill Shankly's decision to sign Big Tony from Chelsea, when quite evidently there were so many cheaper and chirpier options available from any of the city's pet shops (though in fairness to Shanks, Big Tony did go on to sign at least twice for every other manager in the country, so he wasn't alone in his lack of judgement).

No matter. Whatever the reasons for their deep blue love affair with Everton Football Club, the fact was it was every bit as intense as Terry Venables's passion for Alan Sugar or that of any of the fanatics who, every week, thronged the terraces.

All this meant that Aunty Kitty and Uncle Jack would defend to the hilt the Blue realm and attack with relentless vigour the Red one. The ensuing debates and arguments which arose on our frequent away trips to their house which was all of two doors away, would rage incessantly – invoking images of Alec Ferguson returning from holiday to find Arsene Wenger sat in his favourite chair at Old Trafford – though unlike Alec's manic rantings, theirs would usually be limited to good-natured insults and leg-pulls, and were always good fun and, naturally, always about football.

As we would enter their back kitchen past the back door with its peeling paintwork, no formalities would be exchanged. Instead, the banter would fly about immediately:-

"Now listen 'ere young Alan me lad, don't you listen to yer Dad – you be a Blue like us 'cos, don't forget, we're the Lord's Chosen People, not like yer Dad's lot!", Aunty Kitty kicking off the proceedings with a deafening screech (causing me to cover my ears) would make an early threatening sortie into our half of the field to test our defensive mettle, stirring memories of the great Hilda Baker at her lethal best when she starred for the Blues in the late forties.

"'E's already a Red – you'll never change 'im, 'e's gettin' confirmed next Sundee", my father would make a firm Ronnie Moran-like challenge to clear any immediate danger. Unfortunately, the respite would prove only temporary.

"You just lerr 'im stay 'ere for a day or so, we'll purr'im on the straight and narra, won't we, Jack?" Aunty Kitty, by now resembling Matilda the Hun, the former Accrington Stanley centre-forward, in a blue smock, would collect the loose ball and, whooping at full volume, make a frightening charge into the heart of our penalty area, finishing with a strong shot on target, at which point, I would breathe a huge sigh of relief as my father kicked the ball off the line and into touch.

"No chance, I'm not leavin' 'im 'ere with you'se lot; 'e might catch rabies or somethin' – mind you, that's better than 'im becomin' a Blue".

The pressure by now, however, would be relentless. From the ensuing throw in, Uncle Jack would gather the ball, flash one of his engaging Denis Law smiles and dribble menacingly down the wing like a podgy version of Alex Scott, the Everton outside left at his hunched up best.

"Eh, Bert, wot d'yer reckon about Albert Stubbins (popular Liverpool player) bein' transferred to Argentina – yeah, 'e's gone to Fray Bentos – Whey hey!", then ghosting past my father, who was, by then, totally out of position, and laughing heartily at his own joke he would bear down on me, the last line of defence, ready to unleash another jocular volley.

"Eh, Alan, d'yer 'ear about Dixie Dean meetin' Elisha Scott, (the legendary Liverpool goalkeeper from bygone days) as they were walkin' along the pavement in town? Dixie just nodded to say 'ello and Elisha dived into the gutter!".

GOAL!

One Nil to the Blues.

At this point, there would be huge squeals of delight and laughter from Uncle Jack, Aunty Kitty and Dixie the budgie, followed by a triumphant lap of honour round the back kitchen by all three, much to the bemusement of me and the annoyance of my father, who had heard the same old jokes so many times before. Then, with my father striving heroically to get back on level terms, the fiercely fought contest would continue unabated. Generally, it would end up going into extra time, occasionally to a penalty shoot-out. More often than not we would manage to force a replay at our house the next day. All along I would sit and listen in rapt attention as the three of them and "Dixie" the budgie – and now and again, presumably attracted by all the commotion, our neighbours Auntie Nance and Uncle Vic – went at it, laughing at their antics and puzzling as to what Fray Bentos corned beef had to do with football, how a budgerigar could be so knowledgeable about football and why the names of Dixie and Elisha and also lesser known lights such as T G Jones, 'Smiler' Chambers and 'Parson' Jackson always seemed to play a part in their arguments when they had not played for God knows how many years and they did not even merit a mention in my old Arsenal flavoured football annuals.

As we would leave, usually amidst some further light-hearted ribbing and a flurry of Dixie's feathers, as my father attempted playfully to wring its neck, any questions left unanswered would be promptly dealt with by my father on our minuscule walk home, particularly if there was to be a replay the next day and any doubts had been raised about the greatness of our Second Division side. Certainly, as far as I was concerned, the strength of Aunty Kitty's argument against our greatness, together with her and Dixie's deafening screeching seemed merely to re-affirm my resolve that Liverpool were indeed the greatest, despite their lowly status.

Even by this time, in the development of my mantle of redness, I was already beginning to display glimpses of determination every bit as dogged as that of Larry Lloyd and Kenny Burns, at the heart of the Forest defence in the early eighties and there was little doubt that my father's psychology was working potently on me.

All of this is not to say that such psychology was part of any concerted strategy on the part of my father to ensure I became a Liverpudlian. In fact, I do not think any of the brainwashing processes which took place either in Liverpool or any of the other hotbeds for that matter, were borne out of any sense of premeditation or even awareness of what was going on. On the contrary, it was, I am sure, almost entirely instinctive, being no more than simply the manifestation of a vital characteristic inherent in everyone who lived in these soccer spawning grounds, as much a part of them as, say, their kindness or generosity, irritability or short-temperedness or any other of their natural traits.

The thing was, the whole fandom concept just happened to figure so prominently in their every day lives, conversations and psyche that it inevitably cropped up all the time and, in turn, could not help but have a profound influence and impact on youngsters like myself. Our exposure to it meant we all became, in effect, 'chips off the old block' – so much so that even those who were not football-daft were still affected to the point of, at the very least, sticking up for either one team or the other. Nobody escaped absolutely unscathed.

By any sensible criteria, any such experience should, I suppose, be viewed objectively and placed in context, perhaps even rationalised out of our systems. I mean, such intense exposure to anything can hardly be regarded as the ideal way to spend your formative years nor as a desirable preparation for the future realities of life.

The actual reality though is not that simple; the fact is, it's far too late to even begin to consider doing anything about it. Besides, speaking for myself, not even for the most fleeting moment would I want to. The thing is I'll chat with anyone about anything I find interesting whether it be TV, films, religion, politics, music, family, work, piles or whatever. Deep down, however, I am always most comfortable talking football – it's the only thing I'm any good at.

Actually, I'm being far too modest here, for that's not strictly true. I'm sure, if I think hard enough, there are other things. I recall, for instance, one occasion a few years back when I was getting something out of the top cupboard in the kitchen and a large full bottle of OK Sauce fell out and before it had reached the tiled floor of the kitchen and smashed, my hand was there to cushion the fall; in fact, it was my thumb which got there first and the impact of the bottle crushed it and I was in agony for weeks. Deep down, however, despite the intense pain, I was, in fact, quietly delighted with myself. The speed of my reactions had astounded me. I must have looked like Peter Bonetti on a good day (prior to that unfortunate incident in the six-yard box at Guadalajara) – certainly it was the fastest I've ever moved. The pity of it was, of course, that I was in our back kitchen rather than on a football pitch, otherwise, it might have impressed someone else, too. As it was, there wasn't a talent scout to be seen, so my efforts were in vain. There again, though, reflecting on it, I guess like with anything else it's just the way the sauce bottle bounces.

Whatever the likelihood, however remote, of me possessing any other latent qualities, the fact remains that there is still nothing I would rather do than reminisce or theorise about the game or anything to do with it; the size of Roger Hunt's thighs; his slight resemblance to Davy Hickson; his exemplary behaviour which made Bobby Charlton seem like Julian Dicks; the way he used to turn inside defenders; his shooting with either foot but especially his right; his scoring a goal against Northampton with his nose at the Kop end; his breaking our duck against Leicester City and Gordon Banks in 1965; his FA Cup Final header; his goal against Inter Milan; his two goals to clinch the league in 1966 against Chelsea; his selfless running for England; the press always underrating him (even now – if Alan Shearer is worth £15 million, Roger would be worth £20 million – mind you, Jimmy Greaves would be worth £25 million and Michael Owen £30 million and I'm not even that biased); his astonishing display at Old Trafford in 1967 when he was head and shoulders above everyone else on the pitch – the United trinity included; his knighthood by the Kop; my defending him against his critics when he was on his way out; his only show of emotion when Shanks substituted him in a cup-tie against Leicester City; his testimonial when 56,000 were locked in and 15,000 were locked out: Christ, looking back, I think I actually loved him more than my own family. I could talk about him all day and he's not even my favourite Reds player.

At the end of the day, I think it's all about what prevails. I stopped playing five-a-side when I was forty-three because of dicky knees. My mate Bob, who still plays, told me it was really because I no longer had the real desire to play any more and I think he was (almost) right – the dicky knees was probably (almost) an excuse, not a reason. My desire to play had (almost) been spent. The thing is, whatever's inside – whatever drives you – has to come out. You can't feign it. If it's in there, it will prevail. If it's not, it won't. With me and thousands like me, what prevails is our football. Our early years were a continuous high voltage charge of football; the remainder of our lives is merely the legacy of that charge as all the stored up energy is released to sustain us thereafter. It's football all the way and there's nothing we can do about it because it's what prevails, it's what's in us and we couldn't change it if we tried.

One thing in my father's favour at this time, apart, I suppose, from my good fortune in his not supporting Accrington Stanley and his sound common sense in not marrying an Evertonian with a squawking voice like Aunty Kitty, was his physical appearance. With his button nose, dark wavy slicked-back hair and centre parting, he bore an uncanny resemblance to Liverpool's great Scottish winger-cum-centre-forward, Billy Liddell, the Reds' only real star throughout the whole of the Fifties.

True, unlike the great Scot, my father may have lacked a deadly shot in either foot and never ever wore shorts, except when he was playing the Germans in Palestine in 1944; also, my father never sounded remotely like a native Chic Murray though nor did Billy or even Andy Stewart or Rab C Nesbitt, come to think of it. Neither, too, for that matter, did he become, like Billy, a Justice of the Peace after his retirement, though once again when you think back, who did, other than Billy? Nonetheless, despite all of this, as far as we were all concerned, my father was the dead-spit of the Scottish legend; a true Billy Liddell-like and it was this similarity which, I am sure, guaranteed both he and the Reds my unwavering support – I mean, not every young boy has a pretend professional footballer as a dad, though I daresay a pretty strong case could be made for Istvan Kozma junior during his dad's spell with us in more recent times.

Actually, just going back to the bit about Palestine and wearing shorts, it's amazing, once the war was over, how so many Second World War veterans – even all those legendary Eighth Army North Africa 'desert rats' who had worn their own khaki desert gear almost like a badge for the best part of five years – would not be seen dead in shorts. Never so much as contemplate wearing them once they got back home. My own uncle Billy was no exception. He would even wear a collar and tie when sat in a deck-chair at the beach, sometimes even his demob suit. Sounds a bit daft, I know, but that was how it used to be. It makes you realise how much times change, doesn't it? These days most people don't even bother with a suit and tie for a wedding, let alone the beach. Looking back, they really must have had a torrid time of it time of it, those old soldiers – every last one of them a true hero in the face of such adversity. A war of attrition miles from home with no quarter asked or given. Battling desperately for every single square inch of territory in all that heat and sand with scarcely a thought for themselves. And all the time plagued by flies and insects and longing for a solitary cool drink to quench a raking thirst. Sheer hell. And those big heavy demob suits can't have helped them much, either. Not exactly the ideal attire for building huge sand castles and digging deep moats. Or for getting buried alive in sand by the kids. And what about all those melting ice-creams and messy toffee apples and the soggy egg and cress butties.

Weighing it all up, it beats me how any of those guys survived at all at the end of the day, let alone retained their sanity. Still, that's the British bulldog spirit for you. Survive anything when they set their minds to it, those 'desert rats' – even Blackpool beach on a sweltering August bank holiday.

Back amidst the more leisurely demands of the working week, a novel consequence of my father's remarkable "Liddellness" would occur each evening as he returned home after his exacting daily five mile bicycle ride from the English Electric factory (which, incidentally, for those who may have forgotten or for those of the post-Thatcher era who may never have seen one like it, was one of those places where they used to make things).

As he turned the corner of our street, dismounted from his bicycle and took off his bicycle clips, our gang of little scruffbags would badger him for his autograph, pretending he was Billy Liddell. Whether arising out of commendable good humour and patience in spite of his hard day or, more likely, from a slight tweaking of a vain streak, (which never otherwise manifested itself as far as I recall) my beleaguered father, judging by his beaming smiles, actually appeared to relish these rigmaroles, often signing three or four times on each piece of paper, seemingly milking the fantasy adulation, as he feigned the identity of his own Reds hero.

" . . . Billy, Billy! Can we 'ave yer autograph, please, Billy?"

"Sure, son . . . where d'yer want me ter sign?"

"On 'ere, please, dad . . . er, Billy"

"What's yer name, son?"

"Er . . . Alan, Billy"

"Is that one 'l' or two, son?"

"Er . . . one"

"There yer go, son . . . now, d'yer want me ter do yours as well, kiddo? Give us yer pencil and paper, then . . . there yer go . . . and you as well . . . is that the lot then? . . . okay, then lads . . . tara now"

"See yer, Billy."

"Eh, Al, 'ow come yer dad doesn't know 'ow ter spell yer name?"

"Don't know . . . I thought 'e did . . . 'e must 'ave forgot."

The whole 'Liddellness' thing and our ritual, which, for a period, became the highlight of my day and that of our little gang, (and who knows, possibly my father too, since after six years away from home during the war followed by an enforced existence that would have taxed a mule, his life was one of simple pleasures) had stemmed from a chance remark of my mother. She had told me about a particular time when she and my father had been travelling back from town by bus and a drunk had boarded the bus and sat adjacent to them. Insisting that my father was Billy Liddell (in those days, before station wagons and Porsches, even the Stan Collymores of the day used public transport, so Billy's presence on a bus would not have looked out of place), he had adamantly refused to leave them until he had obtained my father's autograph.

By so doing, the drunk was, of course, displaying those same qualities which have stood so many of the finest British footballers in such good stead over the years – biting tenacity, dogged perseverance along with the capacity to sink vast amounts of alcohol. Sadly, however, it seems he lacked even a modicum of perception to complement his other undoubted attributes for quite how the man, no matter how intoxicated and no matter how great the likeness between my father and the great winger, had failed to distinguish my father's pure Scouse tones from Billy Liddell's Celtic lilt is puzzling in the extreme. Maybe he did not know Billy Liddell was Scottish; perhaps he did not know Scots spoke differently from Liverpudlians (patently he had never heard of Chic Murray or Andy Stewart); possibly he was deaf. Whatever, submitting to the drunk's persistent requests and insistence, my father had, in the end, obliged by signing as "Billy Liddell", to which the drunk had responded by saying,

"I knew it was you, Billy".

To my way of thinking, this incident made my father the nearest thing to a real Liverpool player that I was ever likely to encounter on the fringes of the city where we lived. By the time I was old enough to realise that the drunk had obviously been short-sighted as well as hard of hearing since under closer scrutiny, my father's "Liddellness" did not really stand up, it was irrelevant anyway, as Billy Liddell had long retired, and my attention was by then focused on newer Red heroes.

When I come to think of it, with a curly perm and a villa in Malaga, I'm sure my father could have passed for Kevin Keegan.

Looking back, it is significant that even by that tender age it was more natural to develop a fixation with a local footballer than with a film or television star or other media celebrity. I mean, although mass media brainwashing then was nothing like we know it today, we did actually have tellies and there were stars around – Hopalong Cassidy, Andy Pandy, Muffin the Mule and Mr Pastry to name just four – so they could quite easily have dominated our thoughts and aspirations at the time. Also, with all respect to Billy, it was not as if he were a major star in the national sense of say, Stanley Matthews or Billy Wright, or even

Denis Compton, (the footballer, not his white flannelled alter ego, I hasten to add), so the only place we might have had sight of him was possibly on a cigarette or bubble gum card or perhaps an older boy's 'Football Monthly'. No way would Billy have ever been on the telly in the same way as those national stars, though, I must say, if he couldn't have made for more entertaining viewing than Mr Pastry then I'm an Evertonian with red and white underpants.

Undoubtedly then, the intensity of our familiarity and identification with Billy stemmed almost purely from out of our constant exposure to his name in our parents' and families' daily diet of football talk; the very indoctrination processes which were shaping our lives. In all probability, in spite of our little game of charades, none of our little mob would have recognised Billy Liddell even if he had sat next to us on the bus and asked us for our autographs. Indeed, at that age, it is unlikely whether we would have been able to identify any Liverpool or Everton player had we encountered them.

I dare say, in contrast to us run-of-the-mill kids, you do actually get some instances where children of certain famous celebrities – and I'm thinking here of the likes of Keith Richards, Jeremy Beadle, Norman Lamont, John McCririck and similar dubious icons –initially wished their fathers looked more like the local milkman or window cleaner, or the baker or butcher or, in the case of John McCririck, even the butcher's dog. Whatever the case, there is little doubt that what we were all doing in our own little game was by no means an unusual trait amongst other young football fans like ourselves. We, in fact, were simply making our earliest tentative forays along that same path trodden eventually by all fans in using professional footballers or footballing terminology for a host of metaphorical descriptions, (often of the disparaging kind), many of which have seeped into our every day existence, where they subliminally underpin the footballing identity embedded deep into our psyche. Amongst this rich litany, we are blessed with:–

'a gob like Mick Pejic' (actually quite a dish as Blues go), 'legs like Maurice Setters', (where's your horse?), 'hung like Ron Harris' ('Chopper'), 'voice like Alan Ball'(Emlyn Hughes), 'head like Bobby Charlton' (you're never alone with a Strand), 'a gut like Jan Molby' (Sumo), 'a real head-the-ball', 'miles off', 'for a kick-off', 'it was a toss-up', 'pull yer socks up', 'six of one and half a dozen of the other', 'score an own goal', 'he's definitely scored with her', 'on the ball', 'dribble rings round', 'a bit over the top', 'it's only a game', 'fair-play', 'against the run of play', 'start the ball rolling', 'blow the whistle on', 'run of the ball', 'it's a funny old game', 'over the moon', 'sick as a parrot', 'gutted', 'pick the bones out of that', 'get your tits out for the lads', 'Kenny's from Heaven', 'Berger is our King', 'Scmeichel is a twat'.

My father's childhood friend, Ebba Murphy, was a true Blue. My memories of him are especially vivid, no doubt because he was so much larger than life; a colourful character from the top of his shiny pate to the tip of his stubby toe.

Ebba worked with my uncles, Denny and Jack, on the buildings, and was built like one. On Saturdays, shortly after my father had arrived home from work at around midday, Uncle Ebba (as in most close knit communities, almost everyone was Uncle or Aunty) would descend on us like a tropical storm, en route to or from the pub or to the match or both, depending on whether Everton were home or away.

A loud rap on the vestibule door would announce Ebba's tumultuous arrival at the house (front doors, of course, did not require to be negotiated since they were always left open, held in position by a threadbare coir mat). Crashing open the door with a passable impression of Nat Lofthouse barging Harry Gregg into oblivion, Ebba would sweep brusquely down the hall past the parlour to give a deafening thump at the back room door causing it to reverberate like a crossbar struck by a Tommy Taylor header, before bursting in there to join us, his long, beige gabardine mackintosh trailing behind him and seeming, for a moment, to fill the entire room like Jan Molby squeezing into a telephone box. Invariably, he would then make a bee-line for me and proceed to shadow box me for half a minute or so before snatching off his flat cap to reveal his glorious smooth Bobby Charlton-like dome and then sitting down next to my father to light up their Woodbines and put the football world to right.

Sam, another of my father's friends, would arrive soon afterwards, similarly attired to Ebba with flat cap and tightly belted gabardine mac but without quite the same uproarious entrance. The three of them and, occasionally, others too, would then talk for an hour or so (until it was time for them to leave for the match) of nothing but football in a sort of footy fan's forerunner of Football Focus.

In their own little bootroom, all the important issues of any era, past and present, were dissected and analysed – Walter Winterbottom's silly name; the length of Jack Charlton's neck; were Johnny and Arthur Haynes brothers?; why Bobby Collins' head was so big compared to the rest of his body?; did Billy Wright and Charlie Drake use the same barber?; was Ron Flowers a pansy?; how did Jimmy Dickinson get his hair to part so straight?; why were the steps on the Goodison Road terrace only half the depth of the Kop's?; why were Liverpool's floodlights so puny compared to Everton's?; would Tony Kay still mess around with live matches in Walton Gaol?; did Everton dish out purple hearts for bravery or just for kicks?; what was it like to share a taxi with Johnny Carey or kick Harry Catterick?; how big were Alex Young's blisters?; was Jackie Mudie moody?; all of it shamelessly inane but nonetheless vital stuff. I, meanwhile, would watch and listen, mesmerised, though for the most part, naively oblivious to what they were actually talking and joking about.

Always centre stage like some outlandish version of George Curtis on stilts marshalling his defenders would be Ebba, holding sway and commanding attention with his funny anecdotes, witty remarks and bawdy laughter; praising his Blue heroes, rubbishing the Reds . . .

"Eh Bert, did yer 'ear about Phil Taylor an' Johnny Carey (the late Fifties Liverpool and Everton Managers) being interviewed by the newspaper reporter. Anyway, the reporter asks Phil Taylor what were the Red's 'opes for the new season an' Phil Taylor says 'e wants promotion to Division One. So then 'e asks Johnny Carey the same question about the Blues, an' 'e says 'e'd like ter win the league by forty clear points an' the FA Cup Final by ten goals to nil. So the reporter asks Carey if 'e doesn't think 'e's bein' a bit over-ambitious. So Johnny Carey points at Phil Taylor an' says: 'Well 'e started it' . . . "

"Eh, Sam, I see the pair of them are back in Bootle 'Ozzy again. Phil Taylor's gorra bad side again an' Johnny Carey's gorra stiff neck from lookin' down the league at the Reds . . . "

"Eh, Bert . . . "

From time to time during his visits, Ebba, like some superstitious footballer, would perform a ritual which to me would come to represent a test of the strength of my budding allegiance to the Reds. The rituals would happen without any warning. Suddenly he would break off from his conversation with my father and Sam, lower his scrubbed ruddy face into mine, giving me a close-up of his bulbous nose and the random chipped gravestones which doubled for his teeth, and then, breathing fumes of stale beer and tobacco all over me, he would gruffly demand . .
.

"Are you still a Red? . . . When are you gonna see some sense and become a Blue?"

To an seven year old boy, the overpowering hotness and smell of his breath, the rasping tone of his voice and his sheer intimidating Jimmy Scoular-like presence made it difficult to discern the obvious light-heartedness behind his question and so, as far as I was concerned, in comparison to what had been mere skirmishes with Aunty Kitty and

Uncle Jack, these occasions represented the first real examinations of my credentials as a Liverpudlian.

Each time they occurred, I would brace myself, take a gulp of the pungent air and deliver the same response. "Everton are rubbish!", I would hesitantly but, nevertheless defiantly splutter. Ebba would, at first, feign a grimace causing me, no matter how familiar I was with the outcome of the rituals, initially to regret my temerity and then, unable to hold back his amusement at my terrified expression any longer, his face would explode with riotous laughter, his vast cavernous mouth gaping wide open in an unbridled celebration of yellowed teeth and bulging tonsils, like a hippopotamus yawning. Then he would fondly put his massive arm around my shoulders and ruffle the top of my head. My father and Sam would join in the raucous laughter, and I swear I could recall the glint of pride in my father's eye as he acknowledged my stands against the giant Ebba. (Or may be it was just wishful thinking, on my part).

Whatever, it didn't matter, for I had passed my first test with flying colours – red ones, of course. Confronting Ebba Murphy, albeit with my father and Sam on hand to support me and regardless of how contrived it all became, I recall feeling immensely proud and pleased with myself. When the ritual eventually stopped, no doubt because Ebba became bored with it and had not attached quite the same significance to it as I had, I remember experiencing a sense of acknowledgement that I was becoming accepted as a real Liverpudlian.

I had taken on Ebba Murphy and defeated him.

What Ebba's antics had done, of course, in similar fashion to that of all the other Evertonians in my family, was unwittingly to introduce me very early on to the ethos of fan loyalty and fidelity; the fundamental reality which lies at the core of true fandom – one fan, one club for life. To Ebba the whole thing was simply a bit of a laugh but to me it represented a firm expression of my allegiance.

At this stage, remember, I had not been anywhere near Anfield, nor caught the remotest glimpse of any of the Liverpool players, not even Billy Liddell on a bus, and yet my formative sense and qualities of loyalty to the Reds were already becoming firmly established in the most fundamentalist fashion. I, and countless thousands like me up and down the country were as committed, in our own little ways as any budding disciples of the Ayatollah Khomeinei. Such blind and unquestioning loyalty is, at once, quite endearing and, paradoxically, extremely disturbing but, nonetheless, is what true fandom is all about.

Except amidst circumstances of the most extreme intimidation, such redness or blueness or whateverness which we had developed by this time would remain with us for life. At times, it would be like a ball and chain as was our own experience during the Souness regime; at other times like the magic elation of a first love as when a last minute Tony Hateley diving header would snatch victory from certain defeat. For most of the time it would simply mean being a part of something which, however ethereal, you loved and cherished. At all times it meant complete loyalty whatever the joys or pains.

In the light of all this loyalty ethos, it is amusing to hear current Reds' heroes Robbie Fowler and Steve McManaman talking about how they were once Blues but are now devoted Reds. This can only be regarded as absolute twaddle – it simply doesn't happen like that. Either they were never true Blues or else one of these days in a 'Derby' match we are going to touch for our biggest ever tonking with own goals galore raining in from all angles from the two 'Blue' infiltrators in our ranks. It's simply the way it is – just ask Sandy Brown and John McClaughlin, both well known closet Reds.

Uncle Ebba may have been the truest of Blues. His bricklaying buddy, Uncle Denny, an old school Liverpudlian, was an equally staunch Red and acted like a counterweight against Ebba's attempts to convert me.

With his generously angled features, his Brillo-pad topping of swept back, tight, wiry curls, his Frank Carson laugh, and court jester's disposition, Uncle Denny was also a one man riot; a scream; quite simply, the biggest hoot you could ever wish to meet; a cross in looks and flamboyance between Frankie Howard and Leonard Rossiter except that, unlike the former, he was hysterically funny and unlike the latter, he had, at least up to his retirement, – similar to any good 'brickie' – never suffered from rising damp. The expression "act daft and I'll buy yer a coalyard" was coined for Uncle Denny, and helps to explain how he came to acquire, in successive stages over the years, the entire South Yorkshire coalfield. With so much going for him, there was never any way in which any Evertonian in the family was going to get the better of him. When Uncle Denny was around, my Redness was safe. Somehow Uncle Denny could twist things to make it seem we were top of Division One, not struggling to get out of Division Two.

Uncle Denny's visits to our house could never be termed 'run of the mill' – more a full scale friendly madness invasion. If Ebba Murphy was a tropical storm, Uncle Denny was a Liverpudlian whirlwind; a Kansas twister of Hollywood proportions. No seat in the house would be left unsat on by his rampaging posterior, nor any mantelpiece left unleaned on by his marauding arms, nor any square inch of the lino and mats untrodden by his twinking feet. No topic of conversation was safe from his breezy Bootle lilt. By the same token though, none except for football, ever received more than fleeting consideration.

His mastery of the comic touch was always there, as natural as Klinnsman's diving technique. It lay in his bewildering, rapid movements; from one chair to another, from settee to pouffe, from sideboard to mantelpiece, from room to room; his legs crossed first one way, then another, flailing arms folded likewise, then stretched out, then folded again; hands scratching his head, then an ankle, then a knee, then a knee and ear simultaneously in impromptu patterns; half finished sentences, questions with no discernible beginning nor end, a digression here, a distraction there; an infectious laugh; a sudden impulsive grabbing of the listener's arm or leg. At any one time, a dozen assorted topics, half of them about football, would be fighting for space amidst a patchwork quilt of jumbled words and phrases as if someone had him on remote control and was flicking the switch by the second to change stations.

Sitting on the settee with his nose two inches away from mine he would begin a dialogue of sorts:

"Now listen 'ere, young Alan, me lad, I'll give yer a bit of advice"

– then quickly turning to my father –

"Oh yeah, Bert, I didn't tell yer, did I, I bumped into Terry Thingy at the match the other day – e's a corker Terry isn't 'e Bert – d'yer know 'es thinkin' of emigratin' to Australia? 'Ow's 'e gonna' make it to the match from there every week? Oh and by the way . . . "

– then taking some sandwiches from my mother –

"Thanks Ed, 'yer make gear sarnies y'know – yer should be 'ed chef at the Adelphi! What's . . . "

– move to another chair –

"Well, Bert, d'yer think 'e'll play Harrower this Sat'dee or will 'e stick in Bimmo instead?"

– gets up and stands by the sideboard –

"Now what was I tellin' yer, Alan? Oh yeah . . . "

– quick sideways glance at a stain on my mother's pinny –

"Eh Ed, yer've got some doings spilled down yer pinny, ('doings' being his favourite descriptive noun) – Yer know the best thing to get that off Ed, untie the bow, heh, heh, heh. God knows about the stain though? Mind you, 'e should do 'cos 'e knows everythin', heh, heh, heh. I tell yer what Ed; those . . . "

– again addressing me –

"Now, I 'ear yer Uncle Ebba's been tryin' to turn yer into an Evertonian, Alan . . . "

– points at me –

"'E's got too many brains ter be a Blue, 'asn't 'e, Bert? – yer can tell just by lookin' at 'im . . . "

– looks back at my father –

"Oh aye Bert, did yer know about your Agnes and Joe, she's expectin' again – the fifth isn't it? Yer should've 'eard yer mam goin' on at them . . . "

– smiling glance over at me –

"And you stick yer 'ands over yer ears you – you shouldn't be listenin' to this . . . "

– then in a whispered voice to my father –

"Yer know Joe's been sleepin' downstairs at yer Ma's 'cos 'es 'ad glandular fever and Agnes 'as been sleeping upstairs with the kids, well when . . . "

– looks back at me giving me a playful clip across the ears –

"I told you to cover yer ears . . . "

– back to whispered tone to my father which ultimately disintegrates into howls of laughter from the pair of them –

"Well I believe when yer Ma found out, she shouted in to Joe "bloody hell Joe, you mustn't half have a long one to reach up to that back bedroom from there . . . I'm goin' ter get yew neutered" . . . she's a corker yer Ma, isn't she?"

– stands by a different chair –

"Now where was I – oh yeah, now you listen to me, young Alan, if yer Uncle Ebba tries on this Everton lark again, then you come an' see me – I'll sort 'im out big as 'e is – we're not 'avin' you becomin' a Blue . . . "

– now back on the settee looking straight into my eyes –

"Yer see Alan, Evertonians don't know what they're talkin' about . . . "

– now in whispered voice with his hand on my knee, looking shiftily either side as if at any moment some mysterious person might enter the room to listen in –

"The thing is, see, they're all a bit mad and most of them wouldn't know a football from George Formby's banjo . . . "

– now turning round towards my mother in the back kitchen –

"Is that the kettle boilin', Ed? Kay's been on earlies again, y'know? Are you still on piecework – terrible isn't it? Did yer . . . "

– now over on the other side of the room, leaning on the mantelpiece, back to his normal voice, looking once more at me –

"Take yer Uncle Jack fer a kick off – now 'e's a great bloke an' all that but 'e 'asn't gorra clue about footy, 'e still thinks Dixie Dean's playin' fer the Blues, that's cos 'e was the last time 'e went to Goodison, Winston Churchill was still in nappies, an' yer Uncle Eddie's just as bad, armchair supporters, now yer don't wanna end up like them do yer? I'll tell yer this . . . "

– then taking a cup of tea from my mother and handing her an empty plate –

"Aw, ta Ed! Them sarnies weren't 'arf tasty, – yer should be on piecework for them, Ed. Eh Bert, that reminds me, didn't you say Sam was ravin' about that young inside right – what's 'is name? Roger somethin' wasn't it? D'yer think 'e'll . . . 'Lunt' or something like that wasn't it?"

– now back over by the sideboard looking once more at me –

"The thing is, Alan, you're far too clever and good lookin' ter be a Blue – just like me, heh, heh 'oh an' by the way, don't forget to eat yer crusts – that's 'ow I got this . . . "

– pointing to his curly pride and joy on top of his head, then, swigging back his cup of tea –

"Ah, that's the gear that, Ed, any more in the pot?"

– now back once more on the settee, hovering over me –

"And listen, son, yer don't 'ave to worry about all this Second Division lark either yer know, we'll be back in the First Division in no time an' when we do, you just watch, we'll win everythin' – the League, Cup, Boat Race, National – the flippin' lot. There'll be no stoppin' us – straight up and don't forget . . . "

– at last settled back in his chair talking to my father –

"I think 'e should play Harrower yer know, Bert. I reckon even 'e can grab a bagful against them – their defence is pretty suspect at the back."

– then pausing to drain every last drop from his cup –

"Who is it we're playing by the way?"

With such unparalleled tactical acumen, the football world lay at Uncle Denny's mercy – he certainly would have bewildered any opposition. As a player he could have been a cross between Kevin Keegan and Paul Gascoigne – covering every blade of grass on the pitch and talking to each one at the same time. On the coaching side he could easily have become a major national supremo – a sort of Malcolm Allison with tight curls. He elected, however, to stay on the buildings with Uncle Ebba and so football's loss was the building industry's gain; and mine too, much to the dismay of the Evertonians in our family.

All this early exposure to football crazy kith and kin took place in the mythical Seaport area (of Z Cars notoriety), which hugged the docks to the north of the city and which, no doubt, resembled countless other similar places up and down the country, all equally steeped in the traditions of community and football, and all with their own rich sprinkling of Uncle Ebbas, Aunty Kitties and Uncle Dennies.

Within their old terraced streets, these places housed established communities where generations of the same families lived within yards of each other, and each morning at the same time droves of men would pour out from their back doors on foot or bike bound for the docks or the factories, and everyone from children to grandparents, from coalyard to dairy, knew everyone else and all felt a part of the whole; hundreds of people, all on first name terms, all sharing the same cobbled lanes and alleyways, the same shops, the same milkman, coalman and baker, the same ragman with horse and cart, the same local schools, churches, pubs and cinemas. There was a wondrous inertia and atmosphere. No-one moved in or out and everyone played pitch and toss, ate Hovis and wore clogs and flat caps, even the women and children and most of the dogs, too. They were our little villages, and in every case, football was an integral part of their fabric and culture.

For most youngsters, football became the be-all and end-all. We were football daft and played 'footy' (the usual Scouse non-conformist trait of abreviation, applied to football like everything else) from morn till night, at every available opportunity – we lived for it and it consumed us. Everything else simply got in the way.

Of course, from time to time, like any other mortals, we were tempted by other pleasures and occasionally strayed from the righteous path to make push-carts or to play 'Allio' or hopscotch or ball tick or ollies (marbles) or moggy wrestling. In the autumn, we collected bommie (bonfire material). Why, now and again, I have to admit, we even played cricket.

In mitigation, I have to say this latter distraction is not quite as shameful as it might at first appear, for the fact is, there have been many famous footballers who have enjoyed brief flirtations with leather on willow. The unique and legendary C B Fry even went on to represent his country in no fewer than four hundred and seventy eight different sports with his most notable achievement being to captain both the England Rugby Union and Hockey teams simultaneously at separate venues fifty miles apart, causing some sceptics to question the record's authenticity. Denis Compton, an outstanding outside left for Arsenal and England was another footballer who also enjoyed the occasional summer thrash with the cricket bat, managing in these brief sorties

39,000,000 first class runs and 123,000 first class centuries, which wasn't at all bad for a mere part-timer with upwards of half a ton of Brylcream on his head and an ego no bigger than Bob Paisley's, in spite of the repeated bolstering it used to receive from his effortless despatching of countless balls over every boundary rope in cricketdom.

The significance of all this is neither of these heroes ever let their forays outside of football interfere with their first love – and neither did we. No matter what the diversion, it would never be for long, for never far away would be the inevitable football; just like the great CB and Sir Denis, whatever the distraction, kicking a ball always seemed to us to be the natural thing to do.

What it all meant was that life effectively became one everlasting game of football, punctuated only by enforced breaks for sleeping, eating, going on messages, school and church. Little did we know or care at the time how profound an impact it was to have on the rest of our lives; we just got on with living and playing it. It was all so simple and straightforward; all so perfect. A perpetual footy paradise – "Are yer 'avin' a game of footy" the familiar cry.

Games would be played in the street or schoolyard by daylight or streetlight and would involve as many as forty or as few as half a dozen, at which time, we would play "attacking defence" or "three and in". To start proceedings, the sides would usually be picked by two captains – invariably the two best players – taking turns to choose their desired team-mates, though at other times the sides just seemed to evolve without any deliberate selection. Often the numbers would increase as a game progressed as more and more arrived to play. Such latecomers would be greeted by the cry of "youse go puddin' an' beef". This would enable them to be accommodated into the game ensuring strict impartiality and fairness. The important thing was the game never stopped and it was up to the late arrivals to identify their team mates as quickly as they could and then to get on with the game.

Surprising as it may seem, it wasn't only in our street games that such crude methods of selection were employed. At the time, back in the dismal Division Two days, Liverpool themselves used to adopt a similar process for their team selection. They, however, were a trifle more limited in their choice and ended up invariably only ever picking, what my father and Sam used to term, 'puddins', which I took to be some obscure critical reference to the inability of most of the Red's players, again according to my father and Sam, to "knock the skin off a rice puddin'". Still, if nothing else, the whole puddin' syndrome did serve to awaken my own critical faculties and it was not long before I came to realise that footballers existed not only to be idolised but also to be criti-cised and indeed, even called a 'puddin' if and when the circumstances so demanded or, if it just so happened, they were called Pat Rice and were having a bad game.

Back on the street, while there was never a shortage of skilful players it was the winning which was all important. Legs, ankles, heads, egos, old men on bikes, passing strangers, Sarah Vaughn and Billy Eckstein – all were there to be kicked with equal vigour as the balls. Never could we be accused of discriminating. It was a simple case of pummelling like mad the nearest person or thing to you, whoever or whatever it happened to be. Nobody gave a hoot about entertainment or the finer points of the game – there were simply too many games to worry about such things. Indeed, by the time we left junior school in 1962, we had probably played in close on ten thousand of these games which is more than treble the combined career totals of Billy Liddell, Ian Callaghan, Roger Hunt and Kenny Dalglish.

Inevitably, in view of all the games and their intensity, shoes would take a terrible pounding, particularly, with most of us being one footed, the kicking shoe, prompting pathetic futile attempts on our part to conceal the nature of the damage from our irate, penniless parents usually involving the deliberate scuffing of the non-kicking shoe to feign even wear and tear and make it look as if the damage was nothing to do with football. Not surprisingly, worn-out shoes became the order of the day and the shoe repairers, 'Billy Hyams – The Sole Saviours', was one of the busiest shops on the block. Now and again, there would be a pair of replacement shoes from the catalogue. Such occasions could carry their own traumas . . .

"Walk over there ter see 'ow thee feel . . . do thee feel alright?"

"Yeah, mam."

"Not too tight, are thee?"

"No, mam."

"Yer sure?"

"Yeah, mam."

"I hope so . . . 'cos that's the last pair you're gonna get . . . if yer ruin them yer can run round in yer stockin' feet . . . yer not gettin' no more"

"Yeah, mam."

"I mean it . . . you so much as dare look at a ball in them and I'll murder yer . . . I'm warnin' yer . . . d'yer understand"

"Yeah, mam."

– FIRM SMACK ACROSS THE BACK OF THE HEAD –

-"What was that for?"

"That's in case yer even thinkin' of kickin' a ball."

"Ahray, that's not fair. I 'adn't done anythin'."

"Sounds fair enough to me, son. Yer mam's not made of money . . . them shoes don't grow on trees, yer know."

Even worse damage would be inflicted on the balls. These were invariably plastic ones – usually red or white Frido 'plassies' or occasionally the brown or white 'Wembley' versions or, when there was no proper ball, a tennis ball. Leather case balls – 'caseys' – were a rarity and never used in street games. The main problem in all this was the lack of durability of the 'plassies'. Only very rarely would they ever survive more than a few weeks' intense hammering before bursting, usually on the glass covered tops of the surrounding walls.

Now and again our frustration would reach breaking point when new balls burst on their baptism, which was probably the most traumatic and tragic event any of us had, up to then, experienced although I do seem to recall Terry Ferguson also being pretty downcast too, when 'Crusty', his pet tortoise, emerged from hibernation with only its shell intact; a very messy episode indeed.

Ball deaths involving our own virgin Fridos would trigger reactions approaching the utter desolation and pandemonium of an Ayatollah's funeral, as we would all gather around moaning and wailing to await the distinctive dreaded piercing hiss. Such mourning periods would last all of ten seconds before giving way to the explosive release of pent up anger as we would unmercifully hound and barrack the unfortunate soul who was the last to kick the ball prior to its untimely demise. I hated it when it was me and, even now, the sound of a balloon slowly deflating is enough to induce a cold sweat.

The contrast in all this deflation business with the professional game – especially today's version of it – is stark and worth a quick consideration. Indeed, looking back at the enormity of the problems facing us, it makes you realise just how lucky and molly-coddled professional footballers have become over the years. I mean, I must have been to around 1,400 League and Cup matches all told and yet not once have I ever seen a ball burst – the odd few egos perhaps – but never a ball. Now when you think about it, that is some statistic isn't it? Remarkable by any standards. The sad thing is, though, the players these days, just take the whole thing for granted – the grass, the balls. They simply don't know they're born. What's more, even if the impossible occurred and a ball did happen to burst, you'd have a long wait before any of today's cosseted breed of prima donnas would dig into their pockets for a replacement. No way. In fact, I doubt very much whether there would be a single one amongst them who would even begin to know how to go about buying one. Everything would have to be done for them. If that isn't pampered, then I don't know what is. It's nursemaids they need, not agents. Things were never like that with the likes of Dixie Dean and Billy Liddell – they would have known exactly where to buy a new ball (and a tortoise, for that matter); not only that, they would also have cycled like the wind or caught the bus into town to get one, and they would have bought it with the last remnants of their own money too. Now they're what you call footballers.

Back amidst the looming reality of our own deflated balls, every now and again, efforts would be made to mend the punctures by welding them with a hot poker and then reflating the balls using special adapters (which, if I recall correctly, came with the balls when purchased but were always to be found lurking at the back of the kitchen drawer or in the shed). Sadly I am unable to remember a single such venture ending in anything other than miserable failure with the result that, for the most part, deflated ball games became more the norm than their inflated counterparts.

The games with punctured balls required different techniques to those with balls that actually bounced, and tended to suit the less skilful, battering ram types whose sole purpose in life seemed to be to plough forward in relentless, dreadnought-style, sweeping aside everything before them and dispensing with any notions of playing proper football.

The most infuriating aspect of such "dead ball" games would be when one of these exponents of this yard dog style, deliberately stood on the ball to deflate it, flattening it completely, before dragging it, moulded to the shape of their foot, along the ground with them as they lurched forward in uncompromising, bulldozing fashion towards their opponents' goal secure in the knowledge that their crude methods were more than adequate compensation for their complete lack of finesse and dribbling ability, since it was almost physically impossible for them to be dispossessed unless you amputated their leg.

The perpetrators of these unseemly tactics were, in effect, little more than uncultured yobs who ruined the game for everyone else. Naturally, given my own purist views on the game, I held them in deep contempt – unless they happened to be on the same side as me, in which case, of course, I fully condoned their actions.

The worst of the lot in this regard was a lad named John O'Neill. Playing against him was like confronting a two ton runaway wart-hog on heat. He reminded me of Malcolm Macdonald when he was at Newcastle – all sideburns, stripes and pneumatic legs, when his perception of the opposition centre half was as a sort of lushly piled carpeted access corridor to the goalmouth and the poor defender would come crawling off the pitch at the end of the game with countless sets of muddy studprints all over the front of his shirt, the legacy of Malcolms' frantic trampling en route to goal. With both Malcolm and John it was a case of why bother dribbling round someone when you can go straight through them using their chest as a mat; it saves time and energy and you can wipe your boots clean at the same time. The sad thing was, a lot of the time, tactics such as these worked and many innocent defenders suffered in the process and it wasn't to be until the 1974 FA Cup Final that a defender – Phil Thompson – finally came up with a solution to the problem of Malcolm's stampeding buffalo impersonation – don't give him a sniff of the ball and watch him sulk for the rest of the game. Mind you, having said that and taking nothing away from him, I don't think even Phil Thompson could have coped with John O'Neill on one of his maraudings.

Inevitably, with such levels of commitment and competitiveness, everything was bitterly contested and controversy of one sort or another was never far away. From an early age, we became conditioned to the sort of earth shattering wrangles which would come to haunt the game and our fandom in later years – a disputed decision is, after all, the same whether at Wembley or behind the gasworks and so are the reactions which accompany such decisions. I mean if you think the histrionics of Mario Kempes were bad enough when the linesman flagged two of his efforts offside against Peru in 1978 then you should have seen John O'Neill's reaction when we once told him he couldn't play because he was too dirty.

Probably the most controversial issue of our games was the width of the goal posts. At the start of the game, they would be the width of any other compactly folded coat or pullover but, as the game progressed, so did the expanse of the posts, as more and more discarded items of clothing were randomly heaped on each post, until they were almost touching each other.

Disputes arising from whether a shot had hit a post which, in no time at all, could be around half the width of one of Jan Molby's thighs, or whether it should count as a goal, could last throughout an entire game and beyond. Similar altercations would also arise concerning the non-existent cross-bars, goal lines and the limits of the goalkeeper's penalty box and one thing is certain – Geoff Hurst would never have gotten away so easily with his disputed World Cup goal in one of our games – with or without a Russian linesman to back him up.

The most aggravating source of dispute used to arise with those 'prima donna' types who would never take on the responsibility for retrieving a ball which had been kicked over a back entry wall or into someone's back yard – clearly they'd have made ideal professional footballers.

"It's your turn to go"

"Yeah but I never kicked it"

"Yeah but I never kicked it last time and I went"

"Yeah, well I never asked you to".

"Yer lazy get".

"And you, twat gob".

This brief yet extremely courteous exchange would be followed by the inevitable stand off situation with everyone sat down sulking and moping before a further bout of bickering would end invariably with the same old stupid ever willing ones, most desperate for the game to continue, going for the ball, while as far as the others were concerned, every time it would come down to a case of the old Biblical adage of pride coming before the ball which, I suppose, just goes to show that, once established, people's characteristics never really change. Maybe that's why they introduced ball boys at Wembley – I mean, with all due respect to him, can you imagine trying to persuade Rodney Marsh to fetch the ball, even if he had kicked it out of play?

Apart from being an extremely healthy, vigorous and argumentative way of whiling away our early years, what all the wall to wall football did, above all, was to serve to embody the love affair with football so prevalent in areas such as ours. It was, in fact, what hotbeds were all about and nowhere was this more starkly exemplified than with our Sunday Games.

These were huge twenty a side affairs which would start after church at around noon and continue unabated till around ten thirty at night with each of the participants randomly coming and going to grab their respective Sunday dinners and teas but without the game's flow ever being disturbed. With an age range spanning from ten to thirty something, all striving to emulate their Red or Blue heroes, it is probably true to say that at one time or another these games must have involved virtually every able-bodied male in the neighbourhood, all giving total commitment.

In terms of our football development, all this commitment meant that wherever we turned, whoever we looked up to or cast as our role model, they were inevitably some football-crazy lunatic. There literally was no escape – it was an all sides, round the clock, seven days a week barrage of football. Not, of course, that we would have had it any other way but it was little wonder that amidst this football furnace, the first sparks of our football craziness were kindled into a flaming passion that, in its different forms, was to burn brighter than any other. We simply followed the route laid down.

For most of my own generation in Liverpool following this path, the overwhelming urge to play at every opportunity, so powerful early on, did not last as long as it did with our predecessors. As our teenage years wore on, so the form in which our football fever manifested itself began to change; the desire to play, though still present, was gradually overtaken by the watching, worshipping and thought processes of pure fandom together with other base distractions which became ever more enticing the older we became.

Whether all this was due to the ever increasing success of both local teams or profound changes in our bodily composition I'm not sure but thereafter, what I do know is, it was fandom which became a way of life for us, with playing the game more of a spasmodic adventure limited to Sunday League debacles, five-a-sides and the odd kick around on the beach when on holiday, a far cry from the morn til night saturation of our early years.

Still later, when playing fields became simply a fading reminiscence and even a half an hour's five-a-side had degenerated into little more than an unpleasant grind of red-faced breathlessness, all that really remained was our fandom, any serious notions of kicking a ball long since evaporated – which is just as well since 45 year olds do tend to look a bit ridiculous playing 'three and in' with ten year old kids night after night when they get home from work and having to be called in when their tea's ready.

I suppose the thing is that while kicking a ball may have been virtually a primeval instinct within us, at the end of the day what prevails above all is the uncompromising love affair each of us has with our team.

The fascinating aspect of all this is what it is that continues to drive this spirit of undivided loyalty and commitment throughout our life. The early initiation processes into football are easily identifiable and understandable – straightforward impregnation and inbred enthusiasm – but why, when we reach maturity and are able to rationalise things for ourselves, does the flame of something in essence often quite irrational and at times preposterous, still burn so brightly? I mean, it is one thing following AC Milan and Liverpool when they are winning European Cups, but who in their right mind would go and watch Darlington, for instance, week in, week out, rain or shine for the duration of their adult life. Such fandom would seem to defy any reasonable logic as I am sure any Darlington fan would wholeheartedly agree. There must be some other explanation.

One possible reason for the ongoing attachment and for the apparent absence in many cases of any logical thought processes could lie in the very roots which provide the source of our initial indoctrination. It is, I think widely accepted that most people need some sort of constant in their lives, a base to which they know they can always return. For most of us, home, family and friends form a major part of that base but, sadly for various reasons, not all can remain constant – friends, even spouses, come and go, loved ones die, children leave home, very few of us remain in the same house and neighbourhood, in many cases including my own, our neighbourhoods are destroyed, and many folk move away altogether, some even emigrate.

Perhaps then, with many football fans, our fandom is a sort of immovable rock we unwittingly create to forge an impassive link with our past, fulfilling an overwhelming subconscious yearning for a permanent umbilical cord bringing our childhood and formative years into our later life.

Other pursuits, of course, can help to create feelings of well-being but no matter how much we love model railways, fishing in the Tweed, Eddie Izzard, Van Gogh, Bruce Springsteen, guest bitters, Martin Amis, backpacking in Afghanistan, Quentin Tarantino, all night clubbing, Thai banquets or boxing, the Ryder Cup, Family Fortunes or whoever or whatever – none ever manage to recreate the womb-comforting serenity and harmony nor to stir passions deep within us in the same way as fandom with the near spiritual sense of identity and deep connection which seems to lie at its core, affording it such telling parallels with religion. Well, okay maybe Family Fortunes but that's about it.

In the case of Manchester United fans in particular but also those of other teams – my own for one – the deep associations of fandom are often clouded by the glory-hunting of success and it is true that many fans do come along just for the ride. Indeed, for many impressionable youngsters any yearnings they may have harboured for their local team have been all but destroyed by the media and commercial juggernaut of the big clubs. Nevertheless, for the majority of fans – true fans such as our friends from Darlington – for whom the scent of glory can never really be more than just a pipe dream, there has to be some other reason and it could just be that, in later years, fandom becomes the substitute for a life since passed for which many of us still crave.

Certainly, in my own case, I have no reason to doubt that the deep emotional attachment I have for Liverpool Football Club may, in part, be a subliminal substitution for a sense of suppressed longing for a vital part of myself long since destroyed by the Town Hall Planners when they obliterated our little neighbourhood of Seaport. I suppose, though, the odd piece or two of silverware and the occasional flash of genius from Kenny Dalglish may also have had something to do with it.

"One day yer'll play fer the Reds – just you wait an' see. Yer've got footballer's knees."

Even now, thirty odd years after first hearing these immortal words, they still trigger a little flutter inside me. In fact, I doubt whether in all the years since passed, anything nicer has ever been said to me, which I suppose is a bit of a sad reflection when you think about it but, nonetheless, is true to form and certainly nothing I'm ashamed of. Not that that counts for much though.

It was Jimmy O'Toole who had spoken them as we were all strolling back home after one of our Sunday games. Jimmy, who was in his fifties, and one of the many football crazy fanatics who abounded in the neighbourhood, was the local 'wino', a happy, drunken old soul, who used to beam at everyone through a scrunched up concertina of creases and wrinkles; huge banana smiles and grins which split his face in two and made his ears wiggle. He was a far cry from those whom the drink turned nasty and made them want to fight the world. With Jimmy, the more he drank, the more he smiled and the more he smiled, the more he wanted to share his happiness with everyone around. He was certainly no advert for the anti-alcohol brigade for, Walter Mitty apart, I don't think anyone ever looked happier than Jimmy, though I daresay Hereford United's Ronnie Radford might have given him a good run for his money the day he blasted one in from two hundred and fifty yards against Newcastle in the FA Cup.

Most nights Jimmy would share his cheerfulness with us. Friendly bottle in hand and cap perched precariously atop a curly mane he would come to watch us play and with bottle, cap and all, join in for twenty seconds or so of frantic inebriated dribbling action before retiring breathless and in urgent need of further liquid refreshment.

Most likely, this was Jimmy's way of demonstrating that football could be fun and certainly, on a football pitch, I don't think I've ever seen a funnier sight, unless it was the time when Jan Molby, in a kit ten sizes too small and also wearing a flat cap, tried to outrun some sleeky greyhound winger over forty yards down our left flank, after Stig

Bjorneby had been caught out upfield, and because the momentum of his body was too much for his legs which couldn't cope with the trauma of having to run so fast, ended up doing a triple axile every bit as good as anything ever done by Jane Torville. Incidentally, just in case you're wondering, for the record, I've nothing personal against Jan – he seems a real gen bloke and he was a marvellous highly skilled footballer – one of the best ever and also probably our most accurate ever long passer of a ball – it's just that I've no objection to fat comedians on ten grand a week making prats of everyone but I do have a big thing about overweight and unfit so-called professional footballers taking the piss out of loyal fans and their hard earned money – and that's what Jan did, by no means all the time but for some of it and if he looks in the mirror or at some old photographs he'll know what I mean and at the same time, realise why his hamstrings and joints were always inevitably giving way under the strain. And most galling of all – for us and him, and his country – why he never achieved anything like his real potential which was enormous – like him really.

As for Jimmy, he had been a Red for forty years or more. There was nothing he didn't know about the club nor the players nor the ground, nor the history of the club, nor football in general, and what he didn't know he made up anyway and who he didn't know wasn't worth knowing. Jimmy had served during the war with Raich Carter, had gone out with Alex James' cousin, had drunk regularly with Hughie Gallagher, was close mates with Matt Busby and had been shown how to head a ball 'properly' by Dixie Dean and knew all about the steel plate in Dixie's head which had made his headers fly like a Bobby Charlton rocket shot. He even knew personally all the Liverpool and Everton players and had actually gone to the same school as Eph Longworth, the Red's finest ever full back.

Why on earth, with such a track record and with so many famous friends he chose to spend night after night watching us play football is a mystery, though if anyone ever challenged Jimmy about his famous friends, he would simply smile, take a swig of his plonk and smile again. One time he did actually produce a photograph of himself and Raich Carter in uniform to prove his point and certainly it did look like Raich Carter, though in those days, I suppose, everyone in uniform looked like Raich Carter.

Jimmy used to attend every Reds game home and away which was quite a feat, for invariably right up to kick off time, he would still be propping up the bar at the local pub, 'The Queens'. That was Jimmy though, always laying claim to the impossible. Not a team would be picked nor a ball kicked, nor a challenge made without Jimmy having claimed some sort of part in it.

Jimmy's speciality was transfers. He knew about every transfer weeks before they happened by virtue of his inside information.

"Tell yer what, that Bobby Charlton's a bugger fer the rum an' blacks, yer know . . . 'e can't 'alf purrem away . . . we was with 'im an' their Jackie the other night in the 'White 'Orse' . . . legless we were . . . what a night, though . . . I 'ad ter give the pair of them a lift 'ome on me bike, thee were that bad . . . tell yer what, though, Bobby was tellin' me 'e reckons the Reds 'ave purrin' a bid fer 'alf the United squad . . . yeah, 'alf o' them . . . himself, Bestie, the Lawman, Crerand, Stepney, Stiles, Foulksie an' Phil Chisnall an' a few of the other reserves as well . . . 'e reckons it all depends on whether Shanks can get the money together by sellin' Alfie Arrowsmith . . . tell yer what that'd be some transfer if it comes off, yer know . . . like buyin' a new team . . . "

Inevitably, with such big-name contacts within the game at his beck and call, some of Jimmy's outlandish predictions often turned out to be right. Well partly right, anyway. In this instance, the bit about Phil Chisnall, at least. The thing was Jimmy was bound to be right for, by his reckoning, every player in every major club in England and Scotland was, at some time or another, about to be transferred to Liverpool or Everton, so though he was nearly always right, he was also ninety nine per cent of the time, wrong. Not that it mattered to Jimmy though. He just smiled his 'I told you so' smile and basked in the glory of his prediction, and wondered, no doubt, why he had never been offered a job on the Sports Desk of the Sunday People which used to enjoy a similar accuracy rating with their own transfer predictions.

Of course, just like the Sunday People Sports Desk, the problem with everything Jimmy said was that, invariably, it was complete and utter bollocks; never more so than with his flattering observations on my playing ability and footballer's knees. He used to say the same thing to everyone at one time or another. Why, he even used to say the same about himself after one of his own twenty-second, bottle in hand rampages. Yet while the older kids all knew what Jimmy spoke was garbage, we youngsters hung on his every word. The fact that Jimmy's were simply the wistful ramblings of a generously lubricated Hans Christian Anderson meant nothing to us for we never saw beyond his winning smile and his wrinkles and what we wanted to hear.

So when Jimmy told me I'd play for the Reds, I naturally believed him implicitly. I walked as tall as the Spion Kop. He gave me something to dream about. OK, so perhaps my dream did become a bit far-fetched –

scoring three diving headers during injury time on my debut for the Reds against Everton at Anfield to clinch a 3-2 victory and the League title – but if you're going to dream then, just like Jimmy, dream big.

Thus did Jimmy become our perfect model role – expert analyst, happy as Larry Lloyd, always on the ale, football daft, friend to loads of famous footballers and still one of the lads. Jimmy would do for us – what more could a football daft youngster want.

Sadly, one day, Jimmy's liver decided it had had enough and we never saw him again. He had gone to that giant ale-house in the sky where he could drink and talk footy with the angels to his hearts content.

Liverpool meantime had lost their most knowledgeable and best connected fan and we had lost our smiling, wrinkly 'guru'. After that, our football games were never quite the same again for however much Jimmy may have been marinated with booze, the thing was he was even more saturated with football so deep down he really was our 'soul mate'. Even though he didn't actually 'physically' know Raich Carter or Hughie Gallagher or the Liverpool and Everton teams, spiritually he was in touch with them all.

As far as we were all concerned, Jimmy was our link with the Reds and the Blues and the rest of the football world and everything he said was of vital significance making us feel part of the whole. Jimmy had made our heroes seem tangible giving us the chance of feeling as one with them. Budding football fans can't really expect much more than that.

Whether or not it was done deliberately to thwart the increasingly menacing designs of Uncle Ebba and Aunty Kitty to turn me Blue I am unsure, but one Saturday, my father decided the time was right for his seven year old son to start accompanying himself and Sam and Dave – my uncles, not the soul duo incidentally – to the match to watch Liverpool's Second Division 'obscurities'.

It was a decision which at the time, I no doubt cherished, though I have to admit my recollections of those early trips to Anfield are vague and I have only two clear abiding memories. One is of emerging on my father's shoulders from the darkness down under the main stand up the Paddock steps and seeing for the first time Anfield's pitch which suddenly appeared out of nowhere to shimmer like some bright green oasis in glaring contrast to the drab greyness of the stadium terracing and surrounding streets along which we had just walked to reach the ground. (I suppose when you think about it, it was lucky those first games weren't at Filbert Street, for I might have gone round afterwards thinking you played professional football on the beach with donkeys, as opposed to grass with donkeys, that is). The other is of learning that my Uncle Dave actually swore – for example on one occasion he asked me if I wanted a piss – something which he would never have done back home, for if he had my Gran would have killed him for she couldn't abide any form of swearing in the house, particularly if it involved any bodily functions or such like. As for the actual games themselves, I remember very little, though I do recall one bizarre penalty incident involving the Reds' inside forward, Jimmy Melia, who was the Reds' finest ever exponent of premature baldness and by comparison made Bobby Charlton look like the lead singer of ZZ Top.

Reacting alertly to the ref's whistle, following a foul in the box, Jimmy had hastily placed the ball on the spot to take the resulting penalty and stooping down with one hand still on the top of the ball, had sidefooted it into the net past the opposition keeper, and run off gleefully to celebrate his goal, whereupon the referee promptly gave a free kick to the other side for hand-ball by Jimmy whom, I fear, tore off rather more than a few of his precious remaining follicles in his ensuing fit of pique. Thinking about it now though, maybe the referee had never given a penalty at all. Maybe Jimmy had simply mis-read the situation. If that was the case, it wouldn't have been the only time Jimmy got things wrong.

Balding Jimmy apart, I can also just about recall experiencing my first bout of hero worshipping around this time in the shape of the Reds' popular winger Alan A'Court, though with all respect to Alan, I am certain this devotion owed rather more to his name sounding like one of Richard Greene's Band of Merry Men in Sherwood Forest than to his undoubted playing prowess.

Actually just to digress for a second, talking of Alan and Robin Hood and Sherwood Forest reminds me of the time when we were badly cheated out of the League Cup in 1980 in a replay at Old Trafford against Brian Clough's Nottingham Forest by a dodgy penalty decision involving Phil Thompson and John O'Hare. After the game me, Dave Power, Keith, Steve and Jake went for a pint and on coming out we found we'd been drinking in a pub called the Robin Hood, and the worst of it was the ale was like robin's pee and nor was that the only time we've been pissed on by Brian Clough from a great height, though we won't go into that just now.

Useful though all these early excursions may have been in cementing my Redness, my serious initiation came, as it did with most other Reds fans at the time, in the Boys Pen, or the 'Pen' as we termed it, which occupied an enmeshed rear corner of the Spion Kop terracing next to the main stand.

The Pen was truly an awful place. Whilst many other grounds in the late fifties/early sixties had special enclosures for young fans equivalent to the Pen, it is extremely unlikely whether any of them could have come anywhere near matching the Pen's ghastliness.

The Pen was exactly the type of place where today you would actually forbid young lads from attending unless, that is, they had committed a serious criminal offence or had dangerous psychopathic tendencies. To term it a 'jungle' would be an affront to all self-respecting lions, sabre-toothed tigers and orang-utans. William Golding used a watered down synopsis of life there for 'Lord of the Flies' and Anthony Burgess based 'Clockwork Orange' on the antics of some of the Pen's more amiable inhabitants. Those who maintain law and order began to disintegrate only in the late seventies patently never spent a Saturday afternoon on the steps of the Pen. Had they done so, their views on the relative utopia of life today would make interesting reading.

The Pen, in short, was total anarchy.

In 1960 when we were around nine we began our careers in The Pen. By that age, going to the match with your father was considered cissy. Going with your mates on the other hand was definitely the thing to do. So, with entry being just ninepence, the Pen was the only affordable way to watch the Reds whilst at the same time retaining some credibility. Many were the times afterwards when I longed to be a cissy, though don't get me wrong on this score; I'm talking figuratively here. I didn't actually want to be a cissy, it's just that things would have seemed a little safer if I'd have stuck with my father. I suppose what I'm saying is that the Pen was a nightmare for anyone halfway normal, a category which, at that time at least, I just about scraped into.

As far as I could see, there were broadly two types of Pen inmate – thugs and desperadoes. As young scruffs ourselves, we were all reasonably well versed in the usual street and playground escapades. The Pen, however, was ridiculous – Britain's own version of Dodge City.

The first hurdle came on your initial trip up the long winding stepped ramp from the turnstiles where budding racketeers waited to accost you, demanding your money or your life. We chose life but soon learned thereafter to keep our return bus-fare hidden under a brick on wasteland outside the ground whilst half of the time wondering whether that might be where we would end up ourselves if one of the inmates so decreed.

Once inside, there would be other gangs of marauding parasites to contend with, some looking for easy money, others for an easy fight. The problem was the Pen was only ever part full so there was always plenty of room for these gangs to roam around seeking out innocents like us. You prayed for them to find some other poor souls to pick on but regrettably, we seem to have been viewed as an easy target and so, more often than not, we were approached by these budding baboons.

Now adults like to pride themselves in offering the right advice for such circumstances – "stand up to bullies and they will back down" – my dear mother used to say – "they're really nothing but cowards". In fact, bless her, they are just the opposite. They're as hard as nails – tungsten-tipped ones – and any resistance tends to make matters worse as we found out at the cost of repeated confrontations and maulings on our early visits. On one occasion they even took a shine to the shoes my mate Paul was wearing – brand new 'chisel toes' he'd just got from the catalogue. They just took them off him and left him standing there crying in his stocking feet and he had to go home like that and his parents had to carry on paying out each week for his stolen pair and a new pair to replace them, which had to be ones nobody would really like so they wouldn't get pinched again.

Looking back, we must have been masochists to have put up with it all. I mean it wasn't as if anyone ever held a gun to our heads to make us go, so it was all effectively self-induced torture. Yet still we went. Even so, I daresay many people in the game may scoff at all these bleatings. Basically they will say that if it's real terror you're after then look no further than Plough Lane in the late Eighties when Wimbledon came up to Division One and frightened every one to death. To which I'll say bollocks! You only had to go there annually while we had to endure the Pen every fortnight and you also had a referee and a linesman to protect you and you got some respite at half time. Also you never had to walk home in your stocking feet. In fact, the only thing they ever stole off you was three points. There's no comparison, really.

Undaunted by all the Pen's intimidation, but still desperate above all to see our Red heroes, we experimented with ways of mitigating the confrontations, the easiest of which was sticking as close as possible to the solitary police bobby who from time to time patrolled this seething cauldron. We came to look like frightened kids holding their teacher's hand in a playground. At other times, when there was no bobby, like scores of others similarly oppressed, we would spend virtually the whole game in a frantic escape attempt to climb over the Pen's railings into the Kop. The railings must have been twenty feet high and the scene would resemble a mass break out from Butlins. Some actually managed the feat; most of us would get so far and then hang on quivering for dear life for the rest of the game, praying for the final whistle when we could come back down to the safety of an empty pen.

Eventually, thankfully, we found the most a reliable saviour of all; the cousin of one of our lot, who was in one of the gangs, allowed us to tag along with them. From then on, the Pen didn't seem quite such a bad place as we viewed it in relative safety through different eyes and were able to concentrate on the match rather than our backs. Still, it was always a precarious existence and it was a great relief when, a year or so later, extra jamjars, pop bottles and pocket-money at last enabled us to afford to bid good riddance to the Black Hole of Anfield and join the ranks of civilisation on the Kop.

So, at the end of the day, did our nightmare in the Pen teach us anything? (apart from the fact that if fans everywhere had had to go through the Anfield Pen experience then professional football would long ago have ceased to exist due to plummeting attendances – I mean would anyone honestly fancy a guaranteed weekly mugging and actually pay for the privilege?). What it did provide as far as young Liverpudlians were concerned was an unwitting re-affirmation of their faith; basically if you survived the Pen, hung on to your footwear and bus fare, lived to tell the tale and still kept the desire to watch the Reds, then you truly were a fan. Perhaps, then, in that sense, the Pen was not so bad after all and maybe there is some good in everything.

I must admit though, I for one, did not join those who shed a tear when they eventually dismantled the monstrosity and rehoused it, and the pick of its inmates, in Alcatraz, its spiritual home. Then again, as a closet cissy, I would say that, wouldn't I?

In any consideration of football fandom but, most especially, in one where it effectively forms the main theme of what you are writing about, it would constitute quite an anomaly not to highlight the parallels which exist with religious worship. In fact, let's get a bit realistic here, it would be completely nonsensical. Not surprisingly then, in this connection, I share a common ground with many of those who maintain that football fandom is, in fact, simply a surrogate form of religious worship and, clearly, given the intense devotion of some football followers, for someone like myself to hold such a view can hardly be regarded as unexpected or devoid of conviction.

Certainly, whatever the degree of conviction there would seem little else other than football fandom which has an impact and significance comparable to that of religion in the lives of those concerned. Followers of cricket and Rugby League and Union particularly may choose to disagree with this submission, perhaps with some justification – especially those from the rural and mining communities of Lancashire, Yorkshire, South Wales and the South West – but it is difficult to sustain a similarly credible universal argument for anything other than football fandom. The simple fact of the matter is all across the country and, no doubt, the world, most people identify with their hometown club in one way or another and for fanatics, little else in life matters. Blind faith is what they call it.

It comes as little surprise then that even the most cursory insight into both creeds serves to emphasise the links which exist.

Take, for instance, the basic obligations underlying both ideologies. This requires in each instance the unstinting worship of something sacred to the respective followers – in the case of religion, the One True God, while in that of fandom, the One True Team. In either case, as if to serve emphasis to the closeness of this association, the rites of such homage and adoration are celebrated in comparable places of worship used, in the main, once a week on the respective Sabbaths, where the participants don special clothes and the congregations indulge in ritualised singing, chanting and praying.

Rather less overt, though equally significant, is the similarity in both the long term goal of each creed, being in both cases to win promotion to a higher division, and the humble nature of their respective origins – one a stable in Bethlehem, the other a seedy, rundown butcher's meat joint in downtown Accrington, while even the diversity of the various religious tribes – Jews, Buddhists, Moslems, Catholics and so forth, is mirrored in fandom by similar tribal loyalties – Everton, Liverpool, United, City and so on, each with a fierce pride and passion of their own. Finally, though certainly not least, are the precious Guardian Angels common to both sets of followers, one sort with wings and harps, the others often with distinct Scottish twangs and names ending in 'y'.

Given the closeness of all these analogies, it is easy to see why even many high ranking clergymen have admitted to the parallels which are present.

One area where the parallels between both creeds would seem most obvious is in the actual process of indoctrination itself. Speaking personally, however, whilst I have to agree that to be the case, I must admit I found a world of difference between the two and religious worship never came easy to me.

In my case, my parents and my father's side of the family were Roman Catholics, my mother being a converted Protestant which, I suppose, is a bit like when Ray Kennedy followed Bob Paisley's advice and dropped back from centre-forward to become a left sided midfielder. In my mother's instance it was with rather less success than Ray due, no doubt, to the simple fact that she wasn't a natural 'left footer'. The rub of it all was that many of my father's family, inexplicably as it seemed to me, were inclined to display as much fervour in their Catholicism as in their Red or Blue creeds. This, unfortunately, held great sway with my parents and meant that, as well as being raised in the Red Faith, I was also steeped, whether I liked it or not, in the Catholic Faith.

The main problem with this was what being a Catholic entailed for young Catholics lads like myself. In my case it meant being an altar boy, learning the Latin Mass and the Catechism word perfect, obeying the Commandments, mass and communion every day, benediction, Sunday School, Grace at mealtimes, Confession, Novenas, decades of the Rosary, giving up sweets at Lent, processions round the streets half a dozen times a year, Stations of the Cross every Good Friday, an ash cross on our forehead each Ash Wednesday, reading the Catholic Pictorial every Sunday, eating boiled fish on a Friday, (without chips, too), and so on and so forth. All this not only seriously disrupted our budding football careers but, hindsight tells us, would also have precluded anyone of sound mind and disposition from ever contemplating undertaking it of their own volition. Frankly, even the prospect of an hour long Bob Wilson interview on *Football Focus* with Don Howe and Butch Wilkins now seems positively enticing in comparison; though on second thoughts possibly not.

In fact, the saving graces to being a Catholic boy, as far as I could discern, were that every now and then at wedding services each altar boy would receive a tip from the groom, usually around half a crown each, and, six times a year, we would have an extra day off school for a Holy Day of Obligation to which only Catholics were entitled.

Now half a crown in those days was the equivalent of almost three weeks pocket money or a couple of footy matches, and so it was not to be sniffed at. Neither, for that matter was a day off school, since it meant we could play footy uninterrupted all day instead of having to fit it in between school lessons. It struck me, however, that on balance, these two perks, however desirable, were heavily outweighed by the onerous burden of our other commitments, and we Catholic boys most certainly had been at the rear of the queue when the good deals were being handed out, unlike our Protestant friends who, with their scant obligations and responsibilities, seemed to have been right at the front. Indeed if I'm not mistaken I think the whole thing is referred to as the 'shitty end of the stick', a sentiment which I'm sure will be echoed by followers of most Endsleigh League Division Two and Three clubs, as they reflect on their inability to get their fair share of football's ever burgeoning dosh.

What it all meant, of course, as far as we were concerned was that we had to be practically blackmailed into complying with all the demands made on us. The deal was that if we wished to avoid eternal damnation and the horrors of hell, which, by virtue of our indoctrination into the Faith we undoubtedly did, then we carried out whatever was asked of us however unfair it all seemed to be.

The main player in all this blackmail business, lodged at the very core of our budding Catholicism, was the festering monster of mortal sin. With its terrifying images of blackened souls, Satanic evil and outlandish two-footed tackles by demons such as the dreaded Sunderland centre half Charlie Hurley, (who for those who do not remember him made Vinnie Jones seem like Lionel Blair), mortal sin haunted our every breath and the bottom line it brandished never wavered – a soul stained black by mortal sin was condemned to spend eternity in a scalding hot bath with Big Charlie and his fellow demons; clearly a fate far too horrific even to contemplate.

Needless to say, faced with such a prospect, we complied with our obligations and avoided mortal sin in any form whatsoever, taking particular care to steer well clear of the two most mortal sins of all – missing Mass on Sundays and being impure by thought, word or, perish the thought, deed. The gravity of both of these sins was ranked so high that everything else paled. So much so that virtually any other aberrations – murder, serial killing, lying, cheating, stealing, fighting, swearing, disobedience, drawing false moustaches on photographs of Stanley Matthews or even, Heaven forbid, entering Goodison Park, were relegated to the role of mere Venial sins which carried, at worst, a fleeting spell in Purgatory (which was like Hell, only temporary) at best, a quick act of contrition and the slate wiped clean.

Indeed, so great were our fears in all this that I think it is probably true to say there was actually more chance of a genuine football lover being entertained by a Dave Bassett All Stars eleven than of us ever missing Mass on Sunday. We would attend with broken arms, legs, heads or any such like injury, illness or disability. Come hell or high water, rain or shine, or even Charlie Hurley himself, we would be there, religiously. In fact, if it had come to a choice between Mass and a football match which, thankfully, it never did because they fell on different days and at different times, then Mass would have prevailed, such was our implanted terror (of course, if the choice had been Dave Bassett's boys, most of us would have elected to take up the priesthood).

As regards the other dastardly mortal sin, well, suffice to say that, so great was our immortal survival instinct, we even took to peeing with our hands behind our backs, in case of any misinterpretation, up on high, of our actions. We took no chances, entertained no risks. We played a true percentage game – the boring boring Arsenal of the Catholic Faith. As far as our tiny guilt ridden minds were concerned, compared to missing Mass and being impure, little else mattered. By the age of ten, our entire psyche had become saturated with mortal sin, attending Mass, staying pure and the dire prospect of eternal life with the infernal Charlie; truly an enforced indoctrination.

Of course, comparisons to footy in all this mortal/venial sin business are as inevitable as an Auberon Waugh swipe at Liverpudlians. However, as inviting as they may, on the face of it, appear, parallels of any real substance tend actually to have little credence, coming across as all rather facile, and carrying only partial validity.

Obviously, the tempting one is a yellow card for a venial sin and a red card for a mortal sin. As you may well imagine, though, it isn't that simple, particularly in the case of the typical red card offence. Certainly, there are bound to be those who view an Eric Cantona or Julian Dicks stamp or a John Fashanu or Vinnie Jones elbow or even a Paul Ince smile as equally serious offences as missing Mass or even the other unspeakable act and who are we to disagree with such assertions. The point is, however, that is where the comparison runs out of steam for when it then comes to the actual punishment involved we are talking different leagues; different worlds even.

The facts speak loud and clear for themselves in this connection. For a red card in football you get a ban. Now and again, if you're Scottish, a tall centre forward and answer to the name of 'Big Dunc' you may get gaol. And that's about as bad as it gets. Pretty tame stuff (though try telling that to 'Big Dunc' after he's downed a few whiskey chasers). The consequences of mortal sin, in complete contrast, held unimaginable terrors and only those poor second division centre forwards actually unfortunate enough to have been mangled by him, ever really knew the full extent of the punishment that Big Charlie Hurley used to dish out. Sadly, all we know now is that it was so horrendous that none ever survived to tell the tale.

I suppose then, the only way for the football/religion analogy really to work in this context would be for the Football Association to follow the

example of Rugby League and Ice Hockey and sanction the introduction of the dreaded 'Sin Bin'. In this case, though, for the
punishment to equate, the bin would need to be about six feet deep
with huge metal spikes all across the bottom, half filled with molten hot
chip pan oil and with wall to wall video screens switched on up to full
volume blasting out non-stop the latest Gary Newbon interview. Now
that really would be hellish, as I'm sure even Big Charlie's victims would
have to agree. In fact, the spikes and hot oil sound a bit nasty, too.

Back in our little Catholic wonderland, meanwhile, all this preoccupation with mortal sin and Big Charlie was inevitably to have a
profound effect on our everyday lives.

When I was around ten or eleven, I was staying with my cousins at my
Aunty Molly's house around the corner. Aunty Molly was about fifty
years old, a staunch Red and a devout Catholic, who had never
committed any sin, (or so I thought) in her entire life, except she did
admit to once going past Goodison Park on the bus as a young girl.
Every day, she went to Mass and Communion; she said her prayers
kneeling down three times a day, including one for the Reds promotion;
every meal was accompanied, before and after, by Grace; never, under
any circumstances, would she utter a swear word, unless of course
Father Timoney, a big Blues fan, ever tried to tease her about the Reds.
Basically, Aunty Molly was up there with the best of them.

Anyway, the first night there, I developed a tummy ache and told my
Aunty Molly. To my utter surprise, she immediately looked down and
pointed in the direction of my nether regions and, to my shock horror,
asked me asked me outright, " are yer balls okay, Alan?" (as I realised
many years later she actually said bowels, but I had never heard of them
– I was only ten remember – and naturally, in my ignorance, assumed
she had said balls in a mock Cockney accent. As far as I was concerned
in my panic, Aunty Molly, pure as the driven snow, was actually talking
testicles and pointing to them.) I was stunned. 'Aunty Mollys' just didn't
say that type of thing. Then, before I could mutter a response, she
promptly followed it up. "d'yer want me ter rub them for yer, love?" At
this offer my head exploded with profound embarrassment. I went as
red as a Liverpool jersey, coughed, spluttered and ran like the wind
upstairs, rambling incoherently that my pain had miraculously disappeared and quickly hid under the nearest bed, desperately praying she
wouldn't follow me.

My reaction was all to do with the mortal sin thing – if I had been a
Protestant, I would perhaps have been a bit perturbed but hung around

(not literally at that age I suppose) for her to carry out her aunty's duties whatever they may have been. As a Catholic, however, my overwhelming fear of impurity overrode everything and so I hastily fled in terror from a possible mortal sin liaison with my Aunty Molly.

Around the same time as the Aunty Molly encounter, my friends and I came to realise that our oppressive fears concerning mortal sin were not, in fact, confined to ourselves alone but also, unfortunately encompassed our parents' aberrations as we discovered – as you do – the very real link between our existence on this earth and the despicably evil act of impurity. In other words, in order for us to arrive in this God-forsaken place, our parents had actually done it – they had been impure: by deed (and who knows, possibly by thought and word as well). What's more, as it transpires, theirs was a far dirtier deed than we, with our grubby little hands were capable of perpetrating, for they, evidently, had actually done it to each other.

Needless to say, we were all sickened by our findings; mortified, even. It made our previous biggest worry – the pathetic concern we had over the Reds' promotion to Division One – seem all so trivial.

It was not as if discovering such revelations at an early age was altogether alien to us. The fact is, it is a burden that kids from a city such as Liverpool are born with. It's like a form of original sin you can't wash away. Bruce Springsteen once said it's hard to be a saint in a city and he was right. You become a street kid, street-wise with street cred. Whether you like it or not you enter the real world at an early age. By seventeen and a half, for instance, as far as we were all concerned Father Christmas was already little more than a myth, and as for the Tooth Fairy, well she was simply just another vehicle for easy money from our folks. It was very much cynicism in the fast lane, I know, and hard to comprehend if you're not from the mean streets but, believe me, that was the way it was in the jungle where we hung out.

Anyway, faced with our new-found reality we tried as best we could to draw some reassurance from the fact that the Blessed Mary and Joseph must have done the dirty deed to each other, too, which seemed, to us, to have a logical ring to it and also appeared initially at least, to hint at a lesser degree of sinfulness for our parent's transgressions. However, this crumb of comfort was dashed almost at once when somebody's older brother explained to us about the Virgin Mary which, though I have to admit, we found a trifle bemusing did, nevertheless, seem pretty convincing at the time.

As it was, we didn't need to grasp it, anyway. We had our own theories about Mary and Joseph. The way we figured it, Virgin Mary or not,

Mary and Joseph, from whichever stance you viewed it, had been two thousand years ago, so it was highly unlikely in those days whether they would have even known what they were doing, let alone whether or not they knew it to be wrong. Certainly, they wouldn't have been anywhere near as well briefed about mortal sin as we were. I mean they didn't even have goal nets in those days and the 'caseys' they used had laces which could cut your head open if you misjudged a header. So given all that, whatever it was that they used to get up to – even Mary and Joseph – you could hardly attach any blame to them for it. Fair's fair after all. Current generations, on the other hand, could scarcely plead similar ignorance; especially grown up parents who had been taught not to be impure. Their behaviour was inexcusable. As far as we were all concerned, there was no doubt about it – Mary and Joseph were completely innocent but the case against our parents was cut and dried and it all spelt deep, deep trouble.

As if all this wasn't bad enough another gruesome realisation soon dawned. Gradually, it struck us that most of our parents had patently done the wicked deed more than once, since all of us had brothers or sisters, and some both. One of us, in fact, had twelve, which meant his parents had actually done it thirteen times! THIRTEEN TIMES! Once for each Apostle and Pontius Pilate too. Surely there could be no hope for them. God could never forgive that. Even Ally McCloud was never that sinful – though I daresay many of the Scots still stranded over in Argentina since 1978 may dispute that. And such an unlucky number too – you'd have thought they would have stopped at twelve in any case; talk about tempting fate. No doubt they were the sort who even put umbrellas up in the house.

With thirteen kids though, there would have been no chance of putting up any umbrellas in any house. They wouldn't have had the time. Conception to this degree amounts to virtually total pre-occupation with the reproductive function to the complete exclusion of anything else whatsoever. Let's put it in perspective. If only a quarter of the people in Britain conducted their affairs on the same steamy scale, we'd be talking of the world's biggest population outside of China, India and the Maracana Stadium in Rio. That's big. In fact, it's so big that Britain as we know it wouldn't exist. The additional weight would have meant the entire island sinking by around three hundred feet. And that is serious business indeed. For it would have meant every major ground in England other than those in the Pennines and Peak District becoming completely waterlogged. And that quite simply is why footy teams were never intended to all come from the same family and why being impure, especially on the scale we're talking about here, is such a sin.

Reflecting on my own circumstances with regard to this moral quagmire, I thanked God for small mercies that I had but one sister, yet I knew, instinctively, that I would never be able to view my parents in the same light, for they had let me down; and my sister too. They had also let themselves down and betrayed their faith. This was a hundred times worse than swapping clubs or even in later years secretly supporting Arsenal in a Cup Winners Cup Final. Their mortal sins had been of the very worst kind: impure by deed. I could hardly believe it.

My sole consolation was that all my Catholic friends were in exactly the same boat and so I was not alone in my shame. That, however, provided scant comfort and, once more my thoughts strayed to my fortunate Protestant friends and their easy path to eternity compared to ours. Once again, we had pulled the short straw. Once again, they had had it cushy: no mortal sins, no blackened souls, no eternal damnation, no tough away fixtures at Plough Lane. Basically, they could do whatever they wanted to do and it didn't matter. They could even play with themselves to their heart's content and still get to Heaven. It was as if they were almost guaranteed a home draw in every round of the Cup year after year – it was all so unfair.

Shame or no shame, there was still a major problem to be faced; both my parents were staring a relegation dog fight full in the face; they were on a downward path to oblivion, hurtling towards eternal damnation and Charlie the Evil One. To make matters worse, neither of them had been to Confession for years, certainly not since Roger Hunt had broken into Liverpool's first team, and so I was now faced with the dilemma of trying to persuade them to go to Confession and obtain forgiveness without alerting them to the fact that I knew of the terrible things they had done to each other. I would need all the stealth and guile of Jimmy Greaves and the silver tongue of Lawrie McMenemy if I was to accomplish my task. I tried dropping subtle hints . . .

"Eh mam, yer wanna see inside the confessional boxes now they've done them up. Thee look fantastic . . . dead smart . . . .they're like little palaces. Honest ter God, yer've gorra go an' see them."

"Yeah, okay Al, one of these days."

"An' the priests are great now, yer know, mam . . . they're hardly givin' out any Penances, especially Father Flynn . . . the most I've 'ad is one Hail Mary an' a Glory Be."

"Yer must 'ave been a good lad then son."

"No, no . . . it's not just me . . . Tommy reckons it's the same with everyone. His mam and dad went fer their Easter Duty an' thee didn't even gerran Our Father . . . 'e says it doesn't matter what yer've done."

"Do us a big favour, son . . . nip out for us fer some ciggies?"

My enthusiastic efforts were clearly falling on deaf ears and I eventually realised that, sooner rather than later, I would have to confront both of them to tell them I knew of their heinous sins. It was a daunting prospect especially for a young innocent like me but, if we were to stay together as a family in the next life, it was something I would just have to meet head on.

Looking back on it, it really was a tall order I was faced with. In those days children were there to be seen, not heard; talked at, not with; all ears, not mouths. Don't forget, this was pre-'Grange Hill' and light years away from the unexpurgated anarchy of all those precocious little self-opinionated monsters on 'Blockbusters'. Back then you just didn't get young kids telling adults anything at all, let alone how to conduct their lives. Even the remotest little ripple in a family's status quo was guaranteed to induce a shared apoplexy and as far as sex was concerned, well, quite simply, it didn't exist.

Suddenly, when it seemed things could get no worse, they did. Out of the blue, my mother stopped going to Mass. I never found out why; she just stopped. There was no hope for her now; if Big Charlie got hold of her then that would be it, – we would never ever see her soul again.

My poor little mind was demented. Okay, so maybe she had done "that" a couple of times, but she was still my mother and I still loved her more than anything or anyone except Bill Shankly and, around that time, possibly Alan A'Court too, and maybe Tommy Leishman as well, because of the way he ran out behind "Big Rowdy" and his trendy semi-crewcut. I simply could not bear the thought of never seeing her again, knowing she was stoking fires in Charlie's Inferno while the rest of us sat around in Heaven (for by now, as it happens, my father had gone to Confession several times). In fact, what was the point in us going to Heaven at all if she wasn't there – I would rather be in Hell with her than in Heaven without her.

I began to contemplate perpetrating some mortal sins of my own – missing Mass, pulling the pud even, to blacken my soul and elevate my own sinfulness to a parity with hers but fleeting images of Charlie and the eternal hot baths convinced me it was altogether more prudent to save her soul rather than damning my own. Besides, I had forgotten by then how to do such things having become so accustomed to playing the Arsenal way.

And so I tried other avenues. I pleaded with her, begged her to start going again. It was all to no avail. She refused outright, giving no reason for her stance except to say, "one of these days when yer a bit older yer might understand, son". Her mystical standpoint was of little use to me back then, though.

By this time I had become desperate, the pain I felt was unbearable. I can still feel it now. It was every bit as bad as when we'd missed out on promotion on goal average the previous year and that was the worst agony I'd ever known. Each night I would pray and pray for her to come back to the fold before crying my poor little self to sleep in the sheer heartache and terror of being parted from her for eternity. Each night, my pillow would become sodden with tears, as I would re-enact a performance to match that of the seventeen year old Pele when Brazil won the World Cup in Sweden in 1958. It was a pathetic sight; and so was I.

Then one Sunday a few months later, equally out of the blue, she got up early and went to Mass and the following week to Confession, Mass and Communion. She gave no reasons. She just came back; a redeemed, lapsed convert. My relief was immeasurable. I thanked God and once more slept soundly with dry eyes and pillow. For the second time in a matter of weeks my prayers had been answered (the previous week Liverpool had clinched the Second Division Championship, something for which I'd been praying since I first learned all about God and the possibilities of divine intervention). Quietly, I reflected to myself: some God, some Faith, some Prayers, some Team, some childhood.

Long term, all the religious oppression had a rather predictable effect. I simply longed to be like my mother's side of the family, who were all good, sound, easy going armchair Protestants with a simple homespun Red or Blue philosophy, a far less holy and committed bunch than my father's lot and far less hassle for a young lad, hell-bent on following football. Set against such an intimidating backdrop as boyhood Catholicism, anything would have seemed attractive and so, understandably, football became irresistible. My immersion into fandom came to be like a continuous free ride on the Pepsi Max Big Dipper at Blackpool Pleasure Beach, my encounters with Uncle Ebba and Aunty Kitty mere sojourns on a holiday cruise and my daily dose of football the drug for which I craved.

In the end, for me, there could be but one winner in the indoctrination stakes, and ultimately, I chose an earthly paradise of perpetual 'footy' for my spiritual path. Besides, if the truth be known, Charlie Hurley was always a bit on the slow side for my liking.

Of course, the fact that I personally was unable to find a compatible compromise between my two faiths does not carry any real significance apart, perhaps, from highlighting the inherent flaws in my own character. Indeed, many fans I know are perfectly content to combine a zealous love for both their God and their team, a resourcefulness which I applaud wholeheartedly. The same is also true of many footballers who have successfully combined both creeds and can be stoutly heralded as model Christians – "Parson' Jackson, Glen Hoddle, the entire playing staff down at Vicarage Road both past and present, and my own Uncle Tony, spring immediately to mind. I daresay as well that when that final whistle is about to blow I may well – if I get the opportunity – chicken out and invoke the old standby Bjornebye Again Christian escape route to the next life just in case my instinctive hunches have been wrong all along, which is, in truth, usually the case. Whichever road we follow though, whichever passion we pursue – religious, sporting or both – the outcome is usually the same. Once that passion enters your soul, it stays with you for ever. A bit like your vaccination mark, really.

My aunties and my mother-in-law are devout in their Faith. Week in week out they go to their masses or their services, and say their prayers and lavish their praises and then go home to watch their hymn singing and Harry Secombe on the box each of them the whole time harbouring a transfixion profound enough, in its own way, to match any footy maniac's addiction to the people's game. There will be no change of heart there.

And me? Well, with 45 years tucked under my belt since birth, I'm pretty certain that I, too, will always keep my Red Faith even if it did so happen that I did find something better with which to replace it though I must say, that's not exactly a likely occurrence at my age. There again, Wimbledon, remember, were once the most ghastly living thing on planet football yet look at them now – they actually pass the ball to one another – so you can never really be completely sure about anything, I guess. One thing is pretty clear, though, whichever way you look at it, you have to say neither fandom nor religion make for what you might call a balanced sort of existence. Certainly not in this life, at least. God knows about the next though. And if he doesn't, then I'm not sure who the hell does.

The school I attended in Seaport was Our Lady's Queen of the Mersey Catholic Junior School, a rambling mid-Victorian building which used to stand no more than thirty yards from our little terrace house. I use the term 'used to' because, like our house, it too was obliterated from the map by the Town Hall Planners, leaving the resultant debris strewn wilds of our little area of Seaport looking rather like the pitch at Filbert Street after a visit by football's own demolition squad of George Curtis, Maurice Setters and Noel Cantwell. (It was, you may recall, this gruesome Coventry threesome who in the late sixties reinvented the 'sliding tackle' to encompass the total destruction of any object above ground level, living or inanimate, together with the odd few below ground as well, and it would not be at all surprising to find they actually had some connection with the razing to the ground of the Seaport area. It certainly bore their hallmark of leaving absolutely nothing standing).

During my final two years at Queen of the Mersey, our teacher was Mr Bugler, a devout Catholic, who also ran the School Football team. Mr Bugler was, without doubt, the finest person in the history of teaching and although I feel he may have been stretching things a bit far with that submission, I can definitely see where he was coming from. After all, if you don't have faith in your own ability and perform your own Eddie Calvert impressions, no one else will, especially if you happen to be landed with a name like Bugler.

Cutting a marvellous, imposing figure, always smartly attired in light blue shirt, royal blue tie, royal blue short-sleeved V-neck pullover, navy blue slacks and long indigo blue socks, Mr Bugler stood around six feet tall and was undoubtedly of ex-Army or similarly disciplined background. Aged about mid-forties, he was supremely fit with a huge pigeon chest and black Brylcreemed hair, slightly greying at the temples, with a distinctive, precise side parting and a perfect quiff. He also had a prominent hooked nose with a convex bridge which, along with his pigeon chest, gave him a majestic, regal, Eric Cantona like appearance though unlike Eric, Mr Bugler was forever civil, courteous, pleasant and agreeable to all who approached him and to my knowledge, had never attacked a football crowd.

Mr Bugler was a bit of a star, very much the big fish in a little pond. He was also the type of man to whom any young boy would listen and give respect. You would willingly do anything Mr Bugler asked without so much as a second thought. He was the ideal teacher as far as we were concerned – the Matt Busby of the education world. And we were his babes.

Mr Bugler was also, as might be gleaned from his attire, an absolutely avid Evertonian. In fact, Mr Bugler was quite unlike any Evertonian I had encountered up to that time. Not that he had a tattoo of Alec Young on his forehead or anything like that though obviously I cannot vouch for the more remote parts of his anatomy – it was just that whereas most I had come across would carry a healthy and humorous dislike for

Liverpool, Mr Bugler absolutely hated anything to do with Liverpool Football Club. Although he would always maintain his assured dignity and would never lose control or show any outward signs of this deep rooted contempt, the more you were in his company, the more you became aware of the depth and intensity of his antagonism and rancorous feeling towards them. (And this, remember, was at a time when we were Second Division nobodies, posing scarcely a threat to anybody except ourselves. Quite how he was to feel years later, when the Reds were so successful hardly bears imagining. His anguish and suffering must have been unbearable when Emlyn Hughes lifted the European Cup in Rome. There again though, seeing as we now know only too well that Tommy Smith was probably feeling the same way about Emlyn's grinning gob maybe it didn't mean a great deal after all).

With all his deep blue angst and extreme anti-Redness, Mr Bugler just about completed the unbroken football chain which enveloped our little backwater. Along with Sam, the local police sergeant, a rabid Evertonian, Dr Melly, our local GP and a lifelong Red, Mr Heyworth who ran the local sweetshop and cafe and was a Blue, Mr Wilkins, the local dairyman, another Blue and Mr Jenkins, the local coal merchant, a Red, Mr Bugler represented to us youngsters the authoritarian face of the community. With all of them as equally steeped in the whole Red and Blue thing as everyone else, it meant we never actually had contact with anyone of any station who wasn't either a Liverpudlian or an Evertonian. As far as we were concerned it was the norm, the way it was; never could we have remotely envisaged a way of life without football at its core and without everyone obsessed with it and it was not to be until my late teens that I was to meet groups of people to whom football was an irrelevance – a culture shock from which I have never recovered and probably never will.

Stan Marsh was probably the first of this non-footy breed. He was around mid-thirties and had come up to Liverpool from Hampshire to work on the Seaport Dock Project where I worked as a trainee surveyor. Stan hated football but adored cars. If he saw me at the bus stop on his way to work, he used to pull in to give me a lift in his huge cobalt blue Rover Coupe and I'd swagger over, clamber inside and sink into its plush leather upholstery and then, as we drove off, give a sideways smirk at all the other poor sods still waiting at the bus stop in the cold and rain.

Then, one day, he came in his pride and joy – a dinky little black vintage Austin Seven – and pulled in as usual. Now, whatever it may have done for Stan, to me, the love of Stan's life just looked silly as did Stan, sat there in his little dinky car, bolt upright like he had a corner

n the back of his coat. Naturally, I cringed and at first
dn't seen him. I had my street cred rating to consider after
vever, was not into street cred. He casually leaned across
the door. "Come on then, dozy bollocks . . . hop in!" he
ly alerting all and sundry and leaving me no choice but to do
ed. Sheepishly I got in. Everyone at the bus stop was laughing.
me. I was bright red and prayed desperately that none of my
noticed me.

an, meanwhile, proceeded to experience what can only be termed a
otor maniac's orgasm as we chugged embarrassingly along Crosby
Road South in his little paradise on wheels; Stan, in his massive
sheepskin coat with a smug grin as wide as his windscreen, fixed in
permanent mode below his sunglasses and tweed cap; me sinking as low
down into the seat as it was possible to go. Stan, in his own dinky little
way was, of course, simply basking in the glory of a last minute winner
at Wembley in the FA Cup Final, savouring every moment of his lap of
honour along Crosby Road South. And why shouldn't he? He paid his
road tax like everyone else. To me, in contrast, the whole experience was
like being at a crappy Zenith Data First Round second leg cup tie
between Rochdale and Darlington at Spotland Road in torrential rain
at which even Bill Shankly would cock up his nose. In fact, it probably
wasn't that good. Stan, though, understandably, was naively oblivious
to one of the fundamental hotbed realities – namely being in the Zenith
Data is nothing to be smug about unless, that is, you happen to relish
being ridiculed.

Stan went on to complete a three year missionary stint up North,
before thanking God for the M6 and going back down South. I'm pretty
sure that during his time here not once did he ever figure out my enthusiasm for a ball nor my indifference to vintage cars. The significance
escaped him. It always would. I could figure it, though. Quite easily. The
thing was we never grew up with cars. They were never part of our
culture. The way I saw it, if people were meant to have cars, then why did
they bother to invent buses and trains. It wasn't logical. In any case,
nobody by us had a car; they were only for people with money. Everyone
I knew, however, had flat caps and balls of one sort or another. They
came with the territory. I, therefore, was simply following my natural
inclinations. Stan, for his part, was following his. We were just different
vintages. In view of all this, it is hardly surprising that the vagaries of a
community so seamlessly football crazy as ours were lost on someone like
Stan. He was coming from an entirely different direction and would
never have connected even if he had lived as long as one of his cars.

Stan's imperviousness to the spirit of footy was inevitable. So was the fact that anywhere as obsessed with the game as Liverpool was destined to produce youngsters just as besotted. It was guaranteed; like night following day or Nobby Stiles following Eusebio. The only thing that remained in question was which colour those kids would opt for, and like everyone else, the Mr Buglers of this world were naturally to have a say in that.

In spite of his Blue fanaticism, Mr Bugler's objectives at Queen of the Mersey were ostensibly as honourable as those of any other responsible schoolmaster in his position, namely the provision of a good education for his pupils and, of course, the creation of a winning school football team.

The first of these objectives, viewed strictly from an eleven-plus angle, was hardly a rip-roaring success. During our four years in the Junior Boys, the school averaged one eleven-plus pass every two years, which meant two boys out of about a hundred and seventy actually managed to qualify to go on to grammar school. The girls fared more successfully but it would be difficult to sustain an argument that the school was Seaport's answer to Eton Prep School and, however much we loved it, I have to admit, Queen of the Mersey was certainly no seat of academic excellence; when it came to sums and the like, we were Beazer Homes Reserve League.

As it happened, all this academic palaver mattered not one jot. It was hardly even noticed. Nobody, in fact, so much as blinked an eyelid. This was because, in Mr Bugler's second, far more important objective, he was getting perilously close to achieving success. On the football field, the scent of football glory was beginning to stimulate the taste buds of all concerned and this, quite understandably, as those who appreciate such things will know, was to prove sufficient distraction to any of the calamities which may have been taking place in the classroom. As ever, football came first.

It was well known throughout the school that Mr Bugler had been toying for some time with the idea of a youth policy along the lines of the Busby Babes. In 1959 when we were in the second year Juniors he decided it was time to enact, in earnest, his master plan. His goal was to capture the 1961-2 Seaport and District Schools Junior West Championship, three years later. To achieve this, the team needed to finish above arch rivals, St Edgar's, who were always champions while we were invariably runners-up. So, in a constructive and concerted effort to remove our massive inferiority complex to St Edgar's and to reverse the final league table positions, he decided to opt for youth formally revealing to us his gamble for the future . . .

"You will all be aware that we at Queen of the Mersey have tried unsuccessfully for almost a decade to bring home to the school the Junior West Championship. Whilst success is not the be all and end all of sport, nevertheless, it has evaded us at Queen of the Mersey for far too long. Consequently, things are about to change. This year we are introducing a youth policy into the school football team. It will be radical. It will be sweeping. It will mean that current third and fourth year pupils will no longer be selected for the school team. It is something that we know is highly regrettable but we believe it to be an absolute necessity if Queen of the Mersey is to achieve the success we all seek."

Everyone listened, silent and open-mouthed, as the extent of the drastic measures Mr Bugler was proposing began to filter through. In a single ruthless stroke of sporting enlightenment the entire chunk of the team comprising the old guard had been sacrificed for the good of the school; ten and eleven year old boys, over-the-hill has-beens, had paid the price and had been unavoidably discarded onto the scrap heap, replaced by eight and nine year old 'Bugler's Babes', myself included. It was revolutionary stuff indeed; certainly unprecedented in the history of Seaport Schools Football, maybe even all Schools Football, and epitomised the sort of ruthless professionalism displayed by all the truly great managers down the years; an innovation of which, despite its rather harsh treatment of the poor rejects, I am sure even the great Matt Busby himself would have been proud.

Actually I'm not altogether sure if I've got that last point exactly right. Certainly Sir Matt would have warmed to the positive aspects of such a youth policy. After all, he'd done the same thing himself so many times over the years. I doubt, though, whether even Sir Matt would have possessed that added dimension to his character necessary to dump a whole team of redundant ten and eleven year olds into the waste bin without batting an eyelid. To do that for the sake of some higher honour takes someone really special, someone unique and apart from the fray. Someone in fact like Mr Bugler, whose display of single minded foresight and courage at Queen of the Mersey that year, has surely only ever been matched throughout history by born leaders of the calibre of Julius Caesar, Napoleon, Churchill and Remi Moses. To mention Mr Bugler in anything other than such exalted company would be tantamount to insult and Mr Bugler was one of those people whom you never insulted.

Needless to say we did not record much success in the first year of Mr

Bugler's extreme youth policy. In fact, we did not win a single game. This was hardly surprising since, firstly we could hardly run because our kits were too big – we looked like eleven pint-sized Brian Flynns doing Demis Roussos impressions -and secondly, at that age, the two or three year gap reflected amazingly pronounced physical disparities. Despite all our best efforts, most of the time, we were slaughtered.

Regardless of the poor results, Mr Bugler, very much his own man, duly persevered with his 'Babes' with the result that, the second year of his policy was altogether more fruitful. A full year's growth and a corresponding improved mental maturity, meant we were no longer so spindly nor such pushovers. We were also, by then, clearly identifiable as players, no longer merely tiny ferrets scrambling around in huge sacks. The opposition now showed us some respect. Our superior skills did the rest and we duly finished as runners up. Once more, St Edgar's were the champions, but, by this time, Mr Bugler had really got the bit between his teeth and so had we. The following season, 1961-62, was to belong to him and us too. At last we were ready to answer Mr Bugler's call.

During that marvellous unforgettable season, the culmination of Mr Bugler's vision of extreme youth, we were unbeatable. Played 14, won 14, Goals for: 108, Goals against: 6. We were all, by then, ten or eleven year old seasoned veterans, with at least two years big match experience tucked under our belts; wily old campaigners, well versed in all the most important football skills – diving in the box to win a penalty, use of the elbow, time-wasting, professional fouls, the lot. St Edgar's and the other schools were at our mercy; they never stood a chance.

The remarkable thing about it was how far ahead of the times we were. Prior to 1961 there had always been the tough nuts, of course – Jimmy Scoular, Tommy Docherty, Roy Hartle, Skinner Normington, not to mention the Scunthorpe United pair of Edward G Robinson and Jack Palance – but they were all from the hard but fair brigade. We, on the other hand were straight out of the Leeds United school of cold eyed cynicism – yet, amazingly, we were doing our party pieces fully five years before Leeds had even begun to think about them. It was innovation on a grand scale and when viewed alongside the uniqueness of the actual youth policy itself, it makes you wonder just what was really going on in our little corner of Liverpool in the early sixties. Perhaps only Mr Bugler will ever know the truth.

Meanwhile, the man himself could scarcely contain his delight at our success. Fixtures could not come quickly enough for him. He knew we would win every game and easily, too. His star player, 'Amo', saw to that. A diminutive figure, by far the smallest in our side, Amo was gifted beyond all reasonableness, in all aspects of the game; perfectly balanced with whippet-like pace, a mazy dribbler with Bostik-like ball control, an intuitive goal scorer, always with time and space and a lethal shot with either foot. All in all, he was a manager's dream.

Amo also happened to be our main tactic, which would essentially consist of one of us giving the ball to him and then the rest of the team and Mr Bugler standing back and cheering as he would dribble mazily around the entire opposition defence to score. I think that year he scored something like ninety eight of our one hundred and eight goals and made the other ten, including a hat trick in our final game of the season against St Edgars.

Amo eventually went on to sign for Bolton Wanderers. He never made it, though, for he peaked far too early. Sadly that was often the case in those days. Another mate of mine – Georgie Proctor – did the same with Stockport County where they tried to groom him as a centre half, which would have been a sound idea if only Georgie had been able to tackle or head the ball as well as he did everything else. Our biggest local claim to fame was Tony Coleman – the forgotten and unsung left wing hero of the great late-sixties Manchester City team. Tony actually went out with Anita, my cousin's cousin which by implication, I suppose, made me a bit of a mini local celebrity; or at least it would have done if only Anita had managed just once to provide some sign of acknowledgement of my status instead of simply ignoring me every time I waved to her in my attempts at convincing my mates that we were related. Mind you I dare say it might also have helped if she had actually known the identity of the idiot who was always trying to attract her attention. Still, it could have been worse. It was rumoured one of her earlier boyfriends was Paul McCartney, so just imagine the trouble I'd have had touting that bit of reflected limelight if their relationship had blossomed. Fortunately, as Ringo once told me (that's my old mate Ringo Walters by the way, not the one on the drums), Paul couldn't kick a ball to save his life so not surprisingly Anita backheeled him for Tony Coleman and saved me the ignominy of persuading my mates I was related to a Beatle.

Regardless of Bolton Wanderer's judgement, or lack of it, in their eventual rejection of him, it was inarguable that Amo had proved to be our hero in our year of triumph. Yet, as outstanding as Amo's contribution might have been, there was, however, little doubting what really lay behind our success. Quite clearly everything had been down to the revolutionary genius and innovation of Mr Bugler's extreme youth policy. Without Mr Bugler, there would have been no Amo and certainly no championship. For all Amo's undoubted brilliance, it was Mr Bugler who had become the school's saviour; he was the real champion.

Needless to say, the team's triumph was greeted by scenes of euphoria back at the school. It had been twelve years since the school's last success and so everybody, no matter how remote their connection, was determined to milk every last fluid ounce of elation from the victory. Staff, pupils, parents, dinner ladies, Mr Bugler's goldfish, the school cockroaches, in fact, the entire neighbourhood basked and revelled with untold pride and joy in the glory we had bestowed on the school and the area. A new era, a golden age, was dawning for Queen of the Mersey and for us, too. Mr Cane, the headmaster, was so delighted he decided that there would be an official presentation to the team at the school assembly, with a special award to mark Mr Bugler's achievement. It was a momentous occasion for us all.

As we stood, embarrassed but proud, on the podium in front of the rest of the school to receive the trophy and our Green Certificates of Merit, Mr Bugler, with stirring enthusiasm and resolve, spoke for every one of us:

"Let us regard this as the beginning of a long and successful domination of the League by Queen of the Mersey. There is no end to what we can now go on to achieve . . . "

His words were drowned by loud, exultant cheers and rapturous applause as all present celebrated and rejoiced in the long awaited turning of the tide. Even Mr Cane clapped enthusiastically. Mr Bugler, displaying the right balance of pride, dignity and modesty, rightly soaked up the acclaim. We all did. The future was rosy. Academic worries were a million miles away.

The following season, sadly, Queen of the Mersey finished bottom of the league. Amidst all the euphoria, everyone, particularly Mr Bugler himself, had forgotten the fundamental flaw in his three year vision. This was the local Secondary Modern School, St Wilbur's, which, at the end of every three year cycle, would snatch Mr Bugler's Babes, by then too old for Junior School, from their cradle at Queen of the Mersey, leaving poor Mr Bugler without a team and with the task of having to start all over again from scratch.

Mr Bugler's extreme youth policy had undoubtedly been revolutionary and innovative. Unfortunately, it had also been a mite short-sighted and short term. A triennial success story, in fact. Sir Matt Busby never encountered these problems with his youth policy. The odd transfer bid or bout of homesickness maybe – but losing your entire team to St Wilbur's Secondary Modern? Who'd be a football manager?

I am compelled to say all these years later that, despite all his marvellous qualities, there was a more sinister side to Mr Bugler. He had, buried deep within him, an insidious third objective. It was a mission, his own personal crusade, implicit in his every utterance, his every nuance and more deadly than one of Amo's upfield runs.

His mission, to put it quite simply, was to convert every single Liverpudlian in his class into an Evertonian, thereby creating the only one hundred per cent Evertonian class of boys on Merseyside – in the world, even. It was a formidable task, impossible to most, but one that Mr Bugler, with all his outstanding qualities, was only too capable of achieving.

As any football loyalist will know, the age of 9 to 11 is a critical phase in the development of any budding fan. It is a period when team loyalties, only recently developed, are delicately balanced and extremely vulnerable to outside influences which have the capability to sway them one way or the other. The persuasive attempts of family and friends to change those allegiances are one thing and most times can be readily dealt with. The pressure from someone in authority, particularly someone so influential and respected as Mr Bugler presents, however, quite a different proposition altogether and many young fans have lost their faith and fallen by the wayside under such stress.

In this regard you only have to look at those Evertonians turned Reds whom I have previously highlighted – Steve McManaman and Robbie Fowler – to appreciate how readily such a transformation can occur. Now I know they were slightly older and I know, even at this stage, they could quite easily revert back to their true blue colours. When you think of the pressures they underwent, though, it isn't difficult to understand why they changed from Blue to Red. I mean is there anyone anywhere who, subject to a daily verbal bombardment from a raging Ronnie Moran, would not bow to such intimidation; why even Charlie Hurley himself used to wince at the prospect of a head-to-head with Ronnie. So amidst such pressures as inflicted by the likes of Ronnie, the changing of colours loses much of the stigma it might otherwise deserve, in slightly less menacing circumstances.

Though undoubtedly less volatile, our own experience with Mr Bugler mirrored in principle, at least, that of the young Reds players' battle of wills with Ronnie Moran and the strength of our allegiance to the Reds would, in due course, undergo its most stringent examination at Mr Bugler's hands and charms. It was to be intimidation on a scale we could have scarcely imagined, and would make my own earlier brushes with Aunty Kitty and Ebba Murphy seem like teddy bear picnics. So much so, I would come to respect and admire tangibly the courage of the Catholic martyrs who, at pain of death, refused to renounce their faith.

Mr Bugler's methods to achieve his goal were relentless, though quite often covert and imperceptible. He employed a form of psychological warfare, at times subtle and mild, at other times rather more explicit; at all times persuasive and convincing. He applied the greatest pressure upon the Red faction of the football team, Amo and myself being his prime targets. If he could capture the captain and vice-captain of the football team, the remaining Reds would no doubt capitulate. The battle for our souls was about to commence in earnest.

His initial forays and skirmishes consisted of disarming tactics designed to prompt doubts about the sense of remaining loyal to the Reds. In these sorties, he would use to great advantage the remarkable hold he had on us, knowing full well we would always agree with him. He would support this with an irresistible tide of logic, rationally informing us of the sound common-sense for supporting Everton. The strength of his conviction meant there were times when he offered merely the flimsiest pretence of a routine school lesson to camouflage an underlying tirade of blatant Evertonian propaganda . . .

"Today, lads, we're going to look at some interesting facts surrounding our city's two leading football clubs . . . to see, perhaps, if we can unearth some worthwhile conclusions about our two teams . . . It's a sort of local history lesson – quite an important one, too, as it happens. To help us with our task, I've prepared some hand-out sheets which you can refer to as we go through all the facts . . . take one each and pass the rest on.

"Okay, let's start at the top of page one and work our way down the list . . . we'll discuss each aspect in more detail later . . . right then, first and foremost, the mighty . . . er . . . Everton are a first division side . . . Liverpool, meanwhile, are very much a second division side and have been for quite a few years now . . . Everton are universally acknowledged as a better side than Liverpool . . . Everton were the original side in the city, going by the title of St Domingos and still retain their links with the past – this, incidentally, is a fine example of how to preserve your noble traditions and heritage while still managing to rise with dignity to the challenges of the modern sporting world – remember that one lads, it's important for there isn't another team in the land which has managed to do the same . . . .with typical generous spirit, Everton gave Anfield, their original ground, to Liverpool in 1892 – incidentally, lads, another point to note in this context, Liverpool have never given . . . er

. . . Everton anything at all . . . Goodison Park was the first major purpose-built football stadium in England . . . Goodison Park is a much bigger and better stadium than Anfield . . . Goodison Park has huge double tier stands on all four sides while Anfield has two smallish single tier stands . . . Goodison Park has giant latticed steel floodlight pylons – incidentally, lads, some airline pilots reckon they are so high they interfere with flight paths – Anfield has tiny concrete pillars supporting its floodlights – and again, lads, on this point it's important to note that they are not visible above the surrounding roof-tops, contrary to what some . . . er . . . Liverpudlians would have you believe . . . as you'd expect, Everton have a greater support than Liverpool, both on Merseyside and throughout the land and also, as you would also expect, in Ireland with its strong moral and religious traditions . . .

"Everton also have a higher record attendance – 78,299 as against Liverpool's 61905 . . . we . . . er . . . Everton have twice lifted the FA Cup while Liverpool have never done so . . . Everton are nicknamed 'the millionaires' and they are a far richer club than Liverpool and pay far greater transfer fees than Liverpool – by the way, lads, this also accounts for why Everton sign far better footballers than Liverpool . . . Everton are renowned as 'the School of Science' while Liverpool lack any corresponding title . . . Everton teams are celebrated for playing skilful, attractive football while Liverpool are known for more of a 'kick and rush' style of play . . . Everton hold the League's scoring record with the great Dixie Dean's sixty goals in one season . . . Everton's training ground at Bellefield is acclaimed as the best in the business along with Spurs and Burnley . . . Liverpool's training ground at Melwood is quite near to Everton's . . . geographically speaking, that is . . . most people prefer Everton's football kit to Liverpool's.

"Right, lads, I think that's probably enough to be going on with. Certainly for what we're attempting to do. Now, can anyone tell me this . . . say, a complete stranger came to Liverpool . . . let's say for argument's sake, a Martian, and somebody gave him all these facts about our two football teams . . . which team do you think our Martian friend would choose to watch – let's assume, of course, that he's a Martian with a reasonable amount of common sense and good sound moral values – perhaps even a Catholic Martian – and also one who has got a fair knowledge of what football is all about . . . in other words, he's certainly not daft or stupid or a complete heathen . . . anyway . . . let's see . . . Amo – you tell the rest of us what you think . . . "

Now, in the face of this bombardment it was hardly likely that Amo's answer was ever going to be what you would term 'difficult' to predict. In fact, it was an answer that would have been blindingly obvious to even the most rabid Red and, certainly, the Man from Mars, no matter how green he might have been about football or anything else, would have encountered little problem at all in selecting the best season ticket value on offer. Indeed, there may be those who find it hard to understand why, in the face of such sound logic for turning Blue, all Liverpudlians at the time and, in particular, vulnerable kids like myself, did not turn to Everton. In the event, as any true fan will know only too well, the strength of such arguments in themselves didn't present us with even the slightest problem. We had heard them all before and, even at our tender age, had learned to develop a tough outer shell against such forms of propaganda.

Ironically, although it didn't help us one iota back then, for the past twenty odd years – since the early Seventies and Shankly's second great side – the football boot has been firmly on the other foot and it has been the young Blues who have needed to withstand and reject constant Red attempts at brainwashing, for while Everton have enjoyed sporadic success during this time, the Reds have become synonymous with the word. Meanwhile, as we all know only too well, throughout the rest of the country, every fan has had to learn to stand firm against the remorseless Man United bandwagon hype which, I'm led to understand, has now even penetrated the final frontier of the people's game – the Royal Family.

Away from Buckingham Palace, the real problem we faced in maintaining our resistance to turning Blue lay with the person delivering the logic, for Mr Bugler had a silver tongue. Not for him the ranting or raving to which we were accustomed. Not for him the joking or leg-pulling of our families and friends. Mr Bugler relied on a different approach altogether – verbal seduction. His soothing yet authoritative voice first coaxed then convinced and then completely intoxicated us. As we stood mesmerised, his enticing tones enveloped us, tugging us gently, but surely, towards the precipice of a blue abyss. He was a sorcerer weaving a magic spell; a male siren luring us towards rocky blue shores. And finally, all his sophistry and chicanery began to work on us. Bewitched and beguiled, we young Reds yearned to please him.

As he would wobble up to the school gates each morning on his black "sit-up and beg" push bike (in those days, even Mr Buglers still rode bicycles), we would duly flock around him, admiring his dazzling royal blue bike clips and craving the acceptance and the pat on the back or the arm around the shoulders with which we knew he would reciprocate if we were to tell him we had changed our faith and become Blues. His wily ploys had every Red in the class, by then, standing on the very edge of the cliff he had created with only the strength of our Red faith preventing us from plummeting headlong into the deep blue darkness wherein he waited to greet us. And even this was not the end of our torment, for Mr Bugler had still to play his trump card. If we were to manage to hold out against his ultimate subterfuge, it would indeed be a miracle.

Until Mr Bugler, casually and effortlessly, dropped it into one of his enticing monologues about the Blues, none of us had ever heard of any connection between Everton and the Roman Catholic Church nor Liverpool and the Protestant Church. Sure, there had been hints of Everton retaining some links with their religious origins but certainly nothing like this. Nonchalantly, he had supported his statement with the observation that all three parish priests were keen Evertonians, as was Archbishop Heenan. He had even hinted at a link between Everton and Pope Pious.

Now, like every other budding fan, we were all familiar with the Rangers and Celtic religious connotations in Scotland, but never Liverpool or Everton. This was serious fare indeed, not easily dismissed. Our little Catholic consciences, already heavily overburdened with the horrors of mortal sin and the dread of the eternal fires of Hell with which we were brainwashed on a daily basis, began to work overtime. One apparently throwaway remark from Mr Bugler, supported by a subtle disapproving sideways glance at the Liverpudlian contingent in his class, had been more than enough for a seed of doubt to germinate in our minds and grow as fast and large as a Valderama perm.

We asked questions when we got home. The answers confirmed what Mr Bugler had seemingly innocuously told us. Everton was indeed regarded as a Catholic club and Liverpool a Protestant one. Inevitably, we jumped to other conclusions: Our Lady was always in blue and white; the school football colours were to become blue and white; the parish priests, the Archbishop and the Pope were all Blues; probably even our Guardian Angels were Blues. Everything fell into place. All Catholics should be Blues including us. We were in turmoil. Perhaps it was a sin to support Liverpool and not Everton; maybe a mortal sin or even a sacrilege. Maybe supporting the Reds was worse even than missing Mass or being impure. Our shame was complete; our consciences were racked as we succumbed to Mr Bugler's Joker – good old Roman Catholic guilt. Only this was no joke to us. This was life or death. In fact, it was more – it was Supernatural Life Ever After and we all knew only too well the consequence – an eternal hot bath with Charlie Hurley.

It is true time ultimately enables Catholic boys to shake off many of their guilt complexes but, as I have already mentioned, when it has a firm hold, Roman Catholic guilt, particularly in a young boy, possesses sufficient potency to sway the most resolute of minds. There was no escape route; we were Catholics so we would have to renounce our Red faith and become Blues. We all prayed to St Jude, the Patron Saint of Lost Causes, in a final, desperate bid to hang on to our Red faith but knew deep down our Redness had come to an end.

God works in mysterious ways.

Around this time, the school was visited by an African missionary, Father Scragg, who was said to be originally from around the Everton area of the city. Our headmaster, Mr Cane, who, incidentally, possessed the most apt name I've ever known, had prepared us in advance for his talk, informing us that he was one of the Church's leading missionaries and highly respected throughout the Catholic hierarchy. It was rumoured, he told us, that he had even met the Pope. Needless to say, our aching Red hearts sank. The screws were being tightened even more. Even Mr Cane, a far less passionate Evertonian than Mr Bugler, was in on our conversion.

I remember Father Scragg distinctly for two reasons. The first involved a puzzle he gave us to attempt. It was to join nine dots with four straight lines without taking the pencil off the paper and none of us could do it. It involved lateral thinking. Besides, we young Reds had far weightier problems on our tiny, guilt-ridden minds.

The second reason I remember him was far closer to our hearts: Father Scragg, devout Catholic, famous missionary and friend of the Pope, was also a Liverpudlian; a passionate Red; a fervent Kopite. We couldn't believe our luck. Our relief was immeasurable. Audible sighs welled up from deep inside every Red. Huge, beaming Emlyn Hughes smiles broke out on previously glum faces as our pent-up guilt evaporated in an instant. Cheers and applause from all of us echoed around the classroom. Father Scragg seemed pleased, though rather bemused at the euphoric intensity of our reaction.

Mr Bugler, meanwhile, just grimaced, thwarted by divine intervention. He would have to try again the following year with a new batch of Liverpudlians. Knowing him, I am sure, he would be successful. He was, after all, Everton's finest ever missionary, though no match for Father Scragg. There again, would anyone have been. After all, Father Scragg did know the Pope and there aren't many from Liverpool who can say that. Not even Mr Bugler.

Fittingly for such an esteemed teacher, Mr Bugler had still managed, despite all that had gone awry, to provide his pupils with a valuable lesson, one that would always stand us in good stead as football fans. Through his failure to influence our destiny as budding football fans, we were all now aware of a basic fact of life: if Mr Bugler could get things wrong then so could anyone. We were as entitled to our opinions on football as anyone. Such opinions, as we were to find out in later years, were pivotal to fandom; who was the best, who was the worst – teams, players, formations, managers, crowds, wingers, strikers, goalies. Everyone could have an opinion and everyone could be an expert. Just as expert, in fact, as Alan Hansen or Andy Gray, only more biased than they could ever be. And the beauty of it all is that we don't have to don a designer suit and hideous tie. We just flop on the couch with a few cans and a packet of crisps and spout as much garbage as the pundits do. And to think the lot of it is down to Mr Bugler – definitely a star and years ahead of his time. A bit like Martin Peters.

Confirmation of the divine aspect of the intervention to preserve our Redness was to arrive at the six o'clock Mass, at which I was serving as an altar boy the morning after Father Scragg's visit.

The Mass, which in those unenlightened pre-ecumenical times was said entirely in Latin, had proceeded that morning in the uneventful fashion that was the norm, with Father Browney, the slight, bespectacled parish priest, conducting it and delivering his recitals in typically accomplished manner and myself and my fellow acolyte, Tommy O'Neil, who, as it happened, was also my best friend at the time and later best man at my wedding, performing our duties and spouting our responses with commendable alertness and aplomb, given the depth of our bleary-eyed stupor at that unearthly hour. The service had reached the Canon, the central core of the Mass, which is performed, for the most part, independently of the altar boys, by the priest and which even at its most stimulating, would be a valuable cure for insomnia.

The congregation in the church that morning barely filled the first two rows of pews and consisted of a dozen or so nuns from the nearby convent, plus a further half dozen other faithful female souls, all of whom were familiar faces at this particular time Mass. I knelt on the altar steps immediately behind and to the right of Father Browney. Tommy knelt on the opposite side of the altar steps, to Father Browney's left.

The vast, virtually empty church was, as ever at this point, eerily silent save for the monotonous, barely discernible murmurings of Father Browney reading from the Canon Liturgies. As he pressed on with his whispered intonations, I was suddenly aroused from my inevitable steadily enveloping lethargy as I became aware of a different sound permeating from what seemed to be above and behind the altarpiece pinnacle. As it grew noticeably louder, I glanced upwards towards its apparent source and then across at Tommy and Father Browney. If they were aware of the sound, which by then was becoming increasingly distinct and clear to me, they were certainly displaying no outward sign of acknowledging it.

I was, by now, able to clearly distinguish it as the strains of a choir, albeit like no choir I had heard before that day, nor indeed ever since, for it was quite the sweetest, most beautiful and melodic sound imaginable; an exquisite, lilting refrain delivered by voices of matchless quality in sublime harmony. There was little doubt in my mind that I was listening to a heavenly chorus. Truly a choir of angels. The entire performance spanned no more than a minute or so and then, as quickly as it had arisen, it faded and was gone.

Back in the Sacristy after Mass, I cautiously quizzed Tommy and Father Browney about what had happened, though taking care not to disclose the precise nature of my own experiences, in case they thought I was mad and explaining away my ashened complexion as a sick headache. Neither, evidently, had heard a sound during the Canon.

Later, Father Browney gave me a lift home on the rear seat of his push-bike so concerned was he at my deathly colour. I kept the incident to myself and did not relate it to a soul until years later, by which time I had eventually lost my sense of fear at what I had heard that day and could laugh it off.

So what had I heard? What was the divine interlude of music from on high that only I had been privileged to witness? Had it all happened or was it all my imagination brought on by the previous day's excitement and too many early mornings? Had some of the other priests and nuns been impersonating Julie Andrews and her kids in the bath? Had Julio Iglesias wandered inadvertently into the Sacristy or was he still playing in goal for Stockport County's reserves? I don't suppose I will ever know the answer. Some, I dare say, may consider it a form of divine revelation or manifestation. Others, maybe, a divine calling from the Almighty to enter into holy orders and the priesthood, or even to follow Father Scragg on his mission to darkest Africa. I prefer to believe now all these years later, that it was simply, in fact, a complete vindication of the Redness of my faith – a heavenly sign and seal of approval that my indoctrination was complete.

When all is said and done, could the miracle of Queen of the Mersey really, in all honesty, have been anything else as far as any self-respecting football-crazy lunatic is concerned? I mean, the only other time I can ever recall anything remotely as miraculous happening was many years later on the 'Midweek Match' when Hugh Johns actually got a player's name right in his commentary, so it's not as if I'm the sort who goes round jumping to weird conclusions about such things.

All in all then, I think it's probably a safe assumption to make that what I believe I heard did actually happen and that likely as not it was simply God's way of giving me a sign, and I'm sure if most fans think hard and long enough, they too will be able to recall something similar happening to them. After all, most of us really do think we're God's chosen people, so convictions as strong as that must originate from somewhere.

Despite the horrors of the boys' pen and the nightmare of a Catholic childhood, not least my exposure at the altar to celestial phenomena and having to serve mass every morning at a time suited to enmasked stripe-jerseyed burglars and milkmen but certainly not budding football fanatics, our daily itinerary by this time was approaching blissfulness. Kicking a ball and playing would occupy centre stage and take up the maximum amount of time possible; Saturday afternoons would be spent watching our Red heroes or the Reserves, and any other spare time would be devoted to swapping football cards or devouring every statistic and photo in Charles Buchan's Football Monthly or savouring the comic adventures of 'Limpalong Leslie' in 'The Victor', 'Legge's Eleven' in the 'Valiant' and Roy Race, Blackie Grey and Tubby Morton in the 'Tiger'.

Sadly, although we did also manage to squeeze in games of 'shove 'apenny', blow football, 'Shoot' and, when we were old enough for the pub, table football, we were a few years too early to sample the untold joys of 'Subbuteo' and it was not to be until the age of thirty that I was to find out that life was really about gingerly flicking your finger at a miniature plastic weeble. It is a deprivation I would rather not dwell on, for if I'm realistic, it probably accounts more than anything else for most of my shortcomings in adult life. But more of those later.

Then there were our dreams.

In dreams, anything is possible – out-heading John Charles, out-dribbling Len Shackleton, out-passing Jim Baxter, out-tackling Dave Mackay, even, if we were lucky enough in our later years, out-scoring George Best (on the pitch, naturally). Night-long slumbers, mealtimes, morning Mass, school lessons, trips between house/church/school/shops – all would be spent in football fantasy land as an exquisite pass was threaded through a crowded midfield or a thirty yard screamer driven into the top corner of the net past the outstretched fingertips of a despairing 'keeper. Not even TV heroes of the magnitude of Robin Hood, the Lone Ranger, Hopalong Cassidy and Rin Tin Tin could break the stranglehold of footy – even in slumberland.

Some dreams were obvious and predictable, like the recurring one where you come out of the crowd at Wembley in the Cup Final in May to snatch a late winner. Others were plain silly but still kept recurring.

It's a Derby match and the Reds are outclassed and 2-0 down at half time with the Blues in total control. Things look desperate. Myself, Amo and a few others climb over the railings of the boys' pen (obviously somebody must have reduced them in height or given us climbing lessons) down into the Kop and onto the cinder running track behind the goal to lead the Kop in deafening choruses of "two-four-six-eight who do we appreciate" and "one-two-three and a quarter who d'yer think we're gonna slaughter". The Reds players, inspired by such unprecedented vocal support never before heard at a football match, fight back valiantly to win 3-2. At the final whistle, we are carried shoulder high around the ground by the fans and players alike, heroes of the day.

Needless to say, the dream was a good few years before the emergence of the Kop Choir in the early sixties and while no one can dispute that the principle of the idea was certainly sound and, as subsequent events were to prove, visionary even, it has to be said the content was . . . well, let's just say that the notion of a bunch of snotty nosed kids leading 28,000 hairy arsed dockers in the chant of 'two-four-six . . . ' is hardly the stuff of Kop legend. I mean, even the sheer purgatory of an hour long 'Alec Ferguson's red and white army' chant would be preferable . . . maybe not, though.

Some dreams can turn out to be more like nightmares. We are at school the day after the 1960 European Cup Final at Hampden Park between Real Madrid and Eintracht Frankfurt. During the game, Mr Bugler has seen a manoeuvre carried out to perfection by the great European Champions which, in his infinite tactical wisdom – and who dare question it – he considers we are somehow capable of recreating against our arch rivals, St Edgars, in a crucial Junior West Championship decider at Brooke Vale Municipal Playing Fields, Seaport. The worst of it is, he wants it to involve yours truly in an attempt to emulate the great Santa Maria of Real Madrid, who, receiving the ball straight from the kick off, juggles with it momentarily with consummate skill and poise, before delivering an inch perfect chip over the opposing right back for the winger Francisco Gento to run onto. Amo is to be Francisco Gento. The main problem with enacting the move is, of course, that I am not Santa Maria. For a start, I'm not Spanish and don't like girlie names; and for another, I'm basically crap; it would also have helped if my dream legs had not been like lead and I had been physically capable of kicking the ball even half the distance it needed to go. Suffice it to say, the burden of fulfilling Mr Bugler's expectations weighs heavily on my bony little shoulders.

As is the usual case with dreams, the moment of truth never hangs around waiting for long and so, true to form, in this one the morning of the game arrives all too quickly – within a few snores, in fact . As we gather in the changing rooms prior to kick-off, Mr Bugler delivers his usual "Queen of the Mersey expects every boy to do his duty" speech before individually checking with both myself and Amo that we know precisely what we have to do for the manoeuvre. I gulp. Any slim hopes I have up to then retained of Mr Bugler perhaps forgetting about the plan evaporate at that precise moment. Fatally, as he looks me in the eyes, I feign the outward calm and assurance of someone capable of achieving what is expected and nod in the dutiful manner he both invites and expects. That nod has taken me past the point of no return. There is no going back. My pretence means that I have forfeited any prospect of being excused from my assignment and so I now have to fulfil my duty.

In reality, of course, I felt the complete reverse of the way I appeared to Mr Bugler. Inside, I know I can never do it. I am a nervous wreck, waiting in anguished silence, anxiously contemplating the enormity of my task which seems to grow ever more daunting by the second. A tactical move which a day earlier seemed merely a distinct impossibility for me to execute has now assumed the insuperable magnitude of the feeding of the five thousand. I now need a similar miracle. The butterflies which normally float around in the pit of my stomach are now like a flock of seagulls hovering over Anfield flapping their wings incessantly. I feel physically sick; my stomach is knotted, my mouth is dry and my palms leak beads of cold, clammy sweat. I am experiencing the classic symptoms of a human being gripped by fear. But I am only ten years old for God's sake. I should not be suffering this. This is surely not what football is meant to be about. The idea, I thought, is supposed to be one of enjoyment. This, on the contrary, is akin to Purgatory. Besides, I'm dreaming it for God's sake – at the very least I should be able to control the dream, if not the ball. In fact, I should be able to outshine Santa Maria – it's my dream when all's said and done.

Then, suddenly, it's all too late, the climax of the dream is upon me. As we trot out of the relative warmth and refuge of the wooden pavilion and run towards the cold looming reality of the pitch, our leather studs first clattering on the concrete apron, then crunching into the red gravel before sinking into the muddy bog that passes for a pitch, I pray for a merciful end to the torturous ordeal I am suffering.

As it turns out, the initial fears I have had concerning the distance I am expected to kick the ball prove unfounded, for this does not so much as enter into the equation. As the ball is delivered to me straight from the kick-off, I kill it instantly, displaying much aplomb and skill considering my nervous state. Trapping the ball has always been a strong point of my game – patently I'm not your average bog standard British midfielder – "So far so good" – I think to myself – "perhaps Santa Maria is only human after all".

Sighing with relief, I steady myself and with my confidence soaring by the millisecond, begin dexterously manoeuvring the ball for the next crucial stage of the move; the chip over the fullback. As my adrenaline flows, I begin to feel capable of anything. A forty yard precision punt now seems but a mere formality. The blind terror and panic of only moments earlier suddenly seem light years away. I am, after all, a naturally gifted young footballer and my natural instincts, abilities and co-ordination are now pulling me through in my time of greatest need. "What on earth was I panicking for?", I ask myself, "- it's only a dream in any case".

As I drag myself out of the gooey mire, I wonder where it suddenly went all wrong. How I came to stand on the ball just as everything was starting to go so well. Glancing up I can see everyone clapping and cheering, my team-mates in fits of laughter. All except Amo, who is by this time tearing up the wing like Gento, awaiting my inch perfect chip, and poor old Mr Bugler, who is simply holding his head in his hands in shame. I, meanwhile, sit up abruptly in bed in the cold sweat of a nightmare and immediately give thanks to Shanks I'm not at Brooke Vale playing fields.

The beauty of football dreams are those level playing fields – anything can happen for anyone. There is total equality; Georgie Best, Kenny Dalglish and Pele are no better than me; sometimes, I'm better than them. In fact, apart from when I'm trying to emulate Santa Maria at Brook Vale, I'm always better than them. Every time I play I do things with the ball that would bemuse Houdini, David Copperfield and Paul Daniels and make even Maradona gasp in admiration; I'm that good. And the thing is, I have possession of the ball nearly all the time because no-one can get it off me and so I don't really need any team-mates except to hug me when I score and no matter how many defenders are around me, I've always got time and space to display my full repertoire of tricks and the other good thing is it's not only on the deck that I can turn it on. I can also soar like Les Ferdinand and Duncan Ferguson way above Peter Schmeichel's outstretched fingertips and I can also tackle like a cross between Daniel Pasarella of Argentina and Tommy Smith so that even if I do happen to lose the ball, I can get it back almost at will.

The sad thing about most football dreams is that although we spend our lives dreaming them, they rarely come true. You can dream about winning the League or the Cup but even if it transpires that you do, it's never exactly as you dreamt it (Arsenal fans excepted, that is) which in my case is usually to Brazilian type perfection or with a final twist at the end to amplify the joy. For most football fans, of course, coping with such trifling minutiae as style and brinkmanship would seem like perfect bliss if only the main gist of the dreams ever materialised. I mean imagine all those poor Darlington fans as they lie in their beds each night longing for that coveted Wembley FA Cup Final victory so tanta-lisingly tangible in their slumbers but all so remote in reality; it wouldn't matter to them if they actually won the trophy by virtue of the opposition being wiped out beforehand by mad cow disease – just to get their mitts on the Cup would be all their dreams come true at once.

The magic of football, though, is that fantasy and real life can exist side by side. We used to go to Mr Heyworth's shop on the main road, which was split between a sweet shop and a cafe. Invariably, over by the counter of the sweet shop, impressively sipping a glass of coca-cola, the trendy new American drink, with chunks of ice floating tantalisingly on the top, would be Dave.

Dave was thick set, very short, dwarfish even, around twentyish with dark gypsy looks. Also, some people said his legs had been disabled by polio or TB when he was a kid. He always wore a blue and white scarf round his neck and tucked down under his jacket lapels. He never used to talk to us or even look at us. We used to stare at him but never said a thing. Often his mother would stand there with him and they – she mostly, in her foreign accent (they were from Wigan) – would talk for hours on end to Mr Heyworth. The shop was I suppose their 'local' only it didn't smell of stale barmaids, never had any ale and didn't sell pork scratchings.

Whenever we visited the shop for football bubblegum cards or 'Black Jacks', they would always be there in discussion with Mr Heyworth. Dave himself never muttered much in these conversations except to motion to Mr Heyworth to refill his glass, but his eyes always used to burn brightly at the merest mention of his beloved Everton. It would spark him. Between his gulps of coca-cola, he would excitedly tell Mr Heyworth about his dream of his legs getting better and wearing the royal blue jersey. His mother would laugh loudly and, in her clipped tones, tell him, "ee, don't talk soor daft, our Dave . . . yurr soft 'aporth" and Mr Heyworth would kindly say "you never know" – he was that sort of person – and Dave, with his eyes still gleaming, would then smile as if pleased with himself that there was still, after all, such a possibility of his playing for them and, rather smugly, take another mouthful of his iced coca-cola.

I, meanwhile, would stare longingly and enviously as the mysterious dark liquid was tipped down his gulping throat and wonder what coca-cola tasted like and whether or not it was worth sacrificing a large chunk of my pocket money on a single glass of the stuff. Then, I would snap out of my daydream and soberly reflect on the utter ludicrousness of what I had just heard. I mean, who in their right mind would want to play for Everton; especially when you could sip ice-cold coca-cola instead?

Of course, the thing was Dave was simply wishing on a star to be a star. And while he had about as much chance of being one as Jan Molby fitting into a pair of drainpipe Lee Riders, why the hell shouldn't he? It's what every fan does from time to time, isn't it; as much a part of the indoctrination process as biting into your first meat pie? Besides, other Evertonians always used to kid themselves how great they were, so why not Dave, too? I mean, a bit of fantasising never hurt any Blue as far as I am aware.

To this day, I am still not altogether clear what the expressions actually meant, but, from what I can recall, it seems to me most people I knew, or knew of, delighted in being referred to as either 'a good Liverpudlian' or 'a good Evertonian'.

I am not even sure whether such terminology implied the person in question was a good person who just so happened also to be a Liverpudlian or Evertonian, or, whether they could, in fact, be quite a bad person yet still qualify as a good Liverpudlian or Evertonian (and I certainly would not have totally ruled out the possibility of someone like Adolf Hitler being classed as 'a good Red or Blue' provided, of course, that he could have met the criterion of supporting Liverpool or Everton from his bunker in Berlin). What I am sure of is that the accolade seemed to be pretty-well universally applied, very much in a 'they're the salt of the earth' sort of way and I can't recollect ever hearing anybody being called a 'bad one'. Anyone who died, for instance, seemed to secure immediate recognition as one or the other, almost as if they were receiving some sort of posthumous award or honour. At church there might be as many as three or four Requiem masses a week and, at each mass, the priest would invariably crystalise the life of the deceased, largely in terms of their qualities as a Red or Blue. Match attendance was certainly not a pre-requisite for such an epitaph nor it seemed was the degree of the person's popularity within the community. Whether a match-regular or not or whether the church was packed or empty, the same glowing Red or Blue tributes would always be paid by the priest – "You will, no doubt, recall the deceased, whom , as you are all aware, was a good Liverpudlian" (or Evertonian, as the case may be).

A similar degree of pre-occupation with the quality of a person's Redness or Blueness would be evident at weddings or other family 'do's'. It was at these occasions, where you tended to encounter all those distant members of your extended family who lived outside of the immediate locality; the ones who never bought you any birthday or Christmas presents – great aunties, great uncles, not so great uncles, second cousins, and the like. Such gatherings of the clans were lapped up with great relish by all the grown-ups, especially, it seemed to me, by my mother, as she eagerly related to me who was who and what colour they were:

" See 'im over there – that's yer great uncle Harold." my mother would enlighten me, clearly forgetting I had met him over a dozen times before, "'e used ter be a good Evertonian till 'e emigrated to Rock Ferry, (which was actually a small suburb of Birkenhead and, though admittedly separated from us by quite a wide stretch of water, hardly ranked as an emigation, since it was still just about visible over the Mersey from where we lived). An' next to 'im, that's yer great uncle Jimmy – a good Liverpudlian, our Jimmy – in fact, 'e used to play fer them, I think" (which actually meant that someone from uncle Jimmy's old street had once been promised a trial for one of the Red's junior teams – precise recollection of Red's players, past and present, was not my mother's strongest point).

A clash of colours was an inevitable feature of these family gatherings and, with my priorities at that time being focussed almost entirely on footy, it was the part of the evening I most loved. As the drink began to wield its influence and peel away any of the few remaining veneers of sobriety, everyone's true colours would be revealed, until all present had their feet firmly in one camp or the other. There was no neutral ground. At first, the rivalry might limit itself to light hearted argument and debate; occasionally, it went no further than that. Most times, it erupted into a wonderfully boisterous and spontaneous exaltation of our Redness and Blueness, as song followed insult and both Red and Blue factions, young and old, arms draped round each other, defiantly proclaimed their respective allegiances, with neither side giving so much as an inch. With everyone linked by blood and friendship, but divided by colour, the occasions came to represent a celebration of that special football heritage which blossomed in a hotbed such as ours.

Even more riotous, would be the 'do's' held on New Year's Eve, when emotions were running at their highest and groups from neighbouring 'do's' would come and join in the mayhem. In our little block of maisonettes, alone, as many as half the households would be hosting similar open-door celebrations, with revellers coming and going at will. They were chaotic binges, to say the least. At times, the odd few sensible ones attempted to restore some harmony, by outlawing all footy songs. Around midnight, as 'Auld Lang Sign' nostalgia filled the air, they would achieve some success. In the main, though, it was a fruitless task and, for the most part, it was football, not Rabbie Burns, that prevailed. Throughout all the revelries, the only hint of any trouble might occur as a stray Liverpudlian or Evertonian occasionally forgot the words of their favourite songs and would have to suffer a minute or two's indignity as the foil for twenty or thirty others to laugh and poke fun at. Other than that, however, and the odd wild head butt and broken nose, they were always pretty innocuous affairs. Then as the night wore on and fatigue started to set in, the singing and the banter would eventually die out, giving way to fond reminiscence and chat; the out and out gibberish of a drunken night would begin to hold sway. Occasionally, some of it was aimed in my direction:

"They reckon, that if I'd 'ave 'ad the breaks, I could 'ave played fer the Reds, yer know, Alan – it was only the war that put the blocks on it – they reckon the scouts were on their way round ter our 'ouse, when the Germans bombed it – pity, that, yer know."

My tired eyes opened wide, as I surveyed, with sheer incredulity, the huge bulk of one of my more elderly distant relatives, now flopped, exhausted, in the armchair next to me, recounting, with drink in one hand and cigarette in the other, a hard luck story to rank with the best. Feigning polite acknowledgement, I nodded and smiled as you used to do to your elders in those days. Fortunately, I was spared the obligation of any further immediate response by the interjection of another relative

"Ah, behave yerself ! Don't be fillin' 'is 'ead with all that rubbish – yer'd 'ave been lucky to 'ave gorrin' our school netball team, never mind the Reds. Anyroad, yer were too old fer footy." My uncle Eddie would try his best to bring some semblance of reality to a situation, which was already threatening to drift well beyond the realms of football fantasy.

"Whad'yer mean, I'm tellin' yer, if it 'adn't 'ave been fer that bloody 'itler, they reckon, I'd 'ave definitely signed fer them." The wild claims went on, undeterred.

"Ah, don't talk wet! Anyroad, who the 'ell's dis person, who's doin' all dis reckonin', then? Thee must be off their chump. That's what I reckon, if yer ask me."

"Well no-one is askin' you, are they? But, anyroad, I'll tell yer again, just in case yer didn't 'ear me properly the first time . . . "

Now, I'm one hundred percent sure I didn't set out from the start to doubt the validity of what I was being told about this courtship with Liverpool. Nor did my uncle Eddie's instant rejection of the claims have any real bearing on my disbelief. On the contrary, I'd have given my right arm for it to have been true that a relative of mine came so close to signing for the Reds. After all, quite apart from the obvious reflected glory of such a claim to fame, there may have been other hidden benefits, too; old contacts at the club might have been able to arrange a trial for me or, at the very least, been able to get us tickets for the big games; maybe they could even have managed to get me an introduction to Bill Shankly.

No, the real problem was that, even allowing for the couple of dozen 'gin and oranges' she had knocked back during the night, my great aunty Nora's claims that the Reds had been mad keen on signing her were just that bit too hard for even a football daft twelve year old with bright red starry eyes to swallow. I mean, you only had to look at her knees, for a kick off – no way did they belong to a netball player, let alone a footballer.

Mind you, for all that, what's the matter with a little bit of exaggeration, here and there. I can honestly say, it's never done me much harm. Who knows, maybe I even take after my great aunty Nora. I can certainly think of worse people to follow. She was a good Liverpudlian, when all's said and done, even if she wasn't quite good enough to have played for the Reds.

While Seaport was a hotbed of football, there was no written constitution to that effect. Kenny Everett was from Seaport and, it is said in the smoke rooms of many of the local pubs that Kenny never even once played blow football, let alone the real thing. Johnny Price was another.

Johnny's game was ollies and, for a short while every olley season, I would try to emulate him. There were three basic games of ollies – 'Holey', 'Killer' and 'Ringy'. All would be played to an elaborate and precise set of rules, on the various bombed sites littering the Seaport area, any of which provided the requisite barren and grassless, firm yet dusty, surfaces so ideally suited to the game. The perfect surfaces available enabled the appropriate holes to be formed by rotary digging with the heels, rings to be marked and, most important, prevented the ollies, which had been flicked, from rolling too far.

At the very heart of the game of ollies was the flicking technique. The flick was executed with the thumb restrained behind both the second finger and the olley itself. Flicking of the thumb sent the olley zooming towards its target, which would be another olley on the ground. Mastery of the flicking technique was the key, the essence of the whole game. Quite simply, those who could master it became the best players. At times, the power and the unerring accuracy of such players was stunning.

In this respect, Johnny Price was the master. Johnny was a tall, gangling boy – a forerunner of Steve McManaman – who lived around the corner from us. For his olley style, he adopted an unorthodox, flashy, standing upright technique with a sharply defined and bent index finger. He was so good he would be able to hit another olley six or seven feet away, at least, I would say seven times out of ten. Johnny's audacious, gun-slinging Frank Worthington approach was pure excitement and class. He would flick his olley from midriff height and it would fly like a bullet, hitting full on the other olley, which would, at once, be catapulted six or seven feet away, leaving his own olley nestling, still spinning, in the exact spot previously occupied by the one it had displaced.

I was not quite in the same class as Johnny Price. My father had been pretty good in his time and used to try to coach me but, sadly, olley skills did not run in the family. In comparative terms, if Johnny was starring for Barcelona, then my father was Real Sociedad and I was a substitute ball boy for Bacup Borough reserves, ever willing but utterly useless. You see, I never won any, I existed purely to buy them with the last remnants of my pocket money, and then to lose them to gunslingers like Johnny, who probably never had to purchase a single olley in their entire lives, thanks to willing lemmings like myself.

It wasn't that the common or garden ones were expensive – for a 'tanner' you could buy two dozen the transparent glass ollies with the ribbon of colour in the middle. The "shooters", which were multi-colour opaque and the "parrots" single-colour opaque, the most cherished ones, were more expensive but I never knew where to buy them in any case.

The problem was that I used to lose them all so quickly. Come Thursday night, when I received my pocket money, I would go straight round to the 'Posty' (the Post Office shop) to replenish my empty little cloth bag, which my mother had made for me, with thirty or forty new ollies until it was bulging and rippling with its replacement stock. Suitably fortified, I would swagger onto the debris, my confidence bulging, just like my olley bag, and join in any one of the dozen or so games which would be, by that time, in full swing.

Way before nightfall, I would have lost the lot. My pathetic little olley bag, once more, sagging empty. I would then stand around, utterly morose and envious of Johnny, sheepishly peering every so often into his huge, one hundred weight cement bag, half full of the most dazzling assortment of contrasting ollies imaginable, watching his collection grow before my very eyes, knowing that probably several hundred of his many thousands of ollies had once, for one shining moment, belonged to me.

Little wonder, then, that I clung so doggedly to football as my salvation. Ollies was never really going to be my game. Not of course that ollies ever really became anyone's game in any major sporting sense. I mean, you don't even get olley matches on Sky Sports let alone Grandstand or Sportsnight. I think the reason is probably that the ollies would simply be that teeny weeny bit too small to pick out on the little screen or maybe olley matches have just never attracted the same crowds as say curling or bowls or could it be simply that nobody knows how to play ollies any more. Perhaps, when all's said and done, ollies was never meant to be a spectator sport which is a pity because Johnny Price could have been its first major star. Even more's the pity though that Johnny himself never played football, for with his awesome natural talent and co-ordination, he surely would have become the world-class footballer that Seaport never produced. As it was he had to be content with a postman's round in Birkenhead – a tragic waste of talent – though to be fair he could still boast the finest set of ollies either side of the Mersey.

Mind you, though I say it myself, aren't those last comments just so typical of the arrogance which permeates right through football and that includes the likes of myself? I mean what God-given right does football have, always to consider itself *the* game – *the* game of the people, for the people, by the people. Why on earth should Johnny Price's sublime skills be considered a waste simply because they involved ollies, not footy? The whole thing smacks of utter conceit, egotism and complacency; perhaps the very same attitudes which are currently threatening to squeeze all the remaining decency out of the game and turn it into a cesspit for insidious, money-grabbing megalomaniacs to line their slime-ridden wallets.

That, in fact, is why I included this little piece on ollies. To try and show that even in football hotbeds, there should always be room for sport of all shapes and sizes; that even those with little ollies require a platform of some sort or another where they can play 'Ringy' or 'Holey' to their hearts' content. On one condition though – just as long as they don't come anywhere near me because I never want to see another olley for as long as I'm still breathing and possess a season ticket for Anfield.

To many, the late Fifties and early Sixties – ollies and all – will forever evoke sweet memories of innocence and images of a time when life was hard but uncomplicated; caps were flat and gobstoppers round. Back then a sense of community was all. The consensus is that those years represent the last throw of an unblemished age before burgeoning post-Beatles permissiveness and Americana began to suck us all in with tainted false promises, leaving us all wide open to the outright moral fragmentation and greed of the Eighties and Nineties when the blight of self-interest cynically eclipsed almost everything else. Football wasn't immune to this and we witnessed the marginalisation of true fans as commercial interest held sway. In many ways, I suppose, such rosy views of the past are nigh unchallengeable and stand as a testimony to that very innocence which so many of us now crave but sadly so few of us possess in this age of guilt and dishonour. One thing is certain – you don't have to look too far to find evidence why such views are so firmly held.

Take, once again, the ever convenient case of dear old Jan Molby as a barometer to measure this alleged fall from grace. Today, in our current climate of 'anything goes', so far do our standards appear to have plummeted that there are now few, if any, who would blink so much as a solitary eyelash at Jan's appearance on a football pitch, even down in Swansea. Apart, perhaps, from the odd 'Sumo' insult, the reaction would be scant. Certainly there would be no formal protest at Jan's involvement in a game. Contrast the late Fifties. Then, the mere presence on the field of a Danish professional footballer with a Scouse accent so thick and strong that it would make even Peter Reid sound posh would surely have provoked an uproar. Church leaders both here and in wonderful Copenhagen would have been up in arms, questions asked in the House of Commons (the former alehouse on Heyworth Street) and letters sent to Bert Millichip (even then in his late nineties), so vehement the outrage. Evidence enough? Or should we take another example of what is widely regarded as our headlong plunge into moral decadence? Let us look at the situation with jewellery and trinkets as another case in point. Thirty-odd years ago, even wedding rings used to come off before a game. Today, however, the flagrant flaunting of gold, silver and precious stones by player and manager alike around necks, wrists and fingers and through ears, nostrils and nipples make even the glitzy Zsa Zsa Gabor look like some frumpy, old librarian. So besotted has the game become with all its over-indulgence and opulence, it is difficult to know where it will all end.

And yet, when you really look closely at the alleged drop in standards with which we are constantly harangued, do the arguments actually hold water? Are things really so much worse today? Were the Fifties and early Sixties truly such an age of splendid innocence? Is the reality not rather a case of remove the tinted spectacles and exhale the nostalgia, and the alleged innocence of those distant halcyon days of the Fifties is no longer all it may at first seem?

When, for example, Paul McCartney sang in 1967 of 'finger pie' in his beloved Penny Lane, he was not merely exposing a brand new digital phenomenon nor was he celebrating the glory of the dodgy meat pies and mushy peas from his once favourite 'chippy' on the 'Lane'. Rather, he was owning up to the transgressions of the moral code which existed as much in Paul's late Fifties and early Sixties Liverpool as they do now. The simple fact of the matter is the perpetration of mortal sins of the magnitude sung about by Paul had been around ever since the late great Billy Meredith first caught the eye of the ladies on Aberavon pleasure beach in the early Twenties.

So, don't kid yourself that everything was sweetness and light. True, the likes of Shankly and Busby, Mercer and Nicholson all espoused the virtuous aspirations of the era but they were decent men, their integrity plain for all to see. The sobering truth is, the most untainted symbol to emerge from that period – one that was to become the prized possession of every fan – was, of course, the club scarf; the game's last surviving bastion of decency.

Throughout the Fifties and early Sixties, the club scarf had only one design. It was about four feet long, machine knitted wool equally banded in your favourite team's colours, with white frilly tassels at either end which you usually lopped off since they used to look a bit poncey. The scarves were available from Jack Sharps Sports Shop in town and cost an arm and a leg to buy, which is why at our age we couldn't afford one. From around the age of seven or eight, to own a club scarf represented the summit of your life's ambition. It was all we desired. You could stick the FA Cup and its perfect silver symmetry; the real Holy Grail was red and white, soft and woollen, and worn around the neck. You ached for it, and as far as being a fan went, merely treaded water until its arrival.

My moment of deliverance came on Christmas Day 1962. I was 11 years old and completely scarfless up to then. Never has there been a better Christmas present. For the record, my other presents that Christmas were a brand new Frido 'plassie', a second-hand 10-gear Raleigh Blue Streak racing bike about two sizes too big for me inherited from my cousin David, selection boxes and apples and oranges. As far as I was concerned, my other presents may just as well have not existed, for what I had really craved and longed for so much was now mine and was immediately wrapped securely around my scrawny little neck in anticipation of my first opportunity to show it off and to give everyone a sight of the new me.

Needless to say, the scarf really did transform me. It was like assuming a new identity. With my scarf in place everyone would know I was a Red; simply by looking at me everyone would see what I was. Complete strangers passing me on the street would look on in awe as this true Liverpudlian strutted imperiously amidst their ranks. I would now be important. I would now have esteem. Fellow Liverpudlians, old diehards, would nod at me approvingly, welcoming me as one of their own. Evertonians, meanwhile, frustrated at the cruel fate nature had dealt them, would simply grimace, envious that they themselves had chosen the wrong path of fandom. Naturally, it goes without saying that before any of this could take place, the scarf first had to be washed a few times to make sure the colours ran a bit so it didn't look so new, and I looked like an old hand. With that done, however, the scarf was ready for its inauguration.

The daft thing was, for the first six months or so, until we had finally bid good riddance to the Pen and joined the Kop which we did during the following season, there was no way I could risk wearing the scarf to the match for fear of it being whizzed by the Pen's vultures, which in a way sort of defeated the whole object of the exercise, I suppose. As it happens, though, that little restriction turned out to be pretty well incidental because for the rest of the time the scarf virtually never left my neck except under the strongest protest like when my parents used to take my sister and me to the local slipper baths on a Saturday evening for our weekly de-infestation, scrub, spit and polish. Quite simply, the scarf did everything and went everywhere that I did. It ate with me, drank with me, slept and played footy with me, went on messages, went to school, church and visits to relatives, and even survived the odd skirmishes with Aunty Kitty, Uncle Jack and Ebba Murphy. Effectively, it became part of me and me it. In fact, I've never been so attached to anything before or since in my whole life although apart from its innate ability to relay my Redness instantly, to one and all, the scarf displayed no other latent talent to do anything else nor to fulfil any other function. There again, what else can you expect from a piece of coloured woollen cloth.

I dare say, the reason why the scarf became so precious and indispensable also explained, in turn, why it was worn so lovingly and cherished so dearly by every fan; why, just like the club, it became a lifelong attachment. The scarf effectively stood for the club, which was the love of every fan's life. Naturally, it became a symbol of that love, just like any other lover's keepsake. I mean, once the knot on my own love affair with the Reds was tied, I, like any other smitten lover, wanted to be with them the whole time. That I couldn't actually be with them at any time meant I was forced to adopt a substitute. And that is what the scarf became. The next best thing to being with the Reds just so happened to be red, white and fluffy and remained close to my heart. At once it became an outward gesture of my deep affection for the Reds whilst at the same time and, more significantly, the tangible evidence of my belonging and identity. I was a Red and – Second Division or not – proud of it. Others were Blue and equally proud and so on.

On reflection, wearing the club colours, I suppose, made you an honest fan. This was before the days (although they weren't far away) of fans having to hastily hide their scarves for fear of being attacked by marauding bands of rival 'supporters'. I guess this was the beginning of the end for the traditional football scarf. On the other hand, it might have just gone out of fashion for nowadays, of course, the original old red and white scarf looks pretty naff when set against the limitless range of club paraphernalia currently available.

Club scarves now come in an assortment of guises, designs and colours. Indeed, someone knowing no better might swear that, in Liverpool's case, the Club colour was now actually Hibernian green though naturally they'd be wrong (at least, I think they'd be wrong. I hope so anyway, because no-one has bothered to tell me any different.) And what's more, it's not only scarves with which you can now demonstrate your loyalty to the club – there are key rings and Club shirts, underpants, eiderdowns, pillowcases, tablecloths, curtains, rugs, even carpets – maybe even vacuum cleaners to clean the carpets. Ridiculous, isn't it? The whole thing is remorseless – wrapped up in market forces, so they say. Two things are certain though, market forces or not; the Kop in the sixties wouldn't have looked anywhere near as good with 28,000 vacuum cleaners held aloft as it did with all those lovely red and white scarves and I, certainly, have never looked any better than on Christmas Day 1962.

By the way, just for the record, in 1966, my mother knitted me a new all red scarf to match Liverpool's new all red strip. It was about 10 feet long and I must admit, it turned my head and I gave my little red and white scarf away. So much for lifelong attachments, and loyalty, eh.

The most honest person I've ever come across was an old schoolmate named Pete Staunton. Pete, quite simply, could never tell a lie, not even the weeniest, most insignificant little white one. As far as Pete was concerned, the truth was everything. If the gauge of truthfulness is the length of the day, then Pete`s date of birth, without any doubt, was the 21st of June. Oh, and I suppose I should also add that, as you might have expected with someone who never told a lie, Pete had a little button nose that had never once altered in size from the day he was born, which was, really, quite a novelty to behold.

Pete and I attended St. Murphy's College, a Catholic grammar school run by Irish Christian Brothers in the north end of the city. Like any other well adjusted Catholic boys in the school, Pete and I used to spend a large part of any free time we had, rapt in our most popular pastime of carving the names of our favourite footy teams and footy players on the old school desks. Perhaps significantly because it was a Catholic school, or perhaps not, the Evertonians in our class considerably outnumbered their Liverpudlian counterparts and so, consequently, did the inscriptions of EFC, Alec Young, Alex Scott and so on. For every red logo there were, at least, two blue ones. It was something with which I could never quite come to terms, but that's life I guess. Pete, incidentally, was an Evertonian, whose favourite player, for some inexplicable reason, was Brian Harris, the Blues' unfashionable wing half, as clear a case of everyone to their own as I've ever come across.

Of course, carving names and inscriptions on old desks has always been fairly run-of-the-mill practice at most schools and for the most part any new carvings tend to go largely unnoticed, buried amidst the welter of ancient ones, some of them, in our case, dating as far back as Dixie Dean and Elisha Scott. Not surprisingly, I suppose, the same is not quite the case where new desks are concerned and, as we were to find out to our cost, it is a sad fact of life that such artistic inclinations assume a whole new significance when virgin wood is involved, with the margins between art and vandalism no longer so blurred in the eyes of those with any vested interest in the objects being desecrated. So it was with the new ash veneered benches and worktops which St. Murphy's had had installed in the two ground floor lecture rooms for the start of the 1964 Autumn term.

In all fairness, when I look back now, I suppose the new benches in their virgin condition did actually have a bit of an untouchable aura about them, sitting there perfectly upright and gleaming with all the pristine beauty that only untarnished lacquered wood can muster. I daresay, also, their 'do not touch' message was, even then, pretty-well unmistakable and hand on heart, you couldn't really imagine anyone with even the minutest semblance of a brain wanting to inflict any damage on them. It also has to be said that, given exactly the same situation again, most of the lads in the class would, I'm sure, all behave in a rather more civilised way than we did back then. The thing is, though, sometimes people do just get hold of the wrong end of the stick. I mean someone, at sometime, has to carve that very first inscription. At the time we believed that the school was just being extra thoughtful – simply providing us with brand new blank surfaces for our etchings; new canvases to indulge our artistic urges. In our innocence, we responded like men possessed. The entire class beavered away like a Taiwan sweatshop inscribing a copious onslaught of fresh markings. No doubt, the prehistoric cave dwellers had once felt similar inspiration to us, as they daubed away on unblemished cave walls, though it is unlikely even they could have matched our boyish enthusiasm.

By dinner-time, the damage was done and there was scarcely a square inch of worktop untouched. The illustrious names of virtually every Everton and Liverpool star going back to 1890 had been proudly preserved in wood for prosperity. Our efforts had produced sublime results, though once again the Evertonians had secured a strategic victory, which, for me, had slightly soured our accomplishments. Nonetheless, it had been a sterling achievement by any standards and we all sat back to bask in the glory of our work.

Rather surprisingly, the Christian Brothers did not share the sense of satisfaction our artistic binge had given us. Indeed, within minutes of one of them discovering our handiwork, the class was confronted by the alarming sight of a dozen or more demented, red-faced Irish madmen, in full length black cassocks, jumping up and down in front of us, like the cast of Riverdance on burning coals. Had it not been for the impossible degree to which their faces were contorted with rage, the hilarious sight of them all hopping about might have induced us to become as hysterical as they were. As it was, the only emotion we were able to conjure up was that of blind terror.

Now, for those unfamiliar with the delights of education under Irish Christian Brothers, I will provide, at this point, a little snippet of background insight into life under these committed men of the cloth, in order to lend some kind of perspective to our feelings of terror. Not, of course, that anyone should think, for one moment, that what I have to say could ever paint a complete picture but it will, at least, give some idea of what it could be like. You see, rather unfortunately for us, the forte of most Christian Brothers had very little to do with actual education nor, for that matter, even religion or its teachings. It was not that the Brothers were not proficient in these fields for, indeed, the very opposite was the case- they were extremely so. In fact, it is doubtful whether a much better schooling existed anywhere. It is simply that the special gift which had been bestowed upon these holy men just so happened to have had no connection whatsoever with anything remotely cerebral. It was an altogether more physical attribute involving the peculiar ability to pummel, till red raw, the outstretched hand of any pupil unfortunate enough to have committed a serious aberration, such as walking on the cracks in the pavement or forgetting their PE kit. Such bouts of pummelling were invariably administered with a black leather strap reinforced with whalebone and measuring around a foot long, an inch and a half wide and five eighths of an inch thick. A formidable implement in anybody's hands, the strap assumed fearsome significance when tucked into the readily accessed side pocket of a Brothers cassock, from where it could be drawn and wielded faster than Wyatt Earp in his gunslinging heyday at Scunthorpe United. Needless to say, the strap ensured a reign of terror prevailed.

Not surprisingly, therefore, when suddenly confronted by our manic mentors, the real implications of our carvings had hit us like an Ari Haan howitzer. Pangs of deep regret and remorse welled up inside us. What in the name of God had we gone and done? What on God's earth had we been thinking about? The words, 'evil', 'Devil's work', 'vandals', 'savages', 'Visigoths' (whatever they were) reverberated through our heads in pure staccato Irish tones. We quaked. 'Suspension', 'expulsion', 'excommunication', the venomous tirade continued: there was little doubt we were really in for it. Eventually, when the bedlam had subsided enough, one of the brothers, the giant Brother Brinkley, with squared features apparently chiselled out of basalt from the Giants Causeway in County Antrim, addressed us all with some degree of intelligibility.

"Who is responsible for this desecration!" He growled, slowly and deliberately. It was clear from his tone that he did not regard our efforts as a minor misdemeanour; without any shadow of doubt, he meant business. "Anyone responsible for even one letter put their hand up right now."

Not a single hand was raised.

Evidently, the hieroglyphics had appeared as if by magic. Now, if only Brother Brinkley and the others could be persuaded to think along the same lines we might just about escape with our lives. It was a slim hope, though, and, to be perfectly frank, offered us little cause for optimism. In fact, it was pretty obvious our only realistic way out was to stick together; keep mum and sit it out. With forty in the class, there was always an outside possibility, however remote, that we might just get away with it.

Brother Brinkley glared at us from his great height and murmured menacingly: "Cowards!"

He was just in the throws of turning his mountainous body around, towards the other Brothers, no doubt to discuss their options, when disaster struck. There was a sudden movement in the corner of the classroom where I was sat. A solitary arm had been raised. Regrettably, it was the one immediately to my right. I froze. It was Pete's. Oh my god! We should have known. Truthful Pete. Honest and honourable Pete. Tiny, little Pete, who could never tell a lie. Go ahead and drop us all in the shit Pete. What an imbecile; what an absolute dope. Brother Brinkley stared in our direction. He squinted to get a sharper focus on whose arm it was; his brow was furrowed, his eyebrows arched. He looked worryingly confident that his brief war of attrition had just ended and his own arm muscles were about to get some well deserved exercise. Pete's slight frame, suddenly, looked even tinier and distinctly fragile.

"Staunton, eh! Well, boy, what have you got to say?"

"I did it, sir" Pete affirmed naively from beneath the shadow of his wavy black Teddy Boy quiff, which flopped almost as far down as the bridge of his nose, like a bunch of grapes dangling from a vine. His honesty all but radiated out across the classroom. Clearly, the 'cowards' slur had been just a mite too much for his code of honour and integrity to cope with and his cathartic mechanisms had clicked into unique gear.

"Show me which one."

Pete duly pointed out the lovingly carved name of his hero, Brian Harris, and grimaced, stone-faced, just like Brother Brinkley. Then, with a startling impersonation of Gary Cooper at his very toughest, he looked Brother Brinkley straight in the eye, in a cameo right out of 'High Noon' , daring Brother Brinkley to go ahead and punish his honesty. To the rest of us, sat there open-mouthed, it seemed like pretty impressive stuff, from which only the constant twitching of Pete's tiny snout and his miniature stature detracted. Sadly,though, this was to be as far as Pete's tough-guy act was to take him. In less than the blinking of an eyelid, his huge monastic adversary, had risen manfully to Pete's challenge and had promptly grabbed poor Pete by his wispy sideburns, what little there were of them, hauled him out to the front of the classroom, given him three humdingers on each hand with his awesome weapon and then made him kneel down facing the class with the promise of more punishment to come ringing in his ears. The throbbing of Pete's palms was palpable and his face grimaced in agony. From the movies I've seen, I would say the expression was certainly far more dynamic than anything Gary Cooper ever managed.

The rest of us, particularly Pete's cohorts such as myself, now faced a dilemma. We could all see Pete's pain and his watering eyes and we all knew how potent the strap could be, especially when delivered with the anger and relish Brother Brinkley seemed to be unleashing. Also, we all knew that the matter might not end there; that the corporal punishment might simply be the start. Graver consequences may await us and there was certainly no doubting how genuinely frightened we all were about that particular aspect of the nightmare we found ourselves in; I mean apart from deliberate acts of wanton vandalism and the odd impure thought, we were all still good conforming Catholics and the prospect of expulsion or, God forbid, excommunication turned us sick. Yet, despite all that, we were also Pete's mates. However crazy we all considered him to have been for being so honest, there was no way we would let him suffer all this on his own. Besides, now he had started the ball rolling, there was no means of knowing where it would all lead. In any case, as I scanned the scarred worktops, it gradually began to dawn on me that Pete had, in all probability, made the right decision in coming clean, albeit shepherded by his honesty fixation. We, by our silence, had simply been delaying the inevitable; no way would the Brothers have allowed our dumb act to have got the better of them. The more I thought about it the clearer it became that it was the rest of the class, not Pete, who had been the dopes. In this instance, honesty was almost certainly the best policy.

The same thoughts must have occurred to everyone else, for the next few moments witnessed a wholesale admission, like some sort of subdued American evangelical gathering. One by one, the hands gingerly went up. One by one the individual carvings were identified and the punishments meted out, with the Brothers adopting a rota system of flogging to reduce their fatigue. It was not long before the floor was a mass of kneeling bodies, with each boy blowing furiously on each of their smarting hands in futile attempts to relieve the excruciating pain, while their glistening eyes rolled round their heads in complete disorientation. Rather strangely, by the time it got to my turn, it became immediately apparent that something was different.

In a similar fashion to the way he had dealt with the others thus far, Brother Brinkley had manouevered himself along the bench to where I sat, until he hovered over me, threateningly, to examine the inscription I had carved. Amazingly, as soon as he had got himself close to me, his demeanour, so menacing only seconds before, seemed suddenly to dissolve into inexplicable affability. The first traces of a smile began to appear on his craggy face, the only tangible sign so far of any cessation in the oppression which had beleaguered us since the defaced worktops had been discovered.

At first, however puzzling it may have all been, the miraculous transformation appeared, at least, to offer us all some shared respite and, perhaps, some hope that the tide was turning; that the Brothers' anger had reached some welcome saturation point and would now just mellow and die away. Then, though, as I glanced up at Brother Brinkley's rock-hewn features and he smiled down at me and I was able to feel the warmth of his breath on the side of my face, I began to feel distinctly uncomfortable. Something wasn't right. The interlude may well have been giving the others still to come a bit of a break but it wasn't doing me any good. The change of mood had obviously had something to do with me and it made me very uneasy. Why me? Why none of the others? They had scarcely been given anything less than a menacing growl and six of Brother

Brinkley's very best, yet only minutes later, here he was virtually flirting with me, even though I had carried out exactly the same offence as them. I shivered. Hideous thoughts of a sordid relationship with Brother Brinkley flitted through my mind. I recalled snatches of conversations and News of the World headlines about priests and altar boys. The notion repulsed me. Surely not me. I felt distinctly sick. Six of the strap and the possibility of even direr consequences to follow was traumatic enough for any thirteen year-old to withstand, but being propositioned in broad classlight by a Christian Brother, particularly Brother Brinkley with his reeking hot breath and his massive stained cassock, was a thousand times worse and certainly something well beyond my comprehension. This was the type of thing you only read about in a Jane Austen novel. This, though, was Liverpool not the steamy South.

Brother Brinkley, speaking in rather more innocuous tones than before, called out, "Brother Carey, Brother Moriarty, will you come and look at this."

The rest of the Brothers promptly came over. Brother Brinkley pointed at the inscription I had carved.

"Will you look at that."

They scrupulously examined my inscription. Each of them smiled and gave me a warm, reassuring look. One of them, I'm not sure which one, fondly ruffled my hair. Brother Brinkley told me I was a good lad. I smiled back at them, tentatively and watched as they all shuffled back to the front of the classroom in clearly affable mood. What the hell is going on , I thought to myself? The rest of the class, even those strewn across the floor, looked equally dumbfounded. Why should the name . . . ? Then it dawned on me. Of course . . . 'St. John!' . . . surely not.

It was hard even to begin to take it all in.

So Brother Brinkley hadn't fancied me, after all. Thank God for that. Meantime, Reds hero Ian St. John and the Brothers' complete ignorance of anything to do with footy – they were all rugby men – had saved my bacon and also the rest of the class. Expulsion and excommunication had been wiped off the agenda and, for some of us, at least, so, too, had an appointment with the dreaded strip of leather. The Brothers' anger had been quelled by a bit of unwitting creeping. I had defaced their desk just like everyone else and yet, unbeknown to us all, by doing so, had appealed to their spiritual side and found it bountiful. The undoubted thrill that my phantom devotion to St. John The Evangelist had given them meant that nobody could ever accuse these particular Christian Brothers of lacking in the spiritual area, whatever else may be levelled at them.

As for Pete and his honesty, what can you do except admire and applaud it. What a refreshing change it makes, simply to reflect on such truthfulness. I mean, these days it's just so rare to find anything remotely approaching it. Just think, if only a tiny fraction of it was to be found in football, then Eric Hall might now be smoking Wills Wiffs instead of Havanas and, though the tobacco industry might not be too chuffed about it, what a day for the game, not to mention the environmentalists, that would be. Mind you, while we're on the subject, I don't suppose a smattering or two of it, here and there, in this book would do much harm, either, now I come to think about it.

People – though certainly not myself in the aftermath of the desk carving episode – often ask rhetorically ' so what's in a name, huh?', and, to be perfectly honest, in most instances you have to admit it is difficult to challenge the implied assertion behind that question. Even the irritating 'huh' bit at the end. After all, a name, in itself, is nothing really, merely a label providing a convenient means of identification. Take the name away and the person or the place still exists or existed. I mean, if Alexander the Great had been called, say, 'Sidney the Crazy Elephant', it is unlikely such an insignificant change of terminology would exactly have had a major impact on the course of world history or have changed the stirring feats which Alexander achieved. Fine, so as the bangle-festooned Sidney strutted imperiously around Athens in true Ron Atkinson fashion, it might have prompted the odd sarky comment or contemptuous smirk, both of them, incidentally, extremely dicey ventures from what I've read of the 'big fella'. In the long term, though, it wouldn't have altered a thing. Moreover, it would hardly have impinged on us today, except perhaps to have given us a bit more of a giggle in our history lessons or possibly caused us to confuse the intrepid Greek with Hannibal and his tusked entourage.

In football, uniquely, the same principles do not apply. Names, as far as the peoples' game is concerned and, in stark contrast to how it is with life itself, are the be all and end all. Whether, as with those distant historical figures, this has any link with elephants is open to question, though certainly, it is widely held that it is only since the legendary 'white elephant' FA cup final of 1923, when as many as a hundred and twenty thousand of the blighters stampeded and had to be brought under control by a solitary mounted policeman, that the significance of a footballer having the right name has become as huge as the beasts which were herded out of the game that same year.

Take some of the real 'greats' of football down the years – Billy

Meredith, Dixie Dean, Alex James, Stanley Matthews, Tom Finney, Alfredo Di Stefano, Ferenc Puskas, Pele, Luis Del Sol, Johan Cruyff, Diego Maradona, Georgie Best, Denis Law, Bobby Charlton, Kevin Keegan, Kenny Dalglish. What do all of them have in common, apart from footballing ability? What's the one other thing that links all of them and sets them apart from all the rest? You don't have to think too long about it do you? It's so blindingly obvious. A great name; they all possessed a truly memorable name. Each one literally screams out "Look at me, I've got this fantastic name. One day I'll be a world class player".

Okay, so maybe it didn't happen quite so easily as that. Maybe they did also need a modicum of skill to start with. Perhaps, too, they did have to apply themselves to the task. Look at those names, though. They really did have it made, didn't they? It really was on a plate. How could they fail with names like those? Even more to the point, how could they have succeeded without them?

Apply it to your own experience. Imagine the scene. You're in school. The teacher is about to select the school team and you're desperate for a place in it. Your name is Fred Smith and you're not a bad centre forward. The lad in the desk next to you is also quite a good centre forward, too. Ability-wise, in fact, there's very little in it. If anything, you might be ever so slightly the better player. The thing is, his name is Angelo Gordeno Bandana Del Sol. Yes, Luis Del Sol's namesake. The Spanish maestro. The one who used to have the ball tied to his foot and make it talk, some even say sing. Frankly, you may as well forget it. You haven't got a prayer; not a chance. Angelo is going to get in every time. Your only hope would be if one of Angelo's legs was wooden, and even then it would be touch and go whether you'd be picked. In fact, the odds are they'd actually pick Angelo's timber peg before you. Not exactly a fair contest is it?

You could, of course, always change schools or try moving to inside forward, but even then there's no guarantee of being selected, for who's to say you wouldn't be up against yet another big name. Perhaps even one with two wooden legs. Again, it'd be no contest. You'd be beaten before you started. Your best bet is to change your name. Persuade your mother to divorce and re-marry a Spaniard called Suarez. Better still, stick an 'o' on the end of your first name and then squeeze in the latin version of your 'confirmation' name – 'Gus' – for good measure (any pagans will just have to improvise on that last one). Now you really could be in business. Fredo Giuseppe Suarez. That's not a bad combination. Certainly beats Fred Smith, anyday. It's got a ring to it. In fact, if you don't make captain of the first eleven with that little gem, then there's something drastically wrong. As it stands, if you don't attempt some sort of ploy you'll simply end up helping out with the laundry or dubboning smug Angelo's boots.

I'm convinced it's quite often the names of certain players which can keep some clubs in the lower divisions. I've seen it happen time and time again. The whole thing works like a vicious circle and once it starts it can't stop. It spirals out of control. The lousier the players' names, the lower their self esteem and the worse their standard of play. Confidence drains and with some it can become so bad they can actually end up unable to kick a ball to save their life or anybody else's for that matter. Now if they were playing for Spurs in the top division that wouldn't be so bad. They would still get picked for England. But these guys are strictly lower echelon. And it's fatal. Before long, the same negative outlook affects the crowd, too. They get depressed as soon as they see the names in the programme before the game. And who can blame them? After all, they're only flesh and blood and there's a limit to the amount of punishment the mind and body can take. Even diehards weaned on terminal failure can reach saturation point. Just as these poor souls have managed by some miracle of the human spirit to lift themselves from the debacle that was the previous match, they turn with naive optimism to the team sheet only to see the same old crappy names staring back at them game after game.

It's football's own version of 'Celebrity Squares', a glittering megastar in every position, some nobody has ever heard of except for our long-suffering stalwarts. Gloom pervades them once more. It's contagious and spreads like a Rotherham ripple (a bit like a Mexican wave only much smaller with everyone just standing there shrugging their shoulders and grumbling like mad). From fans it envelopes the team who are already suicidal, then back again via the coaching staff and tea ladies. Soon people are moping around the stadium like prophets of doom each clad in one of those sandwich boards proclaiming the end of the world. Directors, of course, will go to any lengths to get noticed.

Meanwhile, the mood of the fans themselves is by now mirroring that of the players. Desperation has engulfed them. Life is barely worth living. They are making straight for the nearest canal. They've had enough. They're off to the Norfolk Broads for some light relief and a nice cooked breakfast.

Amazingly, what most of those lower division managers never seem to realise is, sometimes, all it takes to break the spell is the signing of a few fancy names. The injection of the odd Peter Marinello-like signature can work wonders. Like a magic sponge. It's purely psychological, of course. Nothing at all to do with football. The new players themselves don't actually have to be any good. In fact, it probably helps if they're rubbish. Otherwise, it can easily lead to an outbreak of jealousy amongst the established names. Footballers are temperamental souls. They certainly don't like being upstaged, especially those who have played in a higher division. So, there's no need for any real quality. Too risky. Just so long as the new signings sound the part, then that's all is needed. It's usually more than enough to lift the spirits and reverse the trend.

Probably equally as effective, and far cheaper, too, especially for those clubs on a shoestring budget, is to re-jig the whole thing in-house. Keep it in the family. Simply change the names of half a dozen of the players in key positions (say the goalie, the centre backs, centre midfield and one of the strikers), give each of them a new Alex Lallas hairstyle and false beard, throw in a forged passport and a pair of dark shades and you've cracked it. Virtually a new team. It can save a small fortune on transfer fees and, if you're lucky, no-one will spot the disguises. It's a trick the successful managers used to use all the time in the old days. Herbert Chapman, particularly, used to swear by it. Hardly ever failed.

I must admit, though, just lately it's become a lot more difficult to implement and, sadly, you rarely see it any more. It's the new trend for shaved heads that's to blame. It would tend to distort things too much. From the stands it would make players with bushy beards look as if they've got their heads on upside down; like they're heading the ball with their chin. The purists wouldn't like that. Nor the directors – not squeaky-clean enough. Also, the club sponsors wouldn't be particularly fussed on it, either, since the real W.G. Grace jobs would merely contrive to hide their logos. I suppose it's all understandable when you think of the money at stake. Maybe, in fact, the whole thing has become just another one for the scrap-books, simply part of a bygone era. If so, it won't be the first and certainly not the last to go the same way. Still sad though, all the same, since the odd blag or two wouldn't go amiss in today's game. It might make a welcome change from all the pretentious posing and preening you see these days, which, you've got to admit, is all a bit much, isn't it? Some of them parade around like film stars. And I wouldn't mind but half of them are not exactly 'Tom Cruises' are they? Not by a long chalk. Certainly, the dishy 'Patrick Bergers' of this world are very much in the minority as far as professional footballers are concerned. Put it this way, I don't mean to be insulting but if I was Michael Thomas or Jason McAteer, I'd be inclined to stand well away from Patrick for the team photo. Direct comparisons can be pretty cruel. Now if they were to invest in one of those false beards and a decent pair of shades, they could stand where they liked and no-one would know any different.

The Reds, throughout the Fifties, epitomised one of those outfits who just could not seem to grasp the crucial significance of having the right names within their ranks. People, nowadays, rightly associate Liverpool with glamorous names. It's inevitable. Keegan, Toshack, Dalglish, Souness, Rush, Barnes and so on are wheeled out every time the club is mentioned. Now don't get me wrong, I'm not complaining here. The opposite, in fact. I'm eternally grateful. Believe me, though, it wasn't always so. Like most other fans we, too, lived through all the despair and mediocrity, all the shame and frustration. I mean just look at the names of some of the crowd we had to contend with in the Fifties. It's hard not to blush just to think of them, even for a fleeting moment. All that merciless ridicule we used to get from the Evertonians. And who could blame them? Those names! Bert Slater, Fred Morris, Doug Rudham, Cyril Done, Dick White, Louis Bimpson. I could go on. What a collection. What a nightmare. Whoever assembled that little crew obviously knew sod all about the true art of management. How the hell did we seriously hope ever to get out of the second division with that little lot? There was more chance of Mike and Bernie Winters making you laugh.

The annoying thing was the solution lay there all the time, dormant within the existing players, winking at us season after season, like a floodlight on the blink. Take just one example. Louis Bimpson. Now Louis was not exactly the finest player Liverpool have ever had, although many older Liverpudlians will tell you he was one of the most popular. This was because Louis had the heart of a brontosaurus. Played like one, too, as it happens. Despite his limitations, there was no way Louis would ever let you down. It wasn't in his make-up. Probably something to do with coming from Burscough, I suppose. Sadly, for poor Louis and for us, too, there wasn't a single soul who could ever take Louis seriously. How could they? I mean, when they handed out the names at the local Registry office, Louis's parents were still down at the Wizard's Den in Moorfields, working out their next practical joke. Either that, or else the Registrar was spaced out on hemp at the time. Certainly, whatever the reasons behind the unfortunate choice of name, there was no way any expectant mothers were going to deliver prematurely from the excitement of naming their own babies after him. Unless, of course, Paula Yates had chanced along. Whichever way you look at it, there was no getting away from the fact, 'Louis Bimpson' was just a rank name.

Ironically, taken on its own, Louis's first name did actually have possibilities. You only have to look at the two other Luis's we've already mentioned – Del Sol and Suarez – to see that. The thing is, though, unless you're a 'Cruyff' or a 'Puskas' you simply can't get away with a single title. 'Louis', by itself, just doesn't work. Besides, apart from 'Pele' which was a pure nickname anyway, it's invariably the surname that is adopted. And there was certainly no way 'Bimpson' was ever going to join any elite band of illustrious surnames.

This, then, is where a little spark of inspiration was needed. Just a tiny piece of ingenuity, a paltry surname switch and it might well have saved the day. It needn't even have been anything exotic or foreign. Okay, so a 'Louis Del Monte' or a 'Louis Panatella' would have been a bonus. And a 'Louis Del Sol', well that would have been a dream. They would certainly have had the whole place buzzing. But, really, any name apart from 'Bimpson' would have done the trick. Anything at all within reason. Christ, even 'Armstrong' might have been enough to set things on their way. Regrettably, the Liverpool management appear not to have been able to see past the end of their players' tunnel. Not a single name was changed. Not a solitary fancy signing made. Nothing to lift the despondency. Not even a Rotherham Ripple. Just the same old boring names. Game after game. Season after season. Predictably, the Reds continued to languish for years in their second division backwater, suffering so badly from name blindness that one year their coach driver even joined in the prevailing spirit and took the team for one away fixture to the wrong ground. In fact, he went to the wrong end of the country. Exeter instead of Newcastle. It was scarcely credible and caused an outcry amongst the Reds' fans and directors. There again, to be fair to the driver, I suppose if you've seen one St. James Park, you've probably seen them all. It is only a name, after all, and, let's make no bones about it, the Liverpool management could scarcely complain on that score with their track record.

Thankfully, over the Pennines in Huddersfield, scarcely a shrug of the shoulders away from the ripples in Rotherham, something was stirring. Something which was to change our team and our lives. A craggy Scottish gent was busily honing his football act, preparing to realise a destiny and, at the same time, a dynasty. Bill Shankly knew all about names and could pronounce them better than anyone. He knew their significance better than anyone, too. Before long he was to grasp the opportunity to put his knowledge to the test. Louis Bimpson, Fred Morris and the rest were about to become fond memories. New exciting names were appearing over the horizon. Shankly's horizon. And ours, too. The magic of Ian St. John and Rowdy Yeats would represent the first significant steps in a long term shift in the balance of soccer power in England and later Europe and, as we have already seen, the 'Saint', himself, would go on to carve his name for posterity in the life and on the desk of at least one grateful young Red. Meanwhile, the Red Faith would eventually spread everywhere. Never again would our indoctrination into that faith present a challenge worthy of the name, for there would be no more daunting Blue gauntlets of aunty Kittys or uncle Ebbas or Mr Buglers to contend with. No more crappy names, either. Life was finally changing for the better and becoming a Red was to become as easy as getting past Dick White on the break. Liverpudlians would at long last have something to sing about.

Confirmation

Every Saturday we go
To see the te-ee-eam that you all know
And we cheer them to the top
From the mighty Spion Kop

Two, three, four –

We all live in a red and white Kop
A red and white Kop
A red and white Kop
We all live in a red and white Kop
A red and white Kop
A red and white Kop

(*Sung heartily to the tune of Yellow Submarine*)

The miraculous escape from the Royal blue clutches of Mr Bugler had signified the removal of the last obstacle to the fulfillment of our redness. With Mr Bugler well and truly vanquished, Shanks, St. John and the rest firmly in place and the Boys' Pen thankfully behind us, the Spion Kop now beckoned and we, resplendent in our red and white scarves and eager to be confirmed into the faith, were ready to answer its call.

The Kop in the early Sixties held 28,000 frustrated pop singers under one roof. As the tannoy system used to bellow out the latest songs of Cilla and Gerry, the Beatles and the Searchers, we all joined in singing in the best Liverpool Saturday night pub and party tradition – loud and passionate and full of piss and wind and not necessarily in tune, yet always in perfect harmony especially for Gerry's anthem. Then some Kopites – rumoured to be either Ben Hendry and the Lloyd brothers from the Liver Pub in Waterloo or a mysterious Kopite called Peter Daly whom I know definitely wrote "I am a Liverpudlian" a few years later –

made up new words to some of the songs and used the school playground skipping song "Ee aye addio" for others except "the Farmer" was no longer "in his den" but we were "gonna win the League" and then they mimicked the "Bra-zil Cha Cha Cha" chant from the 1962 World Cup but with "Liv-er-pool" followed by handclapping, instead. And that's how it all started, though though some say the "Liv-er-pool" chant and also the handclapping "St. John" chant were going strong as early as 1961 and some Evertonians will even tell you tell you that "Ever-ton clap, clap, clap" came first, but then they would, wouldn't they, since they hate to be left out of things. As for me, well I've never trusted my own memory over anything so I'll settle for the Boys Pen singing "Two, four, six, eight, who do we appreciate . . . " as the thing which started the ball rolling.

The Kop was a magical place for lads such as myself. We had gazed down across it in awe through the cages of the Pen. Actually, being there felt like you had made it to the epicentre of the universe, the place where everything was happening – you sensed you were part of something new and important.

On the Kop, we became the kid brothers of a huge, densely packed family cutting a swathe through Liverpool society – young scallies to grand dads, doctors to dockers, bus to orchestra conductors. Like young fledglings in the bottom of a nest, we were snug and secure. We were with our own kind; each of us an integral part of a vibrant whole. We sang as one, laughed and cried as one, joked, roared, yelled, bawled, whistled, ranted, raved, swayed, jostled, surged, steamed and sweated all as one, all part of a pulsating embankment of human vitality and energy. Its allure was stark and obvious – if you didn't mind the geriatric smell, that is, for only those on the fringes could reach the toilets; anyone else used a rolled up Liverpool Echo.

I loved every second of it. My indoctrination and my obsession with football was starting to make some sense and besides, at that age, I had a strong bladder so I could stand near the middle and still not need an Echo. Quite simply, for me, nothing else before nor since has come near to the thrill of being a part of the living, breathing Spion Kop during the Sixties and Seventies and it tingles palpably now as I write about it, though I suppose that could be simply because my bladder is no longer quite so strong as it used to be.

I am not altogether sure if the Kop was the biggest 'end' in football – I think perhaps those at Hillsborough, Villa Park and Molyneux may have been as big, if not slightly bigger – but somehow there always seemed to be something different about the Kop which set it apart. So, when we first trod its concrete steps, just prior to the onset of all the singing and chanting and scarves and swaying, even then as young and ignorant scruffs, we knew it was special.

Whether this derived from its unique structural composition which, from the outside, hardly resembled a football ground at all, more an early 20th Century armaments factory or industrial building with its maroon and cream coloured rendered brickwork and concrete encased iron columns and girders and the peculiar rows of cross-braced windows enclosing it, or perhaps from its immense cavernous interior which would act as a giant echo chamber amplifying every noise, it is hard to know.

The almost mythical reputation may have arisen from what we had been told by older family and friends about its atmosphere and history and about their fondness for it, which secured it a position of almost pivotal significance within the broad Liverpool community. Its sports-manship and its roar, spoken of by visiting players in the old football annuals in the same terms as the Hampden roar, may also have been major factors. Kop humour even then was legendary and probably also played its part – such as the time it took the mickey out of Arthur Kagan when the celebrated leader of the Wembley Community singing visited Anfield with his band in the early Fifties (evidently poor Arthur tried half a dozen times to get the Kop to sing along with his band's wartime tunes but the Kop infuriatingly ignored Arthur's instructions and persisted each time in a tongue-in-cheek rendition of 'Yes we have no bananas'. When the hapless Arthur finally relented and got the band to play 'bananas', the Kop, with predictable contrary irreverence, immedi-ately started up with one of the old wartime numbers. It was, no doubt, good fun for everyone except dear old Arthur, who, understandably, walked off a trifle miffed.)

Looking back, it seems clear that any uniqueness or aura which the Kop possessed stemmed not so much from its undoubted physical attributes nor its pedigree but more from the characteristic vitality of its inhabitants and I think 'inhabitants' rather than 'occupants' more aptly reflects that sense of community spirit the Kop invoked. Certainly, the Kop structure gave the Kopites a platform on which they could perform but the essence of the Kop's magic were the Kopites themselves.

In those days, the Kop was virtually 100% Scouse since outsiders had not by then been attracted by the success which was to follow in subse-quent years; the punters were Liverpudlian by team and birthright; there was no dilution, and on a Saturday afternoon, they were out for a good time following their week's work, which for many finished only at lunchtime that day. For many others, the Saturday match was the start of their Saturday night out and many came dressed in their suits ready for the pubs and clubs later on.

All told, most of them were up for the crack; quite simply, they wanted to enjoy themselves. And so the Kop became like one giant local ale house packed solid with 28,000 Scousers ready for a laugh where there was no chance of reaching the bar unless you were a contortionist but, in compensation, you could chat and joke with all the familiar friendly faces who surrounded you and, as a special bonus providing you were as tall as a Harlem Globetrotter, you could watch a decent game of footy.

It was a potent concoction, a natural breeding ground for humour and an outlet for the banter and wisecracks which are right up your average Liverpudlian's street; all in all, a time bomb of exuberance building towards an explosion. When Bill Shankly provided something on the pitch to shout about and simultaneously, the Beatles let the world know that the city was not simply a port of call, the detonation took place.

I suppose in some remote tenuous way it was like being present at the birth of rock and roll when black music fused with white. The Kop simply ignited and, once a fortnight, the chemical reaction fizzled and crackled and lit up the afternoon sky. The match itself became , almost, an irrelevance and the beauty of it all was that, like Elvis' own creation, the Kop at that time was innocently unaware of itself and of what it was unleashing on an unwitting sporting world. For Liverpudlians, there was little doubting it was the place to go.

From Seaport Sands, we would take the No. 33 bus or one of the football 'specials' to Everton Valley, or the train to Bankhall Station and after an uphill trot, enter the Kop on the Lake Street side, walking up the long back entry cum road which ran from the King Harry pub all the way up to the ground past the rows of large old terrace houses either side. The distinctive colours and strange features of the Kop would hit you as soon as you turned into the entry. As you approached it and the crowds thickened and the mounted policemen began to form a sort of seven-man wide queue, all the time, the Kop's dramatic profile filled more of the skyline until, all of a sudden, you were there at the rows of turnstiles. Then came the relief as you clicked your way inside to take your spec on the terraces with your mates amongst all the other Kopites, ready for your Saturday afternoon fix. The time would be around half past one, the kick-off an hour and a half away, the terraces filling up rapidly and the singing and chanting usually already in full swing, especially if it was a 'big' match. For us, it was where life began and ended.

Such profound sentiment may sound a rather dramatic way of stressing the importance of our fanaticism. I can assure you it is not for, effectively, by the age of thirteen or fourteen, it really was the case. Whatever else may have been happening in our lives at that time, we, in effect, existed almost solely as Reds' supporters. Liverpool's promotion and immediate consolidation into one of the best teams in the First Division together with the irresistible allure of the Spion Kop had fired the imagination of every Liverpudlian and we, certainly, could think of nothing else. Days between matches were spent, depending on the outcome of the previous game, in either cock-eyed mouth-watering anticipation of the next game or ceaseless passionate contemplation of the previous one; neither navels, nor novels come to that, entered into it. The match became everything; being a Kopite even more.

By this time, in terms of our indoctrination, we had graduated. Our formal initiation and education into the Red Faith was complete. We were now fully fledged Reds, Kopites to boot. In my own case, the efforts of my father and Uncle Denny, amongst many, had borne fruit, while all those trials and tribulations at the hands of Aunty Kitty, Uncle Ebba and Mr Bugler were now of no consequence whatsoever. What we now all did with our Faith was down to us. It became like any other religion. We could keep it or lapse; relegate it to the armchair or the ale house; nurture or abuse it. There were no rules to go by, no Catechism to follow. Everything was now governed by instinct and the road ahead was unpredictable. Of course, the beauty of it all as far as Liverpudlians were concerned was that our road was paved with silver. Other fans did not have it quite so lucky and the majority had muddy dirt tracks to contend with. Whatever the route however, for the likes of me, there would now be no turning back and for us, the Kop became our spiritual home, the place where we belonged, the mainstay of our lives.

Whether the same applies to all fans who populate their respective ends, I am unsure, but as a former one myself, I am bound to say that the Kopites who massed on the terraces in those days, for all their humour and sense of mischief and fun, were actually a pretty confused and mixed-up bunch; a curious strain of massive paradoxes and contradictions. I mean, it's easy to see how the Kop legend has grown over the years but like anything else, scratch just below the surface and all is not always quite as it seems.

Talk to any Kopite and they will proudly tell you of their beloved 'spec', their own precious two to three square feet of sacred Kop terracing which belonged to them and them alone; the spot where they stood every other week, rain or shine, for more years than Tony Hateley had clubs – for the record, mine was just to the right of the goal on the lower bank midway between the two stanchions four steps below the fourth row of crush barriers. That, at least, was the theory. The reality, of course, in those days, was altogether different.

Imagine a wild New Year's Eve party in full swing with all the patrons manically weaving about every which way to the music, doing simultaneously the Hokey Cokey, the Conga and Auld Lang Syne. Then imagine a couple of thousand of these parties with all the delirious participants suddenly crammed together onto a huge dripping wet stepped concrete embankment littered with crash barriers with the music still playing and the entire mass still frantically dancing away in all different directions, while at the same time, trying their best to get back to the place from where they started and never once managing to do so. Imagine that going on for a crazy cascading two and a half hours with everyone for the whole time in perpetual motion and for most of the time laughing and singing and shouting at the top of their voice and, here and there, some people trying to light a cigarette or take a piss through a rolled up newspaper, and now and again someone fainting and being passed down over the heads of the crowd to the front of the Kop to be treated by a St John's Ambulanceman and all the time everyone sweating cobs. Imagine the sheer mayhem of it all and take my word for it – it was sheer indescribable joy. But don't try and tell me I really had a 'spec' in the midst of all that madness.

Such inconsistencies ran right through the Kop. We were biased – boy were we biased – really biased – partisan to the core. We dished it out to anyone not in a red shirt. We had a chant for everyone. The stick was endless – "Alan Ball, Alan Ball, is it true what Shankly says your worth, Fuck All, oh Alan Ball"; "Hey there Georgie Best, you're a bigger tart than Gordon West"; "Hey there Gordon West, you're a bigger tart than Georgie Best"; "Ee-aye-addio yer dirty big giraffe" (Jack Charlton – who else); "We'll hang Billy Bremner from the Kop by his balls"; "Bobby Moore OBE – other bugger's energy"; "Greasy Vitalis", "Brylcreem" (Bobby Moore) ; "Hey, hey – you, you – gerroff our pitch" (Les Cocker, Leeds United's trainer – for some unknown reason); "Osgood – no good"; "Roll out the barrel" (Johnny Morrisey); "Yer can stick Lou Macari up yer arse, sideways"; "Dougan, Dougan show us yer arse"; "Sha la la la Summerbee, 'oo the fuckin' 'ell is he"; "I'd walk a million miles to the end of your nose, oh Summerbee"; "Yer get more noise from a packet of crisps than yer do from Gwladys Street", "Yer dirty big fat twat" (anyone bulky); "Who's up Mary Brown? Who's up Mary Brown? – Tommy, Tommy Docherty"; "Tina, Tina" (Peter Shilton); "Who were you with last night?" (Peter Shilton and Tina); "What's it like to shag a sheep?" (any woolyback); "What's the weather like up there?". "There's only one Blackpool Tower" (anyone tall); "Pinnochio"; (our own Phil Thompson).

And then a visiting goalkeeper would arrive at the Kop end and we'd cheer and applaud them – every time (except nowadays Peter Schmeichel whom we all hate because he's so horrible and aggressive and such a whingebag). And then Gordon Banks would come and we'd all go ecstatic and chant warmly "Charlie Chan" and "He's the best goalkeeper in the land" and "Charlie" would grin at us and wave fondly. And then Chelsea would come and play us off the park in January 1966 and we'd applaud them off the pitch; and then Ajax in 1967 and Ferenavaros in 1968 would do the same and so would we. And then in 1969 Leeds United arrived.

They basically needed a draw to clinch the Championship. We needed to win to retain an outside chance of the title. Rivalry between the two sides was intense. Leeds had followed Liverpool out of the Second Division in the early sixties and were intent on emulating everything Liverpool had achieved at that time. In truth, they were by then the better side, not quite to the standard of their early 1970's peak but the best in the country nevertheless. We were still a formidable side but quite clearly past our peak. A fiercely fought game ended goal-less and the Leeds players celebrated joyously. They had, after all, won the League title at Anfield, home, at that time, of their keenest rivals.

It was Billy Bremner, their highly gifted diminutive midfielder who prompted his team-mates to run towards the Kop, hesitantly but determinedly. Rationally, of course, they anticipated a deluge of whistles, abuse and jeers as they approached the vast bank of Liverpool fans on the Kop but they didn't really care since they had just clinched the Championship. Instead, the white shirted players stood transfixed and spellbound for what seemed like an eternity, as they were greeted by a thunderous chant of 'Champions' accompanied by a sea of Liverpudlian arms raised aloft, hands clapping warmly and vigorously in recognition of the qualities of the great footballing side that Leeds undoubtedly were.

The sight and sound of a huge mass of crowded terracing towering high above you containing 28,000 voices and pairs of hands thunderously cheering and applauding, when you expected completely the opposite to happen must come as quite a shock, even to Billy Bremner.

It would be rather akin to the wicked witch in a Snow White pantomime receiving rapturous applause from all the kids in the audience as she poisons the apple. She would be some confused witch. So it was with the Leeds players, who, utterly bewildered and disarmed trooped off the Anfield pitch like embarrassed schoolboys caught in the middle of a naughty prank, rather than swaggering off like the unequivocal deserved champions they had just become.

We, meanwhile, had all got a buzz out of it. Okay, so maybe we had just lost the League but when you have just lost something and you can still dig out something to give, it makes you feel better. It's like having a good cry. Looking back, I suppose maybe we did it because we all liked triers and Leeds were definitely in that category – like eleven Joey Jones bursting every sinew. Maybe such sportsmanship is, in fact, simply altruistic. Maybe we did it to get a telegram off Don Revie and Len Shipman, the League President, telling us how great we were – which we did the next day. Whatever the reason, it doesn't alter the basic fact that Kopites were schizoid.

One thing the Kopites weren't schizo about was having a laugh. The Kop tried hard to be funny. Often they succeeded.

In 1965, people used to throw toilet rolls onto the pitch and onto the goals and they would get tangled up in the nets. Before the Man United game that year, the Kop goal was in a particularly bad way looking like the Andrex advert without the dog. Barely had the referee and linesmen started to clear up all the mess of paper when the Kop struck up "Ee-aye-addio, the ref wants a shit". The officials lapped up the lavatory humour. At a testimonial game, the football was particularly one paced – a dire crawl – and everyone was relieved for the half-time entertainment by the marching band. Then the second half began and it was worse than the first and the Kop cried out "We want the band back" and they sounded as if they meant it and probably did. The players meanwhile, enjoyed the only highspot of the night. At another testimonial – Tommy Smith's – the score-line became a bit of a joke, which as any Evertonian will concur was a bit like the Everton team of the period. It was something like 12-8 but nobody knew it precisely. Anyway, the Kop decided to amuse itself. It targeted the Directors' box with more than strong hints that they needed a scoreboard (something which Anfield has never had) "We want a scoreboard" they bellowed over and over again. Next they tried a bit of blackmail – "Everton have got one, Everton have got one" they cried repeatedly. Then on the hoof came the punch line to match the little cameo scenario they had spontaneously engineered by their improvised leg pulling. "They never fuckin' use it, they never fuckin' use it". The game stopped as all the players and the officials and the rest of the crowd laughed themselves silly.

By the early-Seventies, the Kop's reign as the unique institution it had become in the Sixties was drawing to an end. (In fact some of my own mates say that for most ordinary games this was the case as early as 1966, though I disagree). True, there were many occasions after the early-Seventies when the atmosphere was special. In this respect you only have to think of Bruges, St Etienne, Auxerre, Birmingham City when we were 3-1 down, Derby games, most Man United games and Tommy Smith's testimonial. Also the first bit of the Kop's best-ever song – "Poor Scouser Tommy" – and the aria "We're on our way to Roma" – were still to come.

Really though, whilst you could still enjoy the atmosphere and whilst the traditions still remained such as singing only our own songs and applauding visiting goalies and good play by the opposition and never jeering our own team and basically never doing anything that any other crowd did – the Kopites were fiercely protective of their own individuality – if you are truly honest and objective and take away the rose-tinted specs, you have to admit the real spark, the uniqueness, had gone. The Kop was, by then, only too aware of itself and its reputation. The crowd's own performance tended for the most part to be only in response to events on the pitch and, at times, they were even outsung by smaller numbers of opposing fans – something once unthinkable. The unconscious spontaneity and the embracing of Merseybeat which had created the magic in the first place were a decade in the past. True, Shanks was still there and that love affair was still blossoming. However, the Kop had become like Elvis Presley himself – still doing party pieces and still undoubtedly good to watch and giving value for money and often good fun (especially for those seeing it for the first time) but in reality, no longer in peak form, no longer vital, no longer holding that unique mystery and mystique which had established a reputation in the early days as the first and best of its genre.

You only had to compare the respective atmospheres of the big European nights in the Sixties with their counterparts, St Etienne apart, in the later decades when we were actually winning European trophies, to see that clearly something had gone, something had changed. Also by this time, its capacity was constantly being nudged down from its 28,000 heyday – by the time of the Kop's last stand, it was not much more than half that – and it was no longer pure Scouse but becoming like the League of Nations which, though in some aspects, added a bit of novelty – and let's face it, it's a free country and I welcome anyone – in other respects, it further dulled the caustic Scouse edge that had made it what it was.

Essentially, towards the end of the Seventies, the Kop, in many aspects, had virtually become like any of its great imitators – the Shed, the North Bank, the Boothen, the Holt, the Stretford, the Gallowgate Ends and all the others, all of which brings me to my favourite chant. It's to the tune of 'She'll be coming round the mountain when she comes' and it's sparse and simple and it's elitist and it's guaranteed to get up noses but, above all, it is true and I love the pure arrogance of its message to non-Kopites all over the world:

"Oh yer got yer education from the Kop
Oh yer got yer education from the Kop
Oh yer got yer education
Got yer education
Yer got yer education from the Kop"

And what the hell – if you had it, flaunt it, for all it's worth. Besides, there are no other conclusions to be drawn about the edifice that was the Kop nor any more fitting epitaph for the spiritual home of every Liverpool fan, because all of what happened afterwards on stands and terraces everywhere bore testimony to the chant's fiercely proud and simplistic sentiment. Moreover, it is a sentiment which is as true today as it was back then, even though, you have to admit, painful as it might be, that apart from those infrequent surges of unrestrained enthusiasm which seem to be prompted more by sun-spot activity than anything else, the current all-seated Kop has now become more gentile and certainly less entertaining than a Conservative Party over-sixties Lady's Bridge Club Convention in Chipping Sodbury. Mind you, I suppose the bottom line is that nothing lasts forever in this world anymore, not even something as rare and precious and beautiful as the Anfield Spion Kop bellowing out its deafening defiance to all and sundry on a misty Sixties European footy night in Liverpool in Springtime .

"Whoah! You over eighteen, la' ?"
"Yeah."
"'E is, 'onest. 'E just looks young, 'cos 'e's littler than the rest of us."
"Yeah, yer wanna see 'is old feller, 'e looks even younger."
"Ah, go 'ead mate, lerrim' in. Don't be tight."
"Sorry, la', if 'e's over eighteen, then I'm Donald Duck"

"Yer've gorra big enough beak" (barely discernible sideways mutter).

"'E is over eighteen, though mate, 'onest ter God. Swear on me mother's grave."

"What d'yer mean, yer lyin' get, yer ma's still alive."

"Shut it, soft arse. I'm tryin' ter gerrus in, aren't I. Yer soft get. Take no notice of 'im, pal. 'Onest, 'e's gone twenty. Just look at 'is chest if yer don't believe us. 'E's gorra massive tattoo of a g'rilla on it. Go 'ead, show 'im the g'rilla, Stumpy. Take off yer ganzy. Go 'ead."

"Yeah, go on Stumpy, show 'im the g'rilla."

"Yeah, 'e wouldn't 'ave that if 'e was under eighteen, would 'e?"

"Sorry, la', there's no way yiz can come in. No way. Anyroad, the manager's pipin' us now, so yiz 'ad all berra shift, good style."

"But 'e's older than the rest of us. So if yer gonna let us in, then . . . "

"Piss off, I said. Don't yiz understand English. None of yiz are gettin' in . . . It's nothin' Larry. Just some lads pissin'round . . . Now will yiz frig off, before I 'ave ter get nasty. Friggin' pests."

"Oh that's very nice, that is. Which charm school did you go to?"

"Miserable fat twat!"(Further muttered aside).

"Bet yer wouldn't say that to 'is face."

"Too right. Me name's Croft, not soft. D'yer see the size of 'im? 'E 'ad arms like Popeye . . . Right, are we gonna try the Grafton or d'yer fancy a chinky instead or are we stayin' 'ere all night or what? "

"Yeah."

"Yeah."

"Nah."

"Nah."

"Yeah."

"Nah."

"Okay then, looks like I'll 'ave ter make yer minds up for yer . . . "

"Eh you wi' the dicky-bow! Yer miserable fat bastard! Come 'ere if yer think yer 'ard enough."

"Yer stupid get, 'e's 'eard yer."

"Yeah, look 'e's comin' over."

"Ha! Doesn't bother me. I'm the best runner, aren' I? See yiz at the top of the street."

"Aw, I'm not messin', you're dead you, Tommy. Yer know I've gorra sore leg. Yer stupid get."

Most of our nights at the clubs in town used to end up the same way. It didn't matter which club. The Beachy, the Vic, the Mardi, the Cavern, the Babalou. Always a disaster. Start off full of promise and end up a

Limbo of unfulfillment. Like the Reds with Louis Bimpson and Fred Morris.

Don't misinterpret what I'm saying here. It was all our own doing. The clubs themselves were superb, the girls gorgeous in the best Merseyside tradition and the music . . . well, that was the most special of all. This, remember, was the heyday of Motown, Atlantic, Stax, Beatles, Stones, Beach Boys, Cream, Creedence Clearwater, The Box-Tops, Bob Dylan, The Band, The Kinks, Geno Washington and all the rest. Sublime stuff. So, where did it all go wrong?

Well, the first problem was the sound quality. Inside the clubs, it was marvellous. No question. Outside on the pavement, though, wasn't so clever. A bit muffled for the true connoisseur. Not exactly the perfect reception. It was like trying to pick up Radio Luxembourg under the bed-clothes at night. We could only make out the bass line. Half our night would be spent arguing about which song was playing. We became experts. We had to. We had no choice. Not even the tiniest variation in the beat would escape our attention. So adept did we become, there's little doubt we could have made it as top flight A&R men in Memphis. Did you know the bass line on Eddie Floyd's 'Knock on Wood' is the same as Edison Lighthouse's 'Love Grows'? We did. Certainly it used to be to our ears, anyway.

We used to love that one. They used to play it all the time. At the match, too. 'Love grows where my Rosemary goes and nobody knows like me'. We used to take it literally. I think the notion of it struck a chord with us. Trouble was we could never quite work out where it was she went. Though we tried our best to find out and though we all knew only too well it was the object of our weekly excursions into town, the art of 'tapping off' remained elusive to us. Even the odd times we made it into the clubs, we would hardly ever manage it and certainly never with anyone we fancied. The odd boot, maybe, but that would be all. And most of them seemed to live in Speke, which to us was like the other end of the universe.

It wasn't that any of us were what you would call really ugly. I mean George actually resembled a young Malcolm Allison minus the cigar and fedora and his Mick Jagger strut was a sensation. Tommy had the gift of the gab. Billy was magnificently moody, while I was something else at playing hard to get, though for my particular ploy to work it's usually a big plus if somebody's after you in the first place and that was the bit with which I always struggled. I suppose, when you look back, our main problem was there was no ball involved, so the whole thing was all a bit alien to us. I mean if you could trap a girl like you did a ball, we'd have probably managed fine. Well, say, seven times out of ten, anyway. Nine in George's case. As it was, it was more like none out of ten. Making passes was the same. With a ball you knocked it back. With a girl we used to find it was invariably the other way round.

Thursday, Friday and Saturday night were always the same. There'd be Tommy and George and Billy and me, who would always be together. Sometimes, Eric and John Howard, Billy Lewis, Frank, Pete and Walla Hemmings, Joey, Binky and Sharpy, too. On Fridays or Saturdays, that would be when Stumpy and Frankie Amerigo used to join us. Stumpy was three years older than us but about a foot shorter with Juninho features, which meant he actually looked about four years younger. Frankie Amerigo was the same age as Stumpy and not much bigger but, with a wardrobe that included a pink drape jacket, skin tight ice-blue keks with ten and a half inch bottoms, black shirt with white buttons and studded collar and white tie all topped off with a slick black 'Kenton', Frankie looked the part. Not that we ever knew which part, but Frankie certainly did, so it didn't seem to matter. Actually, it was most probably Joe Pesci, but none of us had a clue back then who Joe Pesci was.

Stumpy was the main reason we never got in any of the clubs. It was virtually a foregone conclusion at every one – except the Grafton, which was a sort of 'grab a granny' old style ballroom where you had to be twenty-one to get in. Daft as it seems Stumpy had no problem getting in there, which was far more disconcerting than the knock-backs. If Stumpy looked twenty-one at the Grafton, then *we* must have looked twenty-five, when we were really just teenagers, which means if the same proportions apply today, then I must now look sixty-three; almost retired with a walking stick in the post. Christ, no wonder all the old dears keep giving me the eye when I smile at them at the bus stop.

Not surprisingly, all the knock-backs from both the club doormen and the female club-goers used to have a demoralising effect on us. All except Frankie Amerigo, who seemed strangely to draw a kind of alarming inner strength from it all. Following each rejection, he used to treat us, and anyone else passing by, to a stunning display of what can only be termed artistic virtuosity:

"Hey, no worries. It's sorted. Pay back time will come. The family take care of its own. It's just business. Cabiche! ", he would say over and over again, as we watched him in fond bemusement, while he used to circle round us, first one way then the other in tiny agitated strides, his head bowed slightly with shoulders repeatedly shrugging and his arms stretching wide with hands palmed open expressively, occasionally reaching up with one hand to yank loose his tie or take a frantic drag of his ciggy. They were certainly heady performances and as puzzling as they may have seemed to us back then (we hadn't even heard about spaghetti in those days let alone vendettas) there is little doubt that if Francis Ford Coppola had been watching, then Al Pacino wouldn't have had a look in for the part of Michael Corleone and one of our mates would have become a major film star. The thing was, though, unless you were a Maurice Cole or a Cherie Booth, that sort of break never seemed to happen round our way, so Frankie eventually had to make do with a window cleaning round in Palermo Street, just off Seaport Road.

For the rest of us, especially Stumpy who was becoming increasingly frustrated that not even the presence of the mighty King Kong on his chest could secure his entry to the sleaziest of clubs, it was impossible to share Frankie's sense of menacing inner resolve that all was fine. Time was slipping away from us. So were our chances of 'bagging off' with the right sort of girls. So, too, with it was any credibility we had left. By this time as far as we were concerned fun had become something only other people experienced. Sex, though our machismo would never allow us to admit it, was the same. And the truth was, it was not only the time and the girls which were slipping away. Our entire lives were, too. The 'swinging Sixties' had almost expired and the nearest we had got to it was sharing Tarzan impersonations on an old bike tyre hanging from the lamp-post outside our local pub, the 'Vic'.

Mind you, the 'Vic' was a wonderful consolation for all our angst. True, we may not have felt so back then, but time and distance really do lend enchantment and I realise now that the 'Victoria Hotel' was truly an epic place, a fitting and reassuring backdrop to what is probably the most volatile and uncertain period in anyone's lives.

From the outside the 'Vic' may have appeared like any other grotty little white rendered pub. Which it was. The 'hotel' bit was simply one of those curious British misnomers coined to flatter. Instead, what we had was a typical local watering hole of no particular attraction to any outsider. Hardly the type of pub you would travel miles for. Certainly not one you would find extolled in the 'pub guide books', even if Oliver Reed was editor. Indeed, with its dingy narrow L-shaped bar room, drab bar lounge and tacky flock papered 'Blue Room' front lounge, a stranger might be excused for questioning why anybody would want to drink there at all. Without doubt, anyone sampling the dubious delights of the Walker's bitter on offer might have been inclined to agree with them, especially if they had also been unfortunate enough to have become embroiled in one of those sobering affirmations of local manhood which could be meted out from time to time by some of the 'Vic's' less hospitable patrons.

As we now all know only too well, applying such a limited set of criteria to the adoption of a 'local' can be misleading. The attraction can have little at all to do with appearances, the local bitter or even a 'good hiding' at closing time. If it's good bitter you're after, then you enrol in CAMRA and you certainly don't drink in the same place night after night because you're fond of the wallpaper. If that was the case, you'd simply take a couple of crates of Newky Brown down to B&Q and have done. As for the closing time 'pastings' – well they tended, for the most part, to be optional affairs in any case.

No, your local pub is more than all that. There are emotions involved. Thirsts to be satisfied. Not just a thirst for ale but a thirst to be part of something, too. To identify with your community. Like you do with your football team. It's no coincidence that most diehard regulars used to be men. It wasn't just that women felt uncomfortable in a pub or that men were more partial to drinking. It was more to do with the men's desire to belong. Most women were already satisfied on that score. At the shops, on the street corners, on the doorsteps, in the back-kitchens, outside the schools, they were constantly replenishing their sense of community. Reaffirming their belonging. Their menfolk needed somewhere to do the same. To also be a part of the same community. So, too, did we. In our case we graduated into it. Much in the same way as we graduated into becoming Reds or Blues. It was almost as instinctive. The indoctrination processes broadly similar, though far less intensive and lacking the excitement offered by the occasional good cup run or title chase. It was, quite simply, what you did. What most people did. The fact that you could also get pissed at the same time as you bonded with everyone else was simply a welcome bonus, as was also the piano in the far corner of the bar lounge which became the centrepoint for many a happy, if off-key, night of song and bondage. Or should that be bonding? Anyway, whatever it was, one thing's for sure it didn't involve sex for we'd have definitely been due first shout if it had have done.

Between 1968 and 1972, the 'Vic' became a second home to us. The place where we met and swapped our thoughts and ideas. Mapped out our lives, all of which revolved around each other and football. It was never going to be as intensive a relationship as some of us had with Anfield or Goodison Park. Nothing could come close to equalling those bonds, ale or no ale. Nor did we ever get around to actually sleeping there, though we did end up slumped across its tables on the odd few occasions and once or twice re-enacted, across its carpeted floors, the crawling stages of our early years when we had had only Farley's rusks for company. Nonetheless, the 'Vic' did become our heartbeat. The place we went to every day. If Anfield and Goodison became the shrines where we worshipped once a fortnight, then the 'Vic' was the living room where we simply got on with cementing our friendships and living out our late 'teens' and early 'twenties'. We had no need for other mates or other interests outside the 'Vic'. Nor anything else for that matter. All we needed lay within our cosy little enclave.

Though at the time seemingly boring and aimless, the period now appears like a whirlwind of activity and excitement. An orgy of freedom and indulgence. A time when the entrance through the 'Blue Room's' doors of a bunch of merely ordinary looking females could create as much of a stir as one of Peter Thompson's lightning dribbles down the left wing when he used to beat the same full back six times and the poor guy would end up exhausted, pleading with 'Thommo' to put him out of his misery and centre the ball. Well, okay, so maybe not quite as thrilling as that. But, certainly enough to lend a sense of hope and purpose to an evening which may otherwise have been drifting towards just another trek to the 'chippy' at the bottom of South Road. At least, that is, until such time as someone else had tapped off with the girls and the irresistible aromas of hot pies and battered fish had begun to waft in through the 'Vic's' doors to stimulate our other primary senses.

For a spell of three or four years, this was our life. We were effectively married to each other, the 'Vic' and football. Our families were simply something to be tolerated. Our homes the place we dossed. Workmates and outsiders remained no more than just acquaintances. It was an exclusive arrangement. As soon as those acquaintances, inevitably, became something more; as soon as we began to develop the merest flicker of a life away from the 'Vic', then the balance was destroyed and the bond broken. Naturally, we didn't know it at the time. We were just following our instincts as we had always done. Pretty soon, though, we had become outsiders to each other. Nothing planned or underhand. Nothing tangible. Nothing was ever said. But the drift had started. The absolute commitment had gone. We were no longer mates in the same way. Sad, but for many of us, simply the way it went.

For those for whom getting married, settling down and having children is a sort of pre-determined destiny, it is almost inevitable that the 'Vics' of this world together with all their rich trappings and camaraderie must at some stage take a back seat or be left behind altogether. To be true to the new people in your life, there is really no other way. Anything else can quite easily become a sham. Meanwhile, for those who move away and set up a new life, the split is often permanent and there exists no alternative. As time goes on, roots are automatically shed. Besides, your 'local' is not exactly the same as your team. You are allowed to change it. Most do at one time or another. For one reason or another. In fact, there are some who flit from bar to bar like a swarm of Bosman signings on the lookout for the very best nectar on offer. Certainly, at the very least, you can pick and choose your favourite pubs in a way true football fans can never do with their team, however much some of them would wish to.

There are the lucky ones, of course. The loyal ones who manage to stay the course. Spend their life in the same neighbourhood. Keep the same friends. Sit on the same bar stool. There's little doubt some deserve a medal for their sterling efforts or, better still, a Bell's Whisky Award for loyalty. Like Bob Paisley. Maybe even a Testimonial night at Anfield or Goodison. If not then certainly Prenton Park or Haig Avenue at the very least. Even for them, though, life is not always plain sailing. There is still more often than not a price to pay and the secret regrets of a solitary life or a liver supercharged enough to bend free kicks round walls or an ale gut as big as two or three of Mickey Quinn's put together or a marriage at an end or, perhaps worse still, without an end, mean that nobody escapes scot-free. Not even lifetime regulars.

What can never disappear throughout all this are the memories, fond or otherwise, of those places at which we first supped. The friends. The music. The girls. The fights. The beer. That first packet of smoky bacon flavoured crisps. That very first snatched sighting of a condom machine on the loo wall – a scathing a reminder of your dismal track record with the opposite sex. The aching fondness for what was. And the social skills which we developed there, too. Invaluable skills you couldn't acquire anywhere else. Honed over just a few years, yet retained for all time. Making a pint of Double Diamond work wonders the whole night when you were skint. Casually nudging the jukebox to get your records on first. Rigging the pub 'spot the ball' competitions. Sneaking your own refill when Tom and Irene had nipped out of the Bar. And most useful of all, tilting the table football machine to gain possession without anyone ever noticing. Magic stuff. Such wiles as those can change destinies. Win honours. Championships even – to be precise, the 1968 Victoria Hotel Summer Table Football Championship, when I thrashed Pete Lysaught out of sight to become the 'Vic's' table footy champion. Enough said, I think. I certainly don't want to come across as big-headed, though a championship is a championship when all's said and done, whether on grass or under glass, even if there were only four others who entered for it. Liverpudlians know that as much as anyone. More than most, I suspect, although I doubt if such a prestigious honour would be enough even now to ensure an easy passage into the clubs in town on a Saturday night. It certainly wasn't back then, no matter how hard we tried.

Being a Kopite didn't mean your own education was limited to Anfield. There were also the away trips. We used to hitch-hike all over. Southampton was the worst to get to. There was no link between the M6 and M1 and we'd hitch along the A5 from Cannock and for some reason known only to themselves, drivers round there never gave lifts so you had to do a lot of walking. We'd get to Southampton tired, wet, cold and starving and then we'd watch the match, usually get beaten and set off back to Liverpool and a fortnight later it would be Arsenal then Crystal Palace, or West Ham, or Chelsea, (each time the dreaded A5), then Sunderland, then Leicester, Aston Villa or West Brom, which were easier because sometimes we'd touch lucky with a removal van full of Reds fans and we'd travel and sing all the way in pitch darkness. Once I recall, the tailgate was up and we'd be going down the motorway singing with our legs dangling over and it wouldn't even seem dangerous, though now it makes me shudder to think of it. Then there would be the local away games – Preston, Blackburn, Manchester, Stoke and Burnley, where for some unknown reason thousands of us marched through the town centre singing "HP baked beans they're the beans for us" and for some other unknown reason the locals thought we were funny because, I suppose, it was novel and they were all laughing and some of the old dears joined in for a few strides and it all seemed such good fun and so harmless.

The best away trip of all was to Goodison Park, mainly because it was slightly nearer than the Dell; in fact, it was nearer than Anfield. Derby matches were always all-ticket and we'd get our tickets by queuing up for hours on end at Anfield or Liverpool Stadium a few weeks before the game and on the day we'd go to the match with our Evertonian mates on the No. 68 bus which dropped us right outside in Spellow Lane.

The atmosphere for the Derbies was always special and you took it for granted because it was always the same. Friendly and buzzing with Goodison Road crammed solid with Red and Blue in what, outside the ground always seemed to be roughly equal numbers, milling about trading jokes and insults and swapping Park End for Gwladys Street and vice versa though Park End were rarer and all the time there were the cries of 'any spares'.

The Park End used to have wooden terraces and the principal object of our annual exercise there was not so much to support the Reds as to dismantle the Park End crush barriers by shoving and pulling and yanking them until the base plates worked loose and then wrenching them out and passing them down to the front over everyone's heads and you knew it was a stupid thing to do and, as hindsight tells us, deadly even, but it used to give us all a great feeling of putting one over on the Blues. They had the last laugh, though, when one year, they concreted the terraces and after that we just used to watch the game, waiting for the Eighties when Ian Rush used to score every time we attacked that end.

And then, when we could afford it, there were the overnight trips to London on Lawrensons coaches which I used to love because it was as if you were going on holiday and that represented some novelty to us. We'd leave just before midnight from the Odeon in Waterloo, usually about half a dozen of us, with our bottles of lemo and sarnies and we'd arrive in London at six-thirty in the morning freezing cold because there'd be no heater on the coach, and we'd be utterly shattered because you would never manage to sleep due to a combination of the cold and someone invariably telling jokes for the whole journey. Then we'd get straight on the tube to Green Park and by half-seven, we'd be singing outside Number 10 and by eight o'clock, the Palace and then the police would move us on and tell us contemptuously that we had big voices for little men and you knew then, instinctively, lines were already being drawn.

Then came the bastards who tried to ruin it for everyone else and did so for years.

We saw them first in little clusters in 1967 in London with their shaved heads and braces and half-mast jeans and big boots and they looked just as stupid then as they do now and about 500 of them came into White Hart Lane at the opposite end to where the Reds and Spurs fans were stood side by side in two groups hurling the usual abuse and trying to out-sing each other but essentially in good humour which was as far as it went. Then this mob of sub humans tried to make this entrance all dramatic by walking right round from the opposite end, I suppose, in hindsight, to impress us or frighten us like Indians stalking a wagon train. The police intercepted them and made them walk all the way back the way they had come and they looked really pathetic, but the daft thing was we were all naive about it and didn't have a clue what was happening until they all must have paid again to get in and suddenly appeared at our end and shifted all the real Spurs' fans out of the way and started pushing and intimidating the Reds' fans on the edges with little skirmishes but getting little change because some of the Reds were hard lads and could look after themselves.

Then a couple of the Reds fans must have decided attack was the best form of defence, got up on their mates' shoulders and the four of them pushed and shoved their way right into the midst of the skinheads and the two lads on top above the heads of the crowd were singing and clapping and shouting defiantly at all the skinheads. The skinheads seemed to be taken aback by the temerity of it all for they all just stood and took it and I couldn't believe how anyone could have such bottle but then as they came pushing their way back towards us still singing at the top of their voices I looked at the brutal hardness of the faces of the four of them and knew why. Most certainly they were not from Chipping Norton.

Then the skinheads sensed that their manhood had been affronted and decided it was time to start the real trouble. The big fighting started and before you could say, 'mind the ale lads', it had erupted into a chaotic free-for-all – just like the 'Vic' on one of its quieter nights. We were scared and, like everyone else, ended up hitting out and trying frantically to get out of the way. The police waded in and dragged people out indiscriminately and formed a line to keep the lid on the cauldron and I wondered why they didn't just arrest every skinhead since a blind man could have seen who was to blame.

After that, there was three-way, though not necessarily wide-spread, aggression at most of the big games, except Liverpool and Everton Derbies, with the police piggy in-the-middle. You didn't wear a scarf for certain away games if you had half a brain – the London games, Manchester, Leeds, Newcastle, Villa – because every club had a bunch of nutters hellbent on trouble.

Liverpool's so-called hard-cases were called the 'Anny Road Enders' who in truth were pathetic. Their favourite chant was 'Kopites are Gobshites' and they were probably right because the Kop used to encourage them with chants of 'get into them', and 'Scousers aggro, Scousers aggro' and 'You're gonna get your fuckin' heads kicked in' and the 'Anfield Boot Walk' and 'We don't carry bottles' and I used to think I'd much rather sing 'Anyone who had a heart' along with Cilla like we used to but you knew those days were gone, and it was sad but as much as you wished otherwise, the fact is, times change and things become different.

Intimidation and violence became the name of the game; confrontation and aggression the odious substitutes for fun and humour. Later, the skinheads and boot-boys gave way to more casual looking and organised thugs and then to the so-called 'firms'. Not a single one of them was ever a true football fan. They came only for the 'buzz' of trouble and to inflict pain on others. For all of them, it was strength in numbers like the old street gangs of Glasgow, Liverpool and the East End. Many were nothing but sheep; bits of impressionable kids from the sticks who were witnessing such displays of violence for the first time. Others were just mindless, callous bastards. Despite what people say though, it really was only ever a minority who caused the trouble and none of them knew a football from a testicle. Still, it used to look bad on the telly and all fans got tarred with the same brush and, in fairness, I suppose, you had to admit that not even the true fans – the vast majority – ever really knew where it would all lead to. The more it was distorted it fed on itself and the more it became a trend amongst other loonies who, like sheep, joined in. At the same time, more significantly, it also seemed to become more difficult for the authorities to keep control of the situation and, from time to time, themselves.

We were at Hillsborough, I think in 1969, in that funny far corner enclosure at Leppings Lane next to the stand and the Reds fans were singing and chanting and some stewards in the stand dressed in their sleeveless plastic vests were yelling at the Reds fans to stop singing for some stupid reason and the Reds fans were shouting back at them to go away in customary polite fashion and the stewards became increasingly angry because the chanting continued just the same. The next thing, half a dozen of the stewards climbed over the railings onto the terraces to drag out a couple of the Reds fans who had sworn at them and the fans resisted with equal force. Then all hell broke loose as more stewards and then police came piling in and there was complete pandemonium and fists and feet were flying and two of my mates who hadn't done a thing were dragged out and amazingly through it all there wasn't a solitary Sheffield Wednesday fan to be seen.

The next day, I was right in the centre of a photograph on the back page of the People newspaper and, according to them, I was a football hooligan. I resented it because although I have to admit it was a bad photo of me and made me look uglier than I really am, (if that's possible), it didn't make me a yob.

Years later, we were back at Hillsborough and some Liverpool fans were dressed in Albert Stubbins gear with a banner which I think read 'The Albert Stubbins Fan Club on Tour' and they were in lovely good humour making their way to the ground – you could see it glowing out of them. As they approached the ground, three dour faced bobbies stopped them in their tracks and all but picked a fight with them, seemingly for being too innocuous and happy and they confiscated their banners and baldy wigs and stuff and what was unbelievable was how good humoured the Reds fans remained in spite of the provocation. Looking back, it all makes you wonder just what was really going on back then and for that matter in the lead up to the disaster in 1989. Certainly, there was no need at all for any of the incidents that I witnessed to have occurred and it is undeniable that no matter which way you looked at it, the fans weren't the only idiots at large in those days.

At Anfield, it was never really bad inside – though I do remember when some United fans tried to invade the Kop and mercifully, just about lived to regret it – but outside, the nutters would always hang around, waiting for the away supporters and you could spot them a mile off but the police seemed oblivious.

At times, Utting Avenue near the ground would resemble the Falls Road but with mounted police and meat wagons instead of troops and armoured cars and skirmishes all over the place. Several times, we let fans take refuge in our house, which was just off the Avenue, till everything had died down and once we even had to shelter a Liverpool fan who was from Glasgow and had been chased because he spoke differently to the Anny Road Enders (I wonder what they'd have done to Kenny or Souey or Big Rowdy or the Saint or Jocky Hansen) and I lent him an anorak and took him to Lime Street Station and never heard from him again. It wasn't a bad anorak, either, (so, if you're reading this . . .).

The frustrating thing was that it went on for years before the police woke up and began identifying and targeting the loonies and kept the visiting fans penned in until the crowds dispersed. Then, sadly, the police used to have to escort the away fans to and from the station and the coaches and the loonies would be like hyenas trying to pick off any strays, especially at Lime Street Station and, all in all, football has never produced a more pathetic and dehumanising spectacle than these chain gangs trundling along Scotland Road with most of them just ordinary fans wanting simply to follow their team, yet looking like convicts.

And then you'd hear the loonies bragging about the buzz they'd got and about the noses being split open by a boot and the blood gushing out. You knew half of it was bullshit to impress and you reflected on the faces you'd seen of the attackers and the attacked – and the look on both and you knew what you'd seen on both was fear and that any buzz the aggressors had got had been adrenaline followed by relief. Then you reflected that maybe each generation did need a war to shed the aggression of its male youth but then you felt some reassurance as you remembered that the loonies were only a minority, despite what some would have you believe.

Then in 1985 the loonies finally achieved their Valhalla in Belgium and thirty-five innocuous Italians and one Belgian lay dead. Some tried to blame the authorities and they were right to a point but, at the end of the day, the authorities never did the attacking – it was the loonies and their camp followers. And then some of the vast majority who weren't loonies never went again, while the rest of us chose still to go but had to live with the shame and I can't help but hate the skinheads for what they did to the game we love, even though that probably makes me almost as bad as them but that's the way I feel about it and I pray that their ilk never flourish again at football matches, though I know they're out there somewhere, skulking in the shadows, trying to wage their futile and contemptible supremacy battles, just waiting to ruin everything.

But then you reflect on the way things have changed so dramatically over the last three or four years, particularly the closing of the terraces and the cost of going to a game and you realise the loonies will probably never again be prepared or able to pay to come back on any grand scale or regular basis like before. You wonder whether all the time there was actually a hidden agenda behind the all-seater stadia to raise prices, gentrify and neutralise the crowd and therefore squeeze the vast bulk of the loonies out of the game.

And then you think of all the ordinary fans who love the game but have also been priced out of it and you realise it's they who are taking the rap for what the loonies did. And then you think back to 1963 and wonder what would have happened if the Kop had never started the whole tribal singing, chanting thing in the first place or those Everton fans had never wrecked that first train back in 1962, and you put on 'Que Sera' by Sly Stone and you think "Ah to hell with it, what's the point of thinking so much anyway?".

And then your mind drifts back to 1985 and 1989 and the killing pens and you find you've answered your own question and you realise that some people have paid the ultimate price for their indoctrination and you can't help but feel a bit guilty. Once more you find yourself hating those skinheads for what they did to our game.

The bastards.

Communion

"I'm going to a place where they eat, sleep, drink and breathe football, and that's my place". In 1959, just as my own indoctrination was bearing fruit, it is said Bill Shankly, with that parting sentiment to his players, left Huddersfield for Anfield.

The fandom of Liverpudlians would never be the same again and a barmy spell six years later was to reveal to me precisely what his words had meant.

It was a grey, damp and overcast Sunday afternoon in May 1965, (actually, it was warm, sunny and cracking the flags but the weather was not really of any significance, for everyone was far too elated to pay it any heed.) The magnificent Victorian and Georgian splendour of Dale Street and Castle Street rose majestically above us as my friends and I joined the ranks of the huge crowds thronging every road and thoroughfare, filling every nook and cranny and clinging to every lamp-post and bus shelter in Liverpool city centre to welcome home the victorious Liverpool team, who, a day earlier had lifted the FA Cup for the first time in the Club's history. (And, as every fan will know, in football, unlike being impure, first times are always the best).

We had taken our 'spec' a good three hours or so before the team was due home and secured an ideal position no more than thirty yards from the Town Hall balcony on which the team were to gather. Even at such an early hour the crowd was buzzing.

Immediately in front of us was a man who seemed, at first glance, to represent what we impressionable young scallies all considered, at the time, to be the archetypal Scouser. We nodded to each other in a ritual of silent knowing agreement that he was the genuine article; each of us suitably impressed.

He stood around five feet ten inches (wide, that is), with a weathered face, tough and pugnacious yet with a ready smile and a warm, friendly glint in his eyes, long, thick greying sideburns, a flat cap and an open lumberjack shirt under a faded Wrangler jacket revealing a greying hairy chest, the half smoked stump of a Woodbine lodged behind his right ear and a folded up copy of the previous night's Football Echo under his left arm. He had a voice like a foghorn and a ready line in banter and quips. Patently afraid of no-one except, no doubt, his own mother, he looked like an ideal travelling companion on all those precarious excursions to the Shed, the North Bank or the Stretford End (in those pre-Skinhead days, of course, as hard as it now is to believe, we did actually congregate at such ends. Clearly at that time our sense of danger, survival instinct and basic common sense had not reached even the formative stages of their development).

As it happened, our initial assessment of the man was soon to be proved wide of the mark, for closer scrutiny quickly revealed to us that, in fact, he was not like any ordinary Liverpudlian, nor indeed, for that matter, any ordinary man. For one thing, he actually had three legs. Two of them, granted, were normal ones attached to his trunk in the usual manner, but amazingly, he also had a third one – a long, slender, smooth hairless limb which was unattached and seemingly out of all proportion to the rest of his huge frame and his other two legs. What's more, he had contrived somehow to attach the sole of the foot of this extra limb to the end of a long yard-brush pole handle which, to the open-mouthed incredulity of everyone around, he then proceeded to thrust up into the air, and wave about high above the heads of the rest of the puzzled throng.

The lofted leg was flesh pink in colour and completely naked except for a red ankle sock and a black 'Continental' football boot with two narrow white stripes either side and moulded rubber studs. As the man waved it to and fro, the leg danced with great beauty to the sounds and rhythms of the burgeoning crowd, transfixing the gaze of all around it. Incredibly, it seemed to know all the steps, first a polka, then a rumba, then a quick step, next a fox-trot and finally, an Irish jig. All around were mesmerised. The dancing leg had announced its presence.

Understandably, almost everyone else in the crowd that day had brought with them a scarf, flag, rosette, rattle, banner or, like ourselves, a cardboard cut out of the FA Cup faced with silver foil, all to greet and celebrate the team's great triumph. But an extra leg? Not, of course, that there was any law against possessing such a third lower limb; indeed, far from it. We were still, after all, in a democracy and people were free to make any stand they wanted. It was just that somehow, a leg seemed, well, a bit inappropriate; more suited perhaps to a tailor's dummy convention or an artificial leg throwing contest; certainly not an FA Cup Winners' homecoming. The man was clearly out on a limb.

Not surprisingly, in view of his unorthodox leg-waving antics, the three-legged man very quickly became a great source of amusement, as well as bemusement for the crowd and an obvious target for the inevitable banter of the many wags in the assembled throng.

"Eh la, 'oo d'yer get ter shave yer legs – d'yer think they'd do mine for me?"

"Eh pal, just 'cos yer got yer leg over last night, doesn't mean yer've gorra wave it about, yer know!"

"Eh Jimmy, I've gorra crackin glass slipper 'ere, it'll just do fer that foot."

Apparently unperturbed by the tirade of flak he was attracting, the three-legged man impassively parried every quip which came his way with a wittier one of his own – "Er, will yiz all piss off" – and laughing loudly along with everyone else, simply thrust his immaculate third limb still higher into the air to resounding cheers.

All this time, the crowd had been growing steadily in size and density. The newspapers the following day were to estimate its numbers at between three quarters of a million and a million and certainly, it is difficult to envisage a bigger mass of people – the state funerals of Chairman Mao or the Ayatollah Khomeini perhaps – but this was certainly no funeral, for one thing there was no coffin and for another, no-one sings "We were runnin' round Wemblee with the cup" non-stop for four hours at any Requiem service I've ever attended.

By now, particularly for the younger and smaller constituents of the crowd such as myself and my friends, things were so crushed that the only movement possible consisted of the involuntary swaying to and fro with the crowd and the hypnotic dancing leg to the tribalistic strains of "You'll never walk alone", "Ee aye addio", "She Loves You" and "Yes, we have no bananas". Soon the crushing meant everyone in the throng had become effectively fuse-welded together – human bonding in its ultimate manifestation. Arms were immobilised and legs entangled; elbows embedded deep into ribs; itches tantalisingly unscratched; brows glistened and clothes dripped with the sweat which oozed from every pore; calves ached agonisingly as all stood on tip-toes for gulps of fresh air between verses.

Sadly, supplies of oxygen had become about as rare as entertaining football with Dave Bassett, for by now, the air was a concoction of stale breath, tobacco smoke and pungent body odours. With fully two hours left until the team's planned appearance, the highly prized view of the Town Hall balcony had long since become the exclusive preserve of six footers alone. Mere teenage striplings like myself had sunk way beneath the sight-line deep down into the bowels of the crowd, into a sweltering and airless engine room where the views were non-existent and the stifling atmosphere induced a panting breathlessness.

My own aspect was confined by now to the back of a familiar looking faded denim jacket against which my nose, chin and left cheek were squashed at an oblique angle. As it happens, I was not at all ungrateful for this small mercy since the angle at least afforded me, from my fully submerged perspective, a sight of sorts of the blue skies directly overhead, not to mention the smooth slender pink leg of the three-legged man which was still being waved vigorously in the air, what seemed by now to be hundreds of feet above my sweat-soaked head.

And yet – and this paradox illustrates as much as anything else the blind and primal devotion inherent in fandom, particularly, as we all now know from hindsight how tragically wrong such occasions can go – for all the puffing and panting and pushing and shoving, all the crushing and discomfort, the wringing wet clothes and tired aching limbs, all the sheer, spent exhaustion which threatened to swamp us, this was no claustrophobic nightmare; no trip to hell and back. In fact, (and why else would we go through it?), it was quite the opposite; it became a truly exhilarating and unforgettable occasion, inducing an overwhelming sense of oneness and attachment: the very essence and core of fandom – the shared experience and identity which every fan has been through at some time or another; everyone as one with the crowd; complete strangers as close to each other as it is possible to get – physically and emotionally.

The crushing and discomfort and sodden clothes became the common factors binding everyone together in turn breeding an instant camaraderie and an utterly intoxicating feeling of unity. The accompanying banter: "Er will yer take it easy lads, there's a woman 'avin twins 'ere"; "OK lads, move along the bus please"; Eh lads, will yer make way fer a Chelsea pensioner and his grandfather" and the continuous sing-along seemed to emphasise and underpin the unique appeal of this football communion. It was base instincts from our stone age tribal past – more base than being impure and more fulfilling than eating and drinking – resurfacing in Castle Street, Liverpool on an otherwise bland Spring day.

Never could Bill Shankly have bargained for his prophetic words about Liverpool's football madness to have rung quite so true. What he had said was tinged with exaggeration; now here he was, about to arrive onto a balcony overlooking half the population of Merseyside, with the other blue half at home, waiting for their turn. 'Football hotbed' seemed, somehow, inadequate in conveying what was happening in Liverpool that day; 'football crazy' is undoubtedly what we all were.

All this time, the smooth pink leg had remained aloft, conducting the crowd in the community singing and entertaining one and all with its dancing prowess. Then, at long last, an ear piercing crescendo of noise told me deep down in my lowly station, that team captain, Ron Yeats and his immortals had appeared on the balcony with the Cup. Eventually the bedlam abated just slightly, enough for the bawling Scouse tones of the three-legged man to be heard, finally revealing to all the purpose of his extra limb as he thrust it with even greater vigour towards the balcony:

"We've got the first leg Ron; eh Ron, we've got the first leg. We've got the first leg Ron; eh Ron, we've got the first leg . We've got the first leg Ron, eh Ron we've got . . . "

He repeated this over and over until he was hoarse and had caught the Liverpool captain's attention. The crowd around laughed loudly and applauded his ingenuity and persistence. Liverpool, having won the Cup on the Saturday, were due to play Inter Milan at Anfield on the coming Tuesday night in the semi-final first leg of the European Cup and with it being our first venture into Europe, our three-legged friend wanted Big Ron and his team-mates to be left in no doubts about the priority which lay ahead. He had certainly made his point. If the players lost against Inter Milan, they would not have a leg to stand on.

The build up to the momentous dancing leg episode in Liverpool city centre had all started in rather predictable fashion on FA Cup Final morning: butterflies in the pit of the stomach, mouth completely dry, legs like jelly, nails bitten past the elbow, sweeping waves of optimism instantly repelled by feelings of terrifying, nauseous fear at the prospect of defeat. I had thought to myself, "Christ, if I was feeling like this, God knows how the players must feel". I was merely watching it on the television; they actually had to take their butterflies and quivering limbs on to the pitch with them. Then I remembered. They had Shanks with them. I felt reassured. He would see them all right. Even so, it was a pity the great man couldn't have been at our house to calm me down. And my father too, for he was also a bag of nerves.

I was thirteen, going on fourteen, at the time; my father was older.Like a great many other Reds fans he had waited a long time to see Liverpool win the Cup. The story went, so he and countless others had told me many times, that when we did eventually win it, the Liver Birds would fly away. "Believe that one when I see it", I had thought; "they're tied down with high tension wire" And I wasn't even the sceptical sort, though I did have good eyesight and I'd read about it in a local history book.

We had been a bit disappointed not to get tickets for the game, though not really surprised, since there were only 13,500 available against a demand of ten times that. Most had gone to shareholders and stand season ticket holders. Also, with my father being a simple, straightforward man with no strings to pull or influence to wield, it was unlikely any tickets would materialise. And so, we had simply reconciled ourselves to the fact that there would not be any for us. In any event even if an opportunity of procuring tickets had arisen, it was touch and go whether we could have afforded to have gone to the Final anyway. The fact was, like many others, my parents were always struggling to make ends meet and a Cup Final, no matter how momentous, might well, in the ultimate analysis, have had to be classed as a luxury and outside of their limited means. There again, maybe if had been able to get our hands on some tickets, we'd have simply sold my younger sister into slavery to provide the necessary funds.

Anyway, like most others, I consoled myself with the prospect of watching the TV coverage of the whole match live and although we only had a little black and white Pye television set, in truth, it was not long before this became an exciting and attractive proposition.

For a kick off, it was the first time the Reds had been live on the box (actually, it was the second, but on the previous occasion in 1950, nobody had had a television set so nobody had seen it). Also, the BBC coverage had the added enticement of the marvellous long pre-match build up to the game itself – the previous finals, the road to Wembley, meet the teams, the teams at their hotels, the interviews, the scenes outside Wembley (everyone was bound to say how novel the singing, chanting, dancing Liverpool fans were because nobody had ever witnessed anything like them before – at least not since the Viking invasions of Aethelwulf the Boneless in the eighth century and only Kenneth Wolstenholme had been around to commentate on that). It all made for a truly mouth-watering prospect.

The TV spectacular was to start at 11.45 am and continue unabated until the post-match interviews at around 5.00 pm unless there was extra time. There were also to be extensive interviews before the game with a host of famous Liverpool celebrities – Frankie Vaughan, Billy Fury, Ken Dodd, Arthur Askey, Ted Ray, Jimmy Tarbuck, Cilla Black. "Why", I mused, "did there always have to be a catch?" Still, I supposed, even that was preferable to Dickie Davies over on ITV and settled down to watch the game.

Cup Finals, of course, are one of the great sporting occasions. Rather like the Boat Race, Wimbledon, the Grand National and Question of Sport, the Cup Final has established itself as part of the nation's heritage. So much so that even non-sporting people take an interest.

They are particularly joyous times for the area with a team taking part, especially when that area happens to be one of football's hotbeds. When the team in question have never won the Cup, then something very special is in the air. That was the case in Liverpool in 1965. The area was literally agog with excitement and fervour and the entire Red chunk of the community obsessed with the occasion. Looking back now, it is hard to believe in the midst of all the subsequent success on which Liverpudlians have been able to gorge themselves that there was ever a time when we could have had such an unsatiated thirst for glory, but the simple fact of the matter is that everything has to start somewhere.

Everywhere was awash with Red and White (and needless to say, some Blue and White too, for some Evertonians simply couldn't wait until 1966 for their turn) – doors, windows, fanlights, lamp-posts, walls, roofs, bus-stops, dogs, cats, budgies, offices, factories, whole streets were festooned in Red and White bunting and silver foil replicas of the Cup. Boys and girls too young for the indoctrination process to have even taken root were decked out from head to toe in the team's colours; Red priests and vicars throughout Merseyside offered up prayers for victory; raffles were held in those pubs and clubs that could get their hands on a ticket; coach and mini-bus parties were organised from all over and for the young kids, street parties became the order of the day. It was impossible to escape Cup Final fever. Liverpool was abuzz and on May 1st that year, everyone except for 20,000 or so lucky travelling ticket holders and ticketless chancers sat glued to their TV screens with everything crossed.

As Cup Finals go, the game itself was not the best. The two teams, both brimful with fine footballers – Lawrence, Lawler, Byrne, Strong, Yeats, Stevenson, Callaghan, Hunt, St John, Smith, Thompson for the Reds and Sprake, Rooney, Bell, Bremner, Charlton, Hunter, Giles, Storrie, Peacock, Collins and Johannson for Leeds – largely cancelled each other out. Frankly, it was drab. However, winning the Cup for the first time has the effect of relegating any such minor considerations as performance quality into insignificance. On this occasion, all that mattered to Liverpudlians was the glorious vision of Ian St John in extra time hovering in suspended sideways animation to head the winner past Gary Sprake and spark the continuous choruses of "Ee-Aye-Addio, we won the Cup".

Needless to say, the Ee-Aye-Addio strains were taken up across Merseyside as the armchair legions took to the streets. The scene at our block of maisonettes was no doubt typical. All at once, doors opened as friends, neighbours, mothers, fathers, children, grannies and all poured outside. Wild hysteria saw some celebrants falling off the balconies as impromptu "hokey-cokeys" and "aya Congas" snaked their way deliriously around the yard, up and down the staircases and along the verandahs.

Later that night, all of us whose parents would allow stood outside the 'Vic' and joined in with the countless renditions of "You'll never walk alone", each one seemingly louder and more fervent than the previous, as they filtered through the pub's doors and windows and out into the street. So infectious was the atmosphere that even the local parish priest, Father Taylor, and his beautiful Golden Retriever on their evening stroll – both normally so reserved, came and joined in with us to howl a quick verse or two. Then at closing time, we watched in gaping awe as grown men over-sated with beer and euphoria beckoned us over to join them in their riotous celebrations to jig and dance in huge circles outside the pub doors. What, with all this, and the breathtaking communion and dancing leg to follow the next day outside the Town Hall, it seemed as if things could never, ever, get any better.

Three nights later at Anfield on Tuesday, 4th May 1965 against World Club Champions Inter Milan – uncharted territory for everyone connected with the Club – they did. Liverpudlians experienced their zenith – the consummation of absurd glory. To fans like myself, it was, without doubt, the stuff of soul-trading with the Devil and, for many of us, the Reds' greatest ever performance.

The afternoon of the game we all skipped off school early to ensure that we would get in. Everyone knew it would be a lock-out. Arriving at the ground three hours early the queues were already enormous, so we decided to try for the Paddock enclosure since we feared we would be locked out of the Kop. It proved to be a wise decision. By 5.20 pm we were inside and breathed a huge sigh of relief – all the standing sections of the ground were already crammed tight.

Anfield throbbed with an excitement never experienced before nor since. Fifty-four thousand five hundred souls were crammed inside; half that number were locked outside. The atmosphere defied belief; unparalleled in its intensity, noise and passion. That night, the 28,000 strong giant foaming tidal wave of humanity which for the entire night tumbled, cascaded and crashed all over the terraces of the Spion Kop like the swelling Southern Ocean at Cape Horn, re-defined the parameters of vocal support. From the moment we squeezed in you could not take your eyes off them; the ceaseless swaying and movement like some vast bank of windswept corn drew your gaze and mesmerised you, making it impossible to look away for more than a fleeting second. The Kop was centre stage and determined to lap it up.

Prompted, partly by the sheer inspiration of winning the FA Cup for the first time, partly by the ensuing celebrations, and partly by a genuine apprehension and fear of the unknown – namely a European Cup Semi-Final and whether they would make it to the pub in time after the game – the Kop rose to the occasion with a unique concoction of noise, fervour, style and humour. Joined by the rest of the stadium to wield a four-sided attack, they created an incessant five hour long tumultuous barrage of chants, songs and sheer glorious bedlam; an unprecedented wall of noise that a school friend of mine was able to hear in the city centre three miles away and which no doubt caused the Liver Birds to re-assess their decision to stay put following the Cup Final victory. Giving without any doubt their finest ever performance, they inspired their heroes to reciprocate in ultimate harmony. The chemistry proved potent and irresistible. 'Santa Lucia' was re-written and didn't those poor Italians know it. The unceasing strains of "Go-oh back to Italee" would reverberate round their heads for days afterwards, perhaps for ever.

The Italian World Champions were simply frightened out of their skins by the sheer ferocity of the cacophonous din which greeted their arrival on the pitch. Even they, weaned as they were on hostile Latin crowds, had patently never encountered anything approaching the intensity of the atmosphere at Anfield that night. Running out towards the Kop end they literally froze to the spot, like petrified rabbits caught in the glare of a car's headlight. Simultaneously, Gordon Milne and Gerry Byrne ran round the running track with the FA Cup in a psychological ploy by Shankly to milk the crowd's hysteria. Recovering slightly, the Italians turned tail and fled to the relative safety and calm of the opposite end of the ground, their faces as shock-white as the hair on Don King's head.

In stark contrast, the team in blood-red shirts were inspired to a pitch of frenzy to match that of the crowd. They swarmed like possessed demons all over the poor bemused Italians and proceeded to tear them apart. Once out of the dressing rooms, it had been even worse.

The Reds, in short, were unrecognisable. I mean we all knew they were a good side, probably verging on greatness, but that was by English, not European let alone worldwide standards; and the Inter Milan of Helenio Herrera were World Champions. That night, though, the Reds amazed us all, reaching levels of perfection which no-one thought possible. Beforehand, none of us had known what to expect, partly because we suspected the team might be tired from their extra-time exertions at Wembley and partly since we had no yardstick of our ability against a side such as Inter Milan whose unchallengable pedigree was enough to make even the most blinded die-hard question our chances. Despite our FA Cup euphoria, the 'Doubting Thomas's' amongst us, including myself, secretly feared from what we'd read that our best might not be enough and we might just be cut to ribbons by the World Champions.

How wrong we were. From the first kick the Italians were shredded like strings of spaghetti. Every red pass found its red target, every red tackle shook Italian bones, every red surge tore past white shirted counterparts. What stood out above all was the movement. It was electrifying. At times, it seemed as if the Italians were standing still and, who knows, maybe they were: it looked like somebody had released onto the pitch a couple of dozen supercharged Kevin Keegans on pint bottle shots of 'speed'. Each red shirt seemed to appear in half a dozen places at once.

Thommo and Cally were uncatchable the whole game, haring up and down the wings like, well, like hares and making the legendary Jair look as if he'd just come out of one of my leaden footed dreams. Up front, the Saint and Sir Roger (though he wasn't actually knighted for another year) played like we'd never seen them, tormenting the meanest defence football has ever seen, one whose coach once threatened to resign if they ever conceded more than one goal in a season. In the middle, Stevo and Geoff Strong each discovered a couple of extra yards of pace and poured forward all night. At the back, Big Rowdy and Smithy gobbled up any Inter attacking notions with Smithy for most of the time playing like the scheming number ten on his shirt and full back Chris Lawler, looking like the best centre forward we'd ever had. Ronnie Moran, meanwhile, was pretty baldy even then. As for Tommy Lawrence, I'm not actually sure if he bothered turning up.

Oh, how we battered them and oh, how we sang. Barely a few minutes of red domination had passed before Sir Roger, doing a Tiller Girl pirouette, hooked a little dink from Cally into the Anfield Road

End net. Then after a further battering came a calamity; Inter Milan achieved what, otherwise, that night they found impossible – they had an attack from which Big Rowdy slipped up and Mazzola pulled a goal back. Then it was back to normal service and the battering continued unabated and through it all, so did our singing and chanting and swaying – even in the narrow strung out Paddock where the inhabitants looked like an elongated version of Bud Flanagan's 'Crazy Gang' on the stage at the London Palladium swaying to 'Underneath the Arches', (only we did it for four hours non-stop). Then Cally scored from a free kick move, the execution of which not even Andy Gray with all his gadgetry could ever have managed to figure out, let alone us. Then, the Scarlet Pimpernel with a number two on his back tiptoed his way past the entire Milan defence and smacked one into the top corner but the referee disallowed it on the grounds, if I'm not mistaken, that EUFA forbade any team from scoring three goals in one match against Inter Milan. A dozen attacks later, Tommy Smith came pouring forward to put Sir Roger through to drive a shot against the keeper and in nipped the Saint to poke it into the Kop net. Then the referee took one look at the Kop's manic celebrations and decided, wisely I would say, to ignore the EUFA directive and that was that. Together in the end, fans and players had destroyed the best football team in the world.

That night, in truth, we would have overcome anyone or anything standing in our path; Rommell's Panzer Tank Division; ten battalions of warring Spartans; a fleet of Klingon Warships; Nigel Kennedy and his violin; even Eric Cantona in a bad mood – none would have stood a chance. All would have been annihilated, for together we had achieved the ultimate footballing communion; fans and players entirely as one; the united spirit and power of eleven plus fifty-four thousand backed by half a city; the sum infinitely greater than the parts. The Italians, in reality, never stood a chance. The final score, 3-1, was a travesty of justice; it should have been 400-0, so total was the Red domination.

Eventually, long after the match had finished – by then fully four days after our Wembley exaltation – we reluctantly and unwillingly made our way home, still singing, still revelling, desperate to prolong our high. Sadly, inexorably, it was over; a once-in-a-lifetime thrill.

Since that time, in the wake of every ensuing Liverpool triumph, I have reflected, invariably, on those four glorious days in May 1965. In comparison, everything else, no matter how great or important, fails to compare. That year, all the ingredients crucial for so rich and rare an experience had been present: the unquenchable thirst for glory of all concerned with the Club; a sense of inquisitiveness and trepidation concerning the then unknown Europe; the excitement and novelty of Sixties Liverpool and the first ever singing Kop; a truly formidable football team and a uniquely formidable manager; and, most significantly of all, an overriding sense of anticipation that something momentous was happening to the Club and us all which had never happened before.

The intensity of joy and sense of communion went beyond our wildest dreams. No Liverpudlian could ever have hoped for such an experience: No fan could. And yet, it had happened. Liverpudlians had been truly blessed and we would all take with us to our graves the indelible memories; players, manager, fans and three-legged friends alike.

Meanwhile those who weren't there, I'm afraid, will just have to take my word for it or else dismiss what I have said as the ramblings of a man stranded in a time warp with a propensity for making absurd exaggerations and no doubt getting on non-Liverpudlians' nerves. And why not?

Of course, to relate all this extraordinary communion without embracing the person who made it possible is unthinkable; akin to describing the Garden of Eden without reference to the Almighty.

When Bill Shankly had spoken about coming to Liverpool in 1959 he could just as easily have been talking about Glasgow or Newcastle or Manchester. He had merely encapsulated life in a soccer hotbed. That he had Liverpool in mind, and the Liverpool directors him, had merely been our good fortune. We, and he, had simply been in the right place at the right time; sleeping giants waiting to explode, and, looking back, as far as we were concerned, it is likely only Shankly could have lit our particular fuse.

Shanks was a special blend of enthusiasm, integrity, wit and, above all, innate ability. This gave him a rare charisma which shone through in all he did. In 1913 in the tiny Ayrshire mining village of Glenbuck, a few minutes after Shanks had arrived in this world, the midwife who had delivered him calmly took hold of the mould which had fashioned him and smashed it to smithereens. Since then, no-one else has come within a million light years of emulating him; nor could they, for Shanks was unique, an inimitable and indomitable human being; the ultimate football fanatic.

Modelling himself on some Caledonian breed of tough, wise-cracking New York Bowrie Boy, his rasping Scottish burr was to captivate solitary 'scribes' (as he called the sportswriters) or multitudes of half a million as he did several times on the steps of St George's Hall in Liverpool. Joke or sermon; comic or orator – it did not matter to Shanks nor to us. His every word, his every rolling syllable was at once funny, yet also deeply profound. He moved and inspired us like no-one before nor since. He also made us laugh and chuckle like no-one else before nor since. Whatever he said he believed and so did we. The Kop could spot a phoney a mile off. They could also tell the real McCoy and Shanks was certainly the genuine article. We trusted him implicitly and utterly and though he was often flawed – for example signing Jim Furnell, Phil Chisnall, Jack Whitham, Stuart Mason, not signing Derek Dougan, often playing injured players prematurely, clinging too long to his old favourites like St. John and Big Rowdy when their best days had gone and drinking Earl Grey tea – and ever contrary and inconsistent in his diatribes. Nonetheless, we loved him for it. He, for his part, also loved us. Shanks and the Kop was to become an utterly selfless, committed two-way devotion, unlike anything else in football.

Armed with his canny perception and insight from his deep football knowledge, Shanks had known that with Liverpool he was onto a winner. He had witnessed the passion of the Liverpool crowds during his visits to Anfield as Preston's right-half. By harnessing the collective enthusiasm and latent potential of a city half full of Red fanatics disenchanted with life in the Second Division, he had seen the possibilities for the creation of something special. What transpired was to go beyond even his wildest ambitions and our wildest dreams and neither Liverpool Football Club nor Liverpudlians were ever to be the same again.

Neither too, for that matter, would fandom, for as they had succumbed to Shankly's magic spell and sung and danced to his melody of success, Liverpudlians had also changed forever the face of fandom and the way it manifested itself. Gradually the individual, orderly respectfulness and innocent flat-capped enthusiasm of the massive crowds of the Fifties had given way to the more raucous, collective exuberance of the singing, swaying, chanting kops of the Sixties and beyond; the age of 'ee-aye-addio' had arrived and had gone nationwide.

Love affairs, of course, have always flourished in football and always will. Now it is Zola, Le Tissier and Shearer; before it was Dean, Lawton and Shackleton; Best, Law and Charlton; Bell, Lee and Summerbee; Young, Kendall and Ball; St John, Keegan and Dalglish; Mercer, Cullis, Nicholson, our own Bob Paisley and perhaps, above all, Sir Matt Busby. In all cases, however, the Club always came first no matter how profound the adulation of player or manager.

With Shanks, it was different. As far as the Kopites were concerned,

Shanks and the Club were synonymous with each other, sharing equal billing and devotion – there came to be no distinction, no differenti-ation – Shanks was the Club. As such, he had achieved what no one else in the world of football, neither before or since, had ever done – not even Sir Matt in all his time and triumphs and tragedies at Old Trafford nor Shanks's successor Bob Paisley in all his unprecedented glory at Anfield. Indeed, if anything, the glories under Bob Paisley have tended to dull slightly the memories of just how strong the union was between Shanks and the Kop. Shanks was a one-off, so, in turn, his relationship with the Kop was also a one-off – a marriage for life.

When the Kopites sang their 'Shankly' hymn to the tune of 'Amazing Grace' it was symbolic, probably unwitting, yet also probably subliminal – for in the eyes of most Kopites, Shanks had actually become their worldly Messiah. The photograph of the adoring fans at Shanks's feet at Wembley in 1974 says it all, and in a spiritual sense, if you think back, it truly was becoming frightening territory, so intense was the bond which had, by then, begun to develop.

At the time, of course, it seemed to be simply another outlet of adulation for the Kopites. Looking back and recalling all that intensity and the endless waves of profound draining emotion which spilled off all of us on the Kop on to Shanks, you realise that what was actually going on was continually pushing back the boundaries; reaching ever deeper into the well of human feelings which, in sport at least as far as I'm aware, have never before nor since been tapped on such a massive scale. The way it had become if Shanks had given the nod, we would have done literally anything he wanted without question. Anything. The team was almost secondary. We were all under his spell and our adulation was showing no signs of peaking. In fact, the opposite was the case and the love affair was spiralling wildly out of control, very possibly threatening to overwhelm one of the protagonists with the stresses such intensity can unleash.

It is clear now, certainly to my way of thinking at least, that by 1974 Shanks himself, together with his wife Nessie, had awakened to what was happening. Even he – the final word in football fanaticism – only had so much to give and over the years, he had given away far too much of himself. He was now almost 61 and at that age, two families – one with 28,000 ever hungrier mouths – were too emotionally demanding for anyone. So Shanks called it a day and left his disbelieving flock without a shepherd.

Once the initial shock-waves had abated, it began to appear that his retirement decision had been a considered one. On reflection, however, it seems doubtful whether Shanks, in reaching his decision, had thought through all the ramifications. What now seems more likely is that Shanks found himself being channelled almost helplessly into the unchartered waters of unsuited retirement by prevailing circumstances and pressures – both the usual sort which would affect any 61 year old family man plus those footballing and fan-related ones unique to Shankly.

And so, as the unassuming and lovely Nessie Shankly and her family finally got back what was rightly theirs, their unique patriarch was destined to drift towards a cruel, yet perhaps sadly inevitable estrangement from the only other love of his life – the beloved Anfield citadel which he had so painstakingly created out of virtually nothing. It was to bring him the deep heartache felt by a forsaken lover and an understandable sense of umbrage with which he would never be able to come to terms. A distressingly unfitting humiliation for the Red's – and arguably football's – greatest man. Meanwhile, not even the most distraught of Red fanatics could, at the time, begrudge any choice the great man elected to make. Besides, with the second greatest and most successful manager British football has ever seen still to follow, what was the point anyway. After all, in football, as with anything else, life has to go on.

Towards the end of his career with his life's work at Anfield nearly complete, and with his third Championship just won, Shanks was in front of the Kop, arms aloft, acknowledging our cheers and adulation. Moments earlier, a policeman had contemptuously trodden on a red scarf on the ground (undoubtedly a Boy in Blue). Shanks had promptly bent down and picked up the scarf and proudly and defiantly draped it round his neck, evidently in the process, we are told, admonishing the policeman with the words "that scarf is someone's life".

Retrieving the scarve and tying it around his neck was not simply an act to impress those watching. On the contrary, he was picking up the scarf for one of his mates on the Kop; one of his own. You could see it in his eyes. It could easily have been his own scarf; his own life. The thing was in his own inimitable way, Shanks was simply fulfilling his role as Liverpool's, and football's, greatest ever fan. He knew everything about the fandom which that scarf represented – the same fandom embraced by fans everywhere, including himself. Most of all he knew how vital that fandom was – it was indeed, as he is alleged to have said, someone's life; a part of someone's life force. It meant everything, and so did he. No fans could ever have had more from anyone in the game. Neither for that matter, could the game ever have had more from any fan, and when you think about it, what a jammy shower of bastards we were to have had him, for without him there might have been nothing at all, and then what would we all have done?

And as you look back with an obligatory wry smile, you realise that all the time Shanks had known exactly what he was doing with us. All along he had been dealing in pure emotion. Our emotions. And his, too. Raw and undiluted. From the very start it was him who was in the driving seat, offering us the bait of glory on the condition we could wring each other dry.

From our vantage point on the Kop, it was the best deal anyone could have offered us. Not surprisingly, we bit his hand off. We became willing participants in a destiny he had conjured up. We had to be, otherwise the whole thing wouldn't have worked. True, there may have been a tiny hint of emotional blackmail involved, but so what. Selling our souls to Shanks was small fry compared to the rewards that might lie in store for us. Besides, ours had been a love at first sight. A true love of implicit trust where we had each given ourselves completely to the other. There hadn't really been any decision to make for either of us. It had already been made somewhere else by someone with a far greater appreciation of these things than we or even Shanks could ever have had.

And even now sixteen years after his death whenever I think of the man and I picture his wonderful uncompromising craggy face, that blunted nose and lilting half smile, the shorn hair and shining mischievous eyes and I imagine the unique vibrancy of how he spoke, the utter self-belief and conviction and sincerity behind everything he said, whether inspirational, flawed or outrageous, I cannot do so without feeling a heavy tug on the heart strings and glistening in the eyes, a resurrection of the emotions he once stirred so deeply. And though a rational part of me knows it shouldn't really be like that, since the nearest I ever got to meeting him was from the terraces of the Kop the fact is, it is almost like when I think fondly of my own parents and loved ones, now also gone. In fact, to tell the truth, it's a bit like that final scene in 'Shenandoah' when James Stewart's youngest boy hobbles down the aisle of the church on crutches and, no matter how hard you try to fight it, the tears still well up and you have to bite hard on your lip, just like James himself, so you don't look daft. That was Shanks, though; a writer of one of life's original scripts of which we were all privileged to have been a part.

No wonder we're all such an emotional lot.

Confession

There is little doubt, as far as the football fanatic is concerned, that the communion shared with team or player, or in our case, manager as well, becomes the essential ingredient of life. Inevitably, however, reality at some stage or another shakes off its marker to cast its irritatingly sobering shadow to compel even the most diehard fan to achieve some semblance of existence beyond the clutches of the tie-ups that bind but cannot feed or clothe. I mean, when all is said and done, even Bill Shankly, however hard he may have tried, stopped some way short of one-to-one relationships with his beloved Kopites and, as far as I'm aware, never actually financially supported anyone by paying their 'lecky' bill.

With this in mind, it is hardly surprising that with the exception of the odd few highlights – the OK Sauce bottle/broken thumb incident and a certain table football triumph at the 'Vic' spring immediately to mind -- it is difficult to relate my own existence outside of football to anything other than a drab end of season goal-less draw at Bramall Lane and, let's be frank here, they don't come much more mundane than that.

Now, I'm sure there are some who may regard such an assertion as simply a glib attempt on my part to elicit some sympathy but let me assure you that there really could be no more candid consideration of a life in which the action has been so non-existent, the scoring opportunities so few and far between and those chances that have materialised so recklessly fluffed. The worst of it is, however unpalatable I may find it and however cynically non-Liverpool fans may view such a representation, in my case, even when it comes to footy, the words 'dismal failure' would seem to provide the most snugly fitting cap to wear.

Take my playing career. Whilst to Jimmy O'Toole my ludicrously bony knees may have displayed a hint of Leyton Orient promise, the reality was, I never came within a Pat Jennings punt of fulfilling Jimmy's prophecy of playing for the Reds and, even now, I shudder at the horror of finding this out.

At twenty, at the local amateur club – Marine (Reserves – naturally) –

the manager, Harry Boyle who was Matt Busby's cousin, took me to one side after the dressing room had emptied following an evening training session and with a sympathetic arm around my shoulder, calmly and cruelly hit me with the facts – "let's face it, son" he mumbled in his Scottish drawl, "this isn't going to work".

I recall gazing up at him with typical naivety, about to ask him what it was that wasn't working, thinking perhaps he may have been referring to his fancy new Scottish diver's watch which he dangled over my shoulder on his limp wrist, when he continued "if you want, you can still come along and train with us". Now I may have been naive but I certainly didn't need any more dots joining. The message was clear – there was nothing wrong with his diver's watch and I was no longer wanted. Needless to say, I was devastated.

The sad fact was I had actually peaked far too early in my career. At thirteen, had the opportunity actually existed, I may well have stood an outside chance of making Harry Boyle's first team. The problem was, though, from then on it was downhill all the way. By seventeen, I was only half as good as when I was thirteen. By twenty, I was only a quarter as good. By the time I reached twenty-five, I could scarcely kick a ball straight and by thirty I probably wasn't even as good as Mike Robinson when Joe Fagan signed him for the Reds. Sad as it seems, football, just like ollies, was never going to be my game. It was as plain as the nose on Mike Summerbee's face. In hindsight, my mid-life crisis had actually begun when I was thirteen and that's a pretty traumatic proposition when you think about it, especially when footy is the only thing in your life.

As if all that was not bad enough, my track record as a fan scarcely fares much better and certainly doesn't stand up to close scrutiny. I realise, of course, that in this context, everything is relative and there are some people who consider ten to fifteen games a season as proof of fanaticism to which I can only say a mate of mine, Billy Hall, has scarcely missed a Reds match home, away or Europe since the dawn of time, which sets the standard as far as I'm concerned.

The facts regarding my own fandom are plain: the Reds' two greatest triumphs, the very pinnacles of their history, were Wembley in 1965 and Rome in 1977 and I missed them both. I wasn't there. I watched them on the telly. Now I know there were extenuating circumstances in each instance – too young, no tickets and no money in '65 and newborn babies, no money and no passport in '77 but that, regrettably, is not the point. Any true, self-respecting football maniac would have made it to both. In '77, another mate of mine, Bill Grice, was also skint yet he flogged all his Embassy No. 6 coupons for the train fare to Rome and I know of others who simply hitched just like I used to do. The thing is, neither excuses nor reasons nor circumstances come into it. When it comes to such occasions, you just go. The way I see it, there are times when you simply have to hold up your hands and confess things and when it came to the crunch, I was found grievously lacking.

It's no use either clinging to any notion that if they took place now, things would be different and I would be there – that is no better than a convicted murderer pleading for another chance. The fact is they happened then, they were Liverpool's zenith, I never showed up and, consequently, I'm no better than a part-time supporter – an armchair fan – worse in fact, since they don't claim to be anything better. Besides, for the Rome final, we had the telly in the bedroom so I can't even rightly claim armchair status – some fan, eh!

Damning as those flaws may seem, there is little doubt about my worst failure. It concerns the very faith about which I write and in comparison, my non-existent playing career and dodgy fandom seem but trivial fare. The fact is – and believe me – it is something which haunts me day and night, and always will. I have failed to pass on my faith. The very life force which has sustained me and my forefathers since time immemorial will die with me. I have no heirs (nor graces for that matter). Neither of my children (one nineteen, the other twenty two) are the weeniest bit interested in Liverpool Football Club, nor football in general. They can't stand it. In fact, so pronounced is their contempt for the game that they don't even particularly like Gary Lineker. I mean, I ask you, how can anyone not like Gary Lineker – the man's virtually a saint for Christ's sake – even Nick Hancock likes him.

I am so desperate, I would even settle now at this late stage for them becoming Evertonians. At least then we could perhaps have some decent arguments but no, after twenty years of begging and pleading and even missing out on Rome to look after them, they've turned their backs on their own father, their own flesh and blood. They've effectively disowned me. Needless to say, of course, I blame my wife. She's from South Wales – Rugby country. What's more, she hates footy too. She's sabotaged them. It really is a nightmare. I'm an outcast in my own home.

Of course, the worst is yet to come. I mean, how on earth am I going to face my father and Shanks when I go to join them after that great final whistle blows. How can I possibly explain to them what's gone wrong. Let's face it, you can't. Nobody could. The fact is, I'm guilty of the worst sin any fan can commit. God, I'm really dreading dying.

The thing is, I don't even know where it is I've gone wrong. I thought I'd got it spot on. I did all the right things. Not once did I falter. Every day, I used to dress up the both of them in their little Liverpool kits and their little football boots even when they went to school, and I'd play footy with them for hours and hours on end every day when I came home from work, taking special care to make sure they always practised kicking the ball with both feet not just one, like Bobby Charlton used to tell us in my old footy annuals.

Then, as a special treat each night, after we'd played for two or three hours, I'd take them for walks around the ground which was only just up Arkles Lane, showing them the Kop, the Main Stand, the Kemlyn Road stand, the Anfield Road End and explaining to them all about John McKenna's giant pole, Louis Bimpson and the dark days.

I'd then buy them all the Panini football stickers and even when they were little, I'd sit them up in front of the telly for Match of the Day and even the Midweek Match. Then, when they went to bed, I'd play little quiz games with them, asking them hundreds of questions about all the old Liverpool players and then I'd sing all the Liverpool songs to them till they fell asleep night after night. Why, I even used to make sure all their toys and presents always had some football connection. I mean, there's not many kids who can boast fifteen games of Subbuteo and two hundred and fifty football annuals. No-one could have tried harder than I did. No-one.

And yet, despite all I've done, the pair of them have turned into footy haters. It's a complete mystery. It doesn't seem fair. Maybe it's God's way of paying me back for deserting Him – the last word in divine retribution. Whatever the reason, all I know is it's the worst news of all when your own children betray you; the ultimate failure – the death of a faith.

In the midst of so much personal trauma, I suppose throughout it all, there's one thing I have to be grateful for. That is, still having enough nous to realise pretty early on that no matter what happens in life, no matter how catastrophic the failure, no matter how hard you're kicked, or where you're kicked, at the end of the day, you do just have to get on with things and muddle through. If I'm honest with myself about it, though, I'm sure really it's only the consolation of following the Reds glory trail which has enabled me to pull through.

I mean, imagine if I'd been born in somewhere like Rochdale. No offence to my good friends Brian, Darren, Ann and Tina, all from that neck of the woods, but with so many inherent flaws supporting someone like the 'Cowboys' might well have been enough to push me over the edge. And don't forget there would have been Mike Harding to cope with too, so I dare say all I can do is to be grateful for small mercies. As it was, leaving aside rather more momentous later episodes and the early Division Two days, supporting the Reds has always been, as might be expected, a cinch.

Take the period between 1973 and 1989 to demonstrate precisely what I mean. Those seventeen years saw twenty three major trophies arrive at Anfield – four European Cups, two EUFA Cups, four League Cups, three FA Cups and ten Championships. That's one and six seventeenths trophies per year if my maths are right, which is like one whole trophy and, say, the base of another with all those little silver badge winner inscriptions, every year. It was an unprecedented domination of domestic football whilst, in Europe, it was the only ever British impersonation of Real Madrid, Ajax, Bayern and AC Milan.

During this time, the Reds' football came to be characterised by a peerless passing style and irresistible passion and power which caused the opposition to simply wilt. Success became inevitable and all so sweet. Conveniently, too, that same success also provided an avenue of escape from reality in a city struggling as best it could to survive in so many other respects. Indeed, the contrast between the football and the city was stark – one was blooming, the other fighting for its life amidst a worsening backdrop of adversity.

From the Fifties through the Sixties and Seventies, Liverpool's inexorable economic decline from leading world port had been humanely controlled. What the city patently lacked in terms of its own inertia (it was a seaport not an industrial centre or capital city or such like), and what the port itself suffered by way of isolation from Europe and the death of the great ocean liners, Government policy had sensibly compensated for with meaty alternatives of car plants, civil service headquarters and a new state-of-the-art dock complex. None of this, of course, could prevent the city's gradual long-term descent to a new, more realistic status but, at least a plummeting free-fall was averted and, with its traditionally strong cultural and showbiz links still blossoming, the city, during this time, actually enjoyed an image which leant towards the positive, even if behind the scenes, things were not quite right and for many, life was hard.

The Eighties cynically blew away the flimsy camouflage. Recession and social revolution bit deeply and Liverpool never knew what hit it. Economically and socially, the city was ravaged; its employment structure and prospects decimated. Meanwhile, the city's image became like a badly walloped football, ideally set up on the penalty spot for anyone – in many instances even our own team mates – to boot. Rival fans even got in on the act, ceaselessly taunting both Liverpudlians and Evertonians alike about their social deprivation. By their reckoning, in the midst of our "Liverpool slums", we had slumped so far that we had resorted to actually "eating dead dogs as a treat". It was all wild exaggeration, of course. We preferred cats.

Thank God, through all the onslaughts, one thing remained intact. Football gave the city a lifeline to distract us all from what was really happening, enabling those with nothing to at least get something, losers to become winners, wrongs, if not righted, then at least partially compensated for. The melodrama became tangible and the Red half of the city – the Blue half would have to wait for Andy Gray and Peter Reid to shuffle along a few years later – was able, at least, to relish the ironic splendour of its football team, if not the harsh realities of life.

And so, as the weekend drew near, we would all savour the prospects which lay ahead; a Smith scythe, a Keegan dart, a Toshack header, a Hughes charge, a Thompson nose, a Heighway lope, a Hall scurry, a Cormack back-pass, a Lindsay chip, a Kennedy or McDermott break, a Souness strut, a hard Case, a Lawrenson surge, a Hansen impersonation of Beckenbauer, a Dalglish turn, a Rush strike, a Lee angled pass, a Beardsley shimmy, a McMahon prowl, a Barnes run and cross from the byeline, an Aldridge pounce – it was endless. And so were the honours as Leicester was followed by Moenchengladbach, then Leicester again, then Newcastle, then Bruges, then Wolves, then Rome, Bruges again, Real Madrid, Rome again, then Chelsea, Everton, Everton again and so on and so forth as League followed Cup followed League followed Cup followed League followed Cup followed League followed Cup followed League followed Cup seemingly forever. The glory became almost a birthright. What had started in the Sixties as a trickle had become an irresistible tide of matchless success, attracting new fans by the truckload from all over.

Visiting Anfield became almost like going to a concert to see your favourite artist perform night after night. You got to know every minute detail of the act and all the players and their roles but each time was always different and fresh and never did you tire of watching them. Basically at Anfield, it went like this: the Reds poured forward and dominated the proceedings and, except for a few flukey breakaways, scored all the goals and won most of the games and, for most of the time, played everyone else off the park and provided the best club football you could see anywhere outside of the Copacabana beach.

And the thing was, you simply could not get enough of it. And year after year, the new pretenders would come – Derby, Newcastle, Ipswich, West Brom, Norwich and several times Everton, Man United, Notts Forest, Leeds, Chelsea, Spurs and Arsenal – and the media would go into raptures over them and hail them as the best thing since 'the Matthews feint' or the Cruyff 'funny turn' and then we'd go and spoil the party and bring everyone down from Planet Cuckooland and proceed to beat whoever it was who'd been touted as the next big thing to topple us and we'd simply step in to win yet another League or Cup. We enjoyed a similar, but not quite on the same scale, domination in Europe. And all the time we would stand on the Kop and savour what was going on, and, though every real Liverpudlian knew the score about how good we were because we were watching it week in week out, what we didn't really appreciate was just how privileged we were and how precariously balanced the continual manufacturing of such massive success really was. We simply turned up and tuned in. As far as we were all concerned, that was the deal. That was what life was all about; dead easy.

There, though obvious really, lay the twist to the entire thing. Liverpool's secret recipe. For it never was dead easy. In fact, it was just the opposite. The thing was Shanks, Paisley and the rest may well have endlessly preached about keeping it simple and playing the easy ball. 'It's a simple game', so they would espouse every week to the green-eyed Southern and Manchester media circus. Rather conveniently though, what they omitted to mention was that the simple game is only simple and the simple pass is only simple if some other poor sod has worked their balls off to make the spare man and possesses the tactical awareness to know where and when to run and where and when to pass. In other words, they worked bloody hard at making the game look simple. Meanwhile, I suppose it also helped that the teams invariably consisted of players who would have met Shanks's exacting standards in terms of attitude as well as ability and that most of the time there was also a lacing of inspirational genius to boot.

Okay, so it's got to be said, there may have been occasions when what we witnessed didn't exactly look that hard. You only have to cast your mind back to the visit of Ossie and Ricky fresh from their World Cup triumph in 1978 when we had scarcely an ounce of luck in front of goal and Phil Neal at centre back for a good part of the game, and we still managed to score seven without reply. Now some might say that was easy and indeed a good many did. Yet, that seventh goal near the end of the game with legs tired, stamina sapped and Terry Mac still running full belt eighty yards to get on the end of Stevie Heighway's immaculate cross, is surely all the proof to the contrary that is needed.

So while there may well have been games against inferior opposition, or opposition who seemed to have come along just to admire the view, it all looked so easy – like sacking managers from the Kippax Street Stand or Rushie scoring against the Blues in the Eighties. The truth was Liverpool had achieved that elusive trick of repeatedly and consistently blending good and outstanding players to function at the height of their powers. The upshot was, for a good deal of the time, Liverpool played like they were on fire and for us, every Saturday was Bommy night.

For supporters of many clubs having just one such dream team in a lifetime is too much to expect, for such perfection is so scarce. For Liverpudlians, though, uniquely, they came along virtually to order and starting with the Yeats/St John Sixties side, we have had at least six, all of them tried, tested and proven on an international stage. It was a joke really.

Best was arguably the '78/79 Championship side with the Case, McDermott, Souness, Kennedy axis in midfield, which took a stranglehold on every game it played, if not always translating such supremacy into goals and trophies. Most effective was undoubtedly the early-Eighties vintage of Hansen and Lawrenson at the back, Souness in the middle and, up front, Dalglish and Rush, possibly the most venomous and productive striking partnership there has ever been. Most attractive – though, of course, beauty is in the eye of the beholder – is probably a toss up between the Keegan '74 Cup-winning team and the Barnes/Beardsley late-Eighties side. Favourite ever? Mine was Big Rowdy's Sixties supermen, but then I suppose I'm biased as anyone else would also tend to be who had been so beguiled by the magic European nights of Anderlecht, Inter-Milan, Juventus, Honved and Celtic.

Whatever the respective merits of any of these teams and, it really is a hard one to call, all of them had one common denominator. On their day – and such days were not exactly what you would term infrequent – each of them could lick any of the opposition around, at home or abroad, which, when you think about its implications, is pretty significant, for it means from the early Sixties right through to the Nineties, Liverpudlians have nearly always had a side capable of stuffing everyone else out of sight.

Not surprisingly, constant exposure to the continued excellence and supremacy of the teams was inevitably to affect the outlook of the Liverpool fans. At first, we simply revelled in it all, mesmerised by the irresistibility of what lay before us. Every week it was the Lord Mayor's Show, and boy, did we show our appreciation. Every pass was applauded. Every shot cheered. Every tackle celebrated. Every dribble drooled over. We were in the presence of greatness and we savoured every moment of every match.

Then, around the early Eighties things began to change and go ever so slightly awry. We started to lose our handle on reality and it began to instill a complacency amongst time-served Reds fans which rendered our successes almost mundane. We found we needed more than just the silverware. The successes had to be accompanied by nigh on perfect football. We would sigh and frown at the slightest error. The buzz we demanded could only be provided by faultless winning performances, otherwise we were almost indifferent. The whole thing became slightly crazy but, in the unique circumstances in which we found ourselves, probably understandable, perhaps, even predictable.

Amazingly, like indulgent mothers spoiling their children, the teams seemed to pick up on the vibes and duly obliged us with ever increasing excellence. It all became faintly ridiculous and now sounds all pompous and conceited and it was, but that's what happened. We had become some weird and unique breed of success freaks, obsessed with being the best, insistent on annual success and weekly brilliance. Liverpool had dug its claws ever deeper into our psyche until, at all times, the craving to be simply the best lay just below the surface. The more we won and the better we got, the more we demanded. My experience, I'm pretty sure, was not untypical of what many Liverpudlians went through, and I must confess I can't say I'm really proud of myself for it, though I'm certainly not complaining.

In all other aspects of my life, I had achieved a reasonable degree of maturity and responsibility. I cared for my wife and family, my friends, my home and dog. Together (not the dog, incidentally) we had scrimped and saved and battled our way through difficult, hungry years, making many sacrifices along the way, nursing our family through illness and tending our dear parents in their final years. We had worked hard and long for meagre returns and, apart from footy, had learned not to expect any great material rewards from life. Basically, I suppose we had become what you would term boringly ordinary. In fact, let's not beat around the bush, we had become ridiculously boringly ordinary; boringly ordinary beyond anyone's wildest dreams.

And yet, throughout it all, when it came to anything to do with Liverpool, I, myself, pathetically was still a child; a tiny, naive boy standing with hands on railings, peering starry-eyed, open mouthed and empty headed through the wire mesh cage of the Boys' Pen, gazing longingly at my beloved heroes – some of them twenty odd years younger than me – striding across the Anfield pitch, carrying my life in the Liver Birds on their chests, my ever more demanding aspirations in their boots.

It was as if my normality ceased to exist where the Reds were concerned; as if they had control of my thoughts. Each night, I would still dream of playing for them, the same dream I had had when I was nine years old, for God's sake. The whole thing was pathetic, I know, but clearly it was the way I still wanted it. And let's be honest here, who in their right or wrong mind would have wanted it any other way. We were still winning every thing, still flying high, just as we had done for thirty years. Just as we would for the next thirty.

Something was different though. It occurred gradually but there was a perceptible change. The obsession was still there alright, stronger than ever. So was the desire to win things. So was the buzz when we did win things. But it wasn't the same buzz; it was watered down. And the joy was blunted – only marginally, but you could sense it. You longed for it to be as sharp as when Roger finally beat the Leicester hoodoo or Saint scored at Wembley or Tosh at Wolves or Supersub against St Etienne but it couldn't be. It was being impure without an orgasm; thoroughly enjoyable and much better than celibacy but hardly the object of the exercise.

Then in 1984, we beat the Blues at Maine Road in the League Cup Final replay. Everton hadn't won anything at all since 1970 except for Bob Latchford's 30 goals newspaper prize and, amazingly, as the final whistle blew, rather than feeling elated you felt instinctively sorry for them and you pinched yourself, thinking you were dreaming, not believing your feelings but having no say in it. The fact was you really did feel a tinge of empathy for them and you knew something was wrong.

You knew that had the Reds achieved this victory in the Sixties or Seventies, then your feet would never again have touched the ground and you'd have taunted all your Everton mates for eternity. Yet here you were, a decade or so later, confused and deflated – an Everton sympathiser for God's sake– with fleeting pangs of regret at another Reds victory going through your head. You knew that a lot of it was due to your feeling sorry for your Evertonian family and friends, many of whom hadn't seen their team win anything at all – my mate Mark and brother-in-law Wayne thought silverware was something worn by a pirate with a parrot on his shoulder. You also knew that the whole Red and Blue rivalry was no longer as pronounced as it used to be when you were a kid, probably as a result of the whole 'Scouse solidarity' thing which had arisen since Thatcher. You realised as well that it was bloody stupid to feel like you did.

The thing was you couldn't help it and though that was the worst that it ever got, you knew something had to give. You knew deep inside we needed something or someone to shake us out of our lethargy; maybe even to stop us winning everything; to stop us from being the best; an anti-Messiah, perhaps, to lead us out of the Promised Land.

Cometh the hour. Cometh the man.

Graeme Souness had been one of our greatest ever players – arguably the linchpin around which much of our Eighties success had evolved. As a manager, he was clearly determined to be equally as influential. As events proved, however, there was a fundamental difference. As a player, he fitted in like a trusty old snug football boot. As a manager, as far as we could see, he was like an oversized pair of Doc Martens, a sort of Sidney the crazy elephant trampling over everything we valued. It appeared he was trying to change a system that – possibly Ajax apart – in terms of continuity, was the nearest to perfection the world of club football has yet seen and it turned into a disaster.

Almost overnight, being a Liverpudlian became hard again, just like it had been in those dark days of the Fifties. We all came crashing down to earth with a huge bump. Suddenly complacency was a thing of the past. We were back in a strange, alien environment of football frailty. The Club and Supporters had somehow coped with Heysel and Hillsborough, but neither of us knew how to begin to cope with no longer being the best nor anywhere near the best. For a five year spell we came back to the real world and only then did you realise just how blissful it had really been to feel sorry for Everton in 1984.

It was our team's only true barren patch in three decades, our first true test of loyalty, and we couldn't take it. We were deflated, disenchanted and depressed. As the team listed and drifted aimlessly in the doldrums of its newly created ordinariness, we were engulfed by sweeping waves of pensive melancholy, inconsolable despair and impotent frustration; petrified by the terrifying unimaginable emptiness of a world without honours and glory.

There seemed to be no escape. Neither was there solace to be had in any efforts to cherish the sublime moments of past glories, for as they grew ever more distant in time, it became increasingly clear that, for Liverpudlians like myself, it was only the present that really counted. The past merely emphasised the emptiness of the nightmare we were experiencing, with the giants of yesteryear (Gordon Milne and Brian Hall?) dwarfing Souey's pygmies (Julian Dicks and Paul Stewart?) If a love lost could be replaced only by a love found, then Cupid had well and truly deserted us. We were untouched by love and celibate for the first time since most of us had sprouted pubes.

The worst of it was that the harder Graeme Souness tried (and he certainly did try most probably more than most because he was that type of character) the worse things seemed to get and the more he seemed to alienate a large section of the fans. The players, many of whom put their growing disenchantment with the manager above their responsibility to their real employers – the fans – lost faith and stopped trying, which actually made them worse than Graeme Souness. Then Souness committed hari-kari when, at the time of his heart by-pass operation, he did an exclusive story deal with the newspaper we all despised – the Sun – and by doing so, not only lent a hollow ring to his only success (the FA Cup victory over Second Division Sunderland) – and how high up the glory ladder do time-served Reds place that triumph – but also proved to every Liverpudlian that he wasn't really a Liverpudlian. No real Liverpudlian (honorary or born and bred) could ever have done what he did and from then on it was simply a matter of when he would go.

Despite everything we should have been able to cope with the situation in which we found ourselves. We should have been able to take the events in our stride. After all, most of us were grown men. Our decline should have been suffered with grace and dignity. That it wasn't was down to the very uniqueness of our experience of unparalleled triumphs.

We had been spoilt rotten for thirty years. Whereas most fans were conditioned to failure or the ordinary or, perhaps attuned merely to fleeting and spasmodic, albeit joyous success, we, on the other hand, had been programmed solely for glory. Where other fans' expectations were pitched in reality, we required perfection. For fans of less successful clubs, this deprivation amounted to no more than a case of what you'd never had you never miss. For us, to be starved of our exaltation, was to deny a junkie his regular fix.

Under Souey we had descended into cold turkey, eking out a barren existence pining for Shanks and Paisley and Joe and Kenny; clinging to visions of the Saint keeping the ball up in front of the Kop in the kick in; and Big Rowdy striding across the pitch to knock West Brom's little Clive Clark into the Paddock; and the Scarlet Pimpernel breaking the Blues hearts with the winner at the Kop end when we came back from two-nil down; and Thommo and Cally haring down the wings past Tony Dunn and Shay Brennan; and the Flying Pig as a sweeper; and Stevo doing his Jim Baxter impressions; and Kevin Keegan and his stupid haircut rip rapping his way all over the pitch in his first few years with us when he really was the best player in Europe; and Tosh preening himself for an imminent corner at the Kop end; and Emlyn Hughes all arms and legs and heart no matter what Tommy Smith says; and Tommy Smith himself colliding with the Kop goalpost to kick Allan Clarke's shot off the line; and Tony Hateley with his diving headers an inch off the deck; and "Little Bamber" running through the Giraffe's legs when Big Jack was really looking out for "Big Bamber"; and Gary Sprake throwing the ball into the Kop goal and nobody – not even the referee – knowing what to give and the club Disc Jockey at half time playing "Careless Hands"; and Ray Kennedy and Souey himself and Casey and Terry Mac complementing each other to utter perfection; and Ray Clemence tipping everything around the post or over the bar; and, above all, Kenny being himself, the best ever, seducing us and the ball every week; and Jocky Hansen making defending seem as easy as Stephen Hendry makes potting balls and Mark Lawrensen and Gary Gillespie doing the same ; and the Roadrunner and later, Barnesy and Quasi sending every defence and every crowd the wrong way; and Brucey dropping everything and doing handstands; and the young Rushy in 1981 against West Ham at Villa Park when he was unbelievable; and Johnno doing his Keegan impersonations and Aldo doing his Rushie ones; and Jan Molby when he was a lean and mean 22 stone; and Ronnie Moran and Gerry 'Crunch' Byrne and Geoff Strong and Gordon Milne and Roger Hunt and Bobby Graham and Jimmy Melia and the lovely underrated Gordon Wallace and Alun Evans and Alec Lindsay and Larry Lloyd and Peter Cormack and Jim Beglin and Supersub and Joey Jones and Phil Thompson and Phil Neal and Barney Rubble and Davy Johnson and Sammy Lee, and Ronnie Whelan and Macca and Stevie Nichol and Ray Houghton bursting every sinew – and then it was back to reality and the visions would slip away leaving me feeling like shit.

Before Graeme Souness turned us over, the fading echoes of the Sports Report signature tune on a Saturday evening were the signal for Liverpudlians everywhere to reach for the radio dial, to change frequencies, to switch off and read the 'Footy Echo', watch television, go to the pub, the pictures or bed even. The radio phone in show, Six-O-Six was about to start and we simply didn't listen to it. It wasn't for us.

We called it the "losers' show" and we were winners. We were detached, aloof, above the pack, contemptuous. We had no time, nor place for it. It had no time, nor place for us.

How the fortunes changed. How the tide turned. Suddenly, we were its principal subscribers, jamming the switchboard in our despair, monopolising the airwaves in our desperation; whining, moaning and screaming for the head of the Manager, the Chairman, the Tea Lady, the Club cat, anyone upon whom we could lay the blame for our collapse from grace. Suddenly we were the losers.

Of course, nobody had any sympathy for us. Every other supporter knew the score – we were spoilt rotten, elitist, arrogant, pompous, condescending, patronising, conceited prima donnas who deserved everything that came our way (just like Man United fans now). And they were, of course, absolutely, unequivocally, one hundred per cent, right.

The good thing was though, thank God, the situation could only get better.

Things started to improve with Roy Evans who, thankfully, was not Graeme Souness. For a start he didn't have a lush moustache, nor the personality or temperament to go with such a flamboyant growth on his upper lip. They're better on the likes of Magnum or Burt Reynolds or Souey himself. They make a statement that says "I'm a bit of a star, a bit different" – and they're right too and good luck to them. But for that reason, Roy was better off without one. Roy didn't want to be a star, he wanted the Reds to be the stars. He was a team man. It was his way. Besides, even if he had have grown one, it wouldn't have gone down too well in Bootle, the place where all the best Liverpudlians come from. Anyway, grey ones look a bit silly in any case.

The simple fact of the matter was whether he liked it or not, Roy was dead ordinary and down to earth. He was like a younger Scouse reincarnation of the great Bob Paisley – depths of personality and character and yet certainly not a personality or a character. More important, he wasn't the slightest bit interested in being one. He had bags of humour too, just like Bob, but he wasn't a comic. He was simply one of those hugely hard working, resourceful types with ability and a small ego who hate a fuss and just get on with things – the type who does it while others are talking or bragging about it. Unlike Graeme, Roy never really fitted in as a player but as a manager he semed made for the Liverpool job, because the Liverpool Way, the Shankly and Paisley and Fagan and Moran and Bennett and Saunders and Robinson 'Way' was inside him.

It seemed if we all kept the faith, it would pay off. The system would produce the results and Roy's genius would be to simply let it all happen.

You could see signs of it in the passing, running and teamwork of the younger players; Robbie Fowler and Steve McManaman and Jamie Redknapp and Jason McAteer and Rob Jones and Stevie Harkness and Dominic Matteo and Jamie Carragher and Michael Owen. Help the man in possession, keep the ball and when you lose it, close down the opposition and get it back as soon as you can. Pass and run, create an opening and stick it in. It sounds dead simple, and so it is if you've got outstanding quality players who all work for each other and play to a system. The occasional touch of genius doesn't go amiss, either.

And so, after five years of being shaken about in a bottle of mediocrity it seemed we were gently being restored to sanity. Normal service was gradually being resumed. Our dreams were returning, our nightmares fading. While the players returned to the reality of hard work and toil to reclaim lost territory, we hopefully were leaving behind five bleak years and preparing to re-enter a stratosphere of glory. We would once again be able to pompously turn off the radio at the sound of *Six-0-Six* and get on everyone's nerves.

Sadly, it didn't quite turn out as planned. Sure, Roy was all the things we had hoped he would be. Or nearly all but, unlike Shanks Bob and Kenny he wasn't a genius. He was talented, loyal, dedicated, hardworking and a Red through and through – unfortunately the record shows that was not enough. To be the greatest team on the planet also requires the greatest players and the greatest manager on the planet, or certainly something approaching it. Under Roy that wasn't the case.

We first knew it against Man United at Wembley in 1997 and the situation never really improved much from there on. In fact, the tinkering which followed made it worse. In the end Roy had to make way. So now we've got the Frenchman and the Scouser. And naturally we've all praying that Gerrard and Thommo will do us proud.

And in years to come, they will count their medals and move aside and let someone else in. And if they're all the rage at that time, then the new manager may well have a lush moustache (or a foreign accent) but if they're not, then the Reds won't let history repeat itself. Meanwhile, me and Pete and Al and Mike and Breda and Gary and Billy and Alan and Joe and Jim and Bill and Sid will sit every other week in our little seats in the stand and purr at every move and thank God for the likes of Gerrard and Thommo. Pete will no doubt continue to be the nicest guy you could ever wish to meet, while Al will worry for England, Mike will set up the Jamie Redknapp Appreciation Society and Billy will simply remain one of the Reds most ardent fans, ever.

And if we've won, then during the time in between games, we'll talk to each other about how great we were and analyse every aspect of the last game and the faults and merits of each of the players and the opposition and we'll phone the Liverpool chatline to find out any snippets and get impatient and slam the phone down as the guy prattles on about nothing simply to eat up your money and then we'll watch the telly and listen to Radio Merseyside and City and Five Live and read the papers and magazines scouring for scraps of praise of our heroes and spend the rest of the time dreaming of the next bit of magical football with a lovely warm glow of satisfaction deep down inside to get us through the week.

And if we've lost or played poorly, we'll be miserable and whinge and moan and drown our sorrows and hope it gets put right but then by the time of the next game, we'll be full of optimism once again. And that's how it is. Oh, and in the meantime, we'll all be delighted to feel sorry for the Blues. And as for me, well, I'll try my best to be the most contented of all of them because having just made a clean breast of everything, never again should I have the need to purge myself. Sadly though, some things are easier said than done, especially where football and me are concerned and the reality is life doesn't always work out as you would hope, so I don't suppose I can really vouch for how I'll be from one minute to the next, let alone the long term future. Unpredictability, I think they call it, something I was born with; just like footy, really, I suppose.

Penance

"Tommy Smith couldn't play."

The lacerating insinuation leapt off the page and threatened to slash my jugular; my favourite-ever player after Kenny wiped off the football map in no more than a paltry few seconds finger action on the keyboard; a legend of the game dismissed in less time than it takes Paul Ince to snarl at a linesman. Even worse was to follow, for the book's author had then gone on to compare Tommy with Ron Harris. Yes, Ron "Chopper" Harris; he, of the Bridge and the Portobello Road. The absurdity of it all was beyond belief. As far as I was concerned, insults of such magnitude amounted to high treason.

Without so much as drawing a snatch of breath, the first vitriolic slurs of outrage had already left my lips and I had reached for the pen, ready to pour out my anger onto the page. Tommy Smith, the 'Iron Man' of Anfield – he of the astute tackle and the crunching pass – had to be defended. The record had to be put straight and who better to do it than me. In fact, who else would want to do it but me.

Amazingly, the perpetrator of this typed assault had been none other than an Arsenal fan; a patron of the North Bank. The utter cheek of it. A camp follower of Tony Adams, Steve Bould and Martin Keown daring to dismiss one of our greatest ever players: a supporter of one of football's philistine acts venturing to condemn an artist like our Tommy; then daring to mention Chopper Harris in the same breath. It was heresy, sheer unadulterated heresy.

Tommy Smith may have been tough, he may have been rough, he may even have perpetrated the odd crude lunging tackle or two, in fact, the very odd crude lunging tackle or two, but above all, Tommy Smith was a class act with the deftness of a ballerina, the beauty and toughness of teak and the skill of a Clodoaldo. Okay, so perhaps not *the* Clodoaldo but certainly one of his distant cousins at the very least. Tommy may not have been quite so handsome as George Best – mind you, have you seen Bestie lately – and he may not always have looked the part, but make no mistake, as sure as Viv Richards could bat, Linford Christie run and Fred Astaire dance, Tommy Smith most definitely could play football. Chopper Harris, meanwhile, good old pro that he was, in comparison to our Tommy, never rose above the rank of mere journeyman.

Between 1964 and 1971, Smithy, a tank of a man with the heart of a lion, the tackle of a bulldozer, the balance of a trapeze artist and the touch of a master, took on and matched the best attackers in Europe and was denied possibly 50 or 60 England caps only by the presence of the world's finest ever reader of the game, England's finest ever defender, Bobby Moore (note, I didn't say Britain's finest, not with Hansen, Lawrenson and Dick White around). Had the vogue in those days been a footballing central defensive partnership (as introduced into this country ironically by Bill Shankly in the early Seventies with his pairing of Emlyn Hughes and Phil Thompson/Smithy himself), rather than the more traditional footballer/stopper partnership, then Smithy, rather than vying with Bobby Moore for the White No. 6 jersey, would undoubtedly have partnered him and earned more than his solitary cap won against the Welsh. Neither Jackie Charlton nor later, Brian Labone, Moore's regular partners at the heart of England defence, would ever have had a look in. Nor, in later years, would Norman Hunter, Roy McFarland and Colin Todd for that matter, unless as Tommy's partners that is.

In mitigation for his Smithy blind spot, the author responsible for the attack on Tommy was probably too young to have witnessed Smith's golden years. Nevertheless, off the letter went on a swirl of red mist, no doubt straight into his waste bin, presumably alongside one I had despatched to him twenty four hours earlier expounding the literary genius of his book. Who was it who said Kopites were schizoid? No doubt, it must have been me or someone like me.

Such over reaction has become sadly typical of the way I now am. It is the route along which my particular fandom has led me; the price I pay for my indoctrination; the penance for my sins. Some fanatics escape with merely being tortured by the performances of their team. My legacy has become a round the clock Alf Garnett watchdog service in their defence and is now part of me. Radio or television programmes, newspaper reports, magazine articles; the fortunes of my team, the city, the country, the world, the universe; an adverse comment here or there; any or all are enough to trigger me off and set me down the paths of retribution and righteousness. If I feel strongly about something, one way or the other, I will react, needing to put right the wrong, to do my bit, to assume the responsibility. More often than not the telephone is in my hand and my finger is dialling in a frantic attempt to contact the person responsible, maybe to praise, though more usually to criticise and set the record straight over whatever it is that has prompted my reactions.

Occasionally, in the midst of all my reactive behaviour, I am fortunate enough to track down my quarry, often only through sheer persistence or ingenious methods of subterfuge which I have been forced to devise and perfect over the years, since most sensible persons understandably try to avoid intense idiots like me. Such immediate contact can be at once rewarding and therapeutic.

Armed with a tirade of facts and meticulous detail, I take a sharp breath and splutter an introduction before launching into a reasoned pummelling of my adversary who, taken off-guard, may scarcely recall what it is they have stated or written that has caused me to become so infuriated. My aim is to discredit their argument while proving my own. My tenacity stands me in good stead and often my onslaughts are successful.

Any such success is invariably due to deeply held convictions and thorough knowledge of the subject matter, which is almost always my football team, the city of Liverpool or its people. Often, my prime motivation is the contempt in which I hold the perpetrators of what has been written or said. These are usually the opinion mongers of the media who tout their provocative prejudices with distortions of the truth, twisted round to suit. At times their vitriol strips away all sense of humour and perspective, leaving me bitter and gnarled with nerves jangling. Any affability I possess disappears at once, my tongue comes out of my cheek and out of the closet comes a side of me altogether more solemn. Understandably, the going becomes rough and not exactly palatable.

One such notable opponent was a journalist on the London Evening Standard. The subject matter of the piece he had written could not have been any more emotive as far as I and, for that matter, any other Liverpudlian, was concerned and what transpired will serve to highlight my reactions at their most extreme at the time they happened and provide a particularly revealing insight into the credibility of certain journalists and the depths to which they will sink to fabricate a story which might justify bigoted and often ill-informed views.

I had come across the article purely by chance having visited London on a business trip the week following Hillsborough. I had just boarded the return Manchester Shuttle from Heathrow. The evening newspapers were handed out free. Settling into my seat and fastening my safety belt, I hurriedly glanced through the newspaper and almost immediately spotted the article which could hardly be missed on account of its prominence.

Headlined 'Private Grief, Public Circus' and featuring material clearly aimed at appealing to an emerging anti-Liverpool prejudice as typified by some of the ill-founded and, to Liverpudlians, offensive responses to a terrible tragedy, the article callously vilified the outward expressions of sadness in the city of Liverpool. In particular, the processions of people and the shrine of flowers, scarves and mementoes, covering the entire Kop end at Anfield had been discredited as superficial posturing and mawkish sentimentality, dismissed as a veneer of grief, stage-managed for the consumption of the world's media; and moreover, a selfish and wicked intrusion into the real grief of the bereaved. Concluding his desecration of Liverpudlians, he had alleged that numbered amongst those filing around Anfield in the endless processions were likely to be those very animals who at Hillsborough had urinated on and picked the pockets of the dead and perhaps had been responsible for the disaster. This, he had informed us, was the ultimate hypocrisy.

It is difficult to envisage a more contemptible piece of writing, nor one so untimely or utterly unwarranted; guaranteed to maim already wounded feelings.

As I read the article – still in a state of emotional trauma over the tragedy – I literally could neither comprehend nor believe the words I was reading. Nor could I even begin to contemplate the motives behind the writer's vicious allegations and odious distortions. I began to shake with a deep welling rage, consumed by anger. My feelings ran away with me and I became so enraged, I found myself actually wanting there and then to slay the evil author of that odious bile; to avenge the dead for his unnecessary wanton desecration of their memory and the living for his gratuitous defamation of their characters. His words had turned me into a snarling monster, hell-bent on vengeance and retribution. Whether I would ever have been capable of enacting my outrage is now academic yet while there is little doubt such over reaction is shameful, I find it hard even now to conjure any regret for the way I felt.

My fingers fumbled for the release catch of the seat belt. I would leave the plane, catch the tube to the newspaper offices and confront him. It was too late. Trying to calm myself I took some deep breaths and tried to reflect for a moment. Perhaps I had misread the article or misinterpreted it. It was easily done, by me especially. Mouthing the words, I re-

read it; slowly and meticulously. There was no mistake. I had not imagined a single insult or slur. They were all there. And others, too, which I had not fully taken in on my first reading.

Rather strangely at this point, my anger beginning to quell. It was giving way to feelings of great sadness. I found myself feeling sorry for myself and my fellow citizens and especially the families of the dead. Tears filled my eyes. I wiped them quickly. How could anyone think this? How could anybody write this or, worse, be allowed to write this? The editor? He must have sanctioned it. Why? How? All we had done was show compassion. Couldn't we be left in peace to mourn and pay our respects with some dignity? Why intrude into our world and then crucify us in print?

My mind filled with scrambled visions and thoughts of the disaster as I fought desperately to gain a perspective of sorts on the article and the man who had written it, to reconcile his motives, to understand why he had felt the need to rub salt into our open gaping wounds. I looked up at the plane's ceiling and my eyes welled up once more.

I suddenly became aware of the other passengers around me, all of whom had copies of the same newspaper. They were talking, laughing, reading, yawning. Some of them must also have read the article and yet they appeared to be unaffected. The centre seat next to me was unoccupied. The man in the next but one window seat beyond was respectable looking, elderly, grey-haired and bespectacled in a dark pin-striped suit. I watched him as he turned to the article. I waited for his reaction, praying it would mirror my own, giving me someone else to connect with; something which I so desperately needed. He glanced at the article for perhaps ten seconds or so and then turned the page.

How could I be suffering such trauma while he, and apparently others around me, were oblivious, unmoved. I felt isolated, alone. I could sense waves of paranoia gripping me, invoking grave doubts and misgivings regarding my feelings about what had happened. My confidence in my beliefs, my principles, began to drain. Perhaps the article was right. Perhaps it was nothing more than mawkish over-sentimentality: the flowers, the scarves, the personal mementos. Maybe I was over-reacting, being too emotional, not seeing events as they really were. Maybe we all had been. Maybe our response had actually been wrong. What if we were all intruding on the private grief of the bereaved, fooling nobody but ourselves that we, too, were grieving? My heart sank. I felt vulnerable, exposed, cheapened.

I became aware of the man next to me beginning to suspect something was wrong with me. I forced a smile to reassure him, though

I cannot explain why I felt obliged to offer him reassurance when it was me who was suffering and his interest in me was, no doubt, limited only to a haughty indignation at my involuntary fidgeting. What I did know was I needed to think clearly; think the whole thing through again. For what seemed like an age I felt unable to conjure up a single positive thought in defence of our response, despite the outrageous things I'd read. It was as if my emotions had been frozen.

I politely declined the offer of a drink from the smiling air hostess. Then, as she moved on down the aisle, I thanked God as a familiar, comforting memory flashed in to my mind. I recalled my Aunty Josie's present, a twelve inch high statuette of a dark-haired Liverpool footballer, given to me the Christmas just before she had died, when I was about nine years old. As kids, my friends and I had always made fun of it, for it resembled nobody who had ever pulled on a red shirt, nor any other colour shirt, as far as we were aware, (rather like the photograph of the player on the front cover of a Sixties Liverpool programme who some said looked like Alan A'Court but to us never looked like any player we knew.) Besides, only Italians had jet black hair and to our knowledge, none had ever represented the Reds. Nevertheless, in spite of its appearance, I had always treasured it. It was around thirty years old. About twice the age of the majority who had perished at Hillsborough. It now stood guard on the Kop steps, watching over the carpet of flowers covering the pitch in silent tribute to those dead. I had placed it there on my old "spec", amongst the tens of thousands of scarves and similar precious mementoes, ironically, only a few yards away from a similar but much larger statuette of an Everton footballer, no doubt placed there by an Evertonian. The two figures had stood together on the Kop, motionless, facing the pitch, representing Reds and Blues alike, paying our respects, shoulder to shoulder in sorrow.

The image made me relax. I could sense the beginnings of a warm glow of comfort returning inside. It enabled me to focus once more on what had happened; how we had responded. How the whole city, rich and poor, young and old, Red and Blue, in the midst of the tragedy's aftermath, had pulled together. The doubts I had entertained only seconds earlier were clearing, my misgivings were being rapidly dispelled.

The indifference of the people around me no longer mattered. I knew the score. What could this journalist possibly know about us, about our city and our community. How could he begin to know how we felt, how we hurt, how we mourned for the bereaved and the people who died.

The statuette was but a tiny tribute, a small gesture, to signify how my family and I felt, to show we cared; for the bereaved and the dead; for those who might still die; for all the unimaginable suffering they had had to endure before death. Neither sentiment nor mawkishness came into it. It was simply a collective show of caring.

I had been at Leppings Lane. I knew of three people who died: the young son of our insurance man, the teenage son of a builder I had known, a teenage boy from the next street to our own. A close colleague's two friends had gone to the match, never to return. He had seen them off. He would never see them again. All this was real. It was tangible, heart-wrenching. My stomach knotted. Sadness once more engulfed me. Tears again welled in my eyes, though this time it was not for myself. My heart ached for those poor souls. Mine were the emotions of a member of a community that shared a communal grief. I had known personal grief. Within the previous three years, my sister and I had buried our father and mother. We missed them badly. The feeling now was similar. It gnawed, it numbed, it pained, it hurt. It was grief. Most certainly it was grief.

I vowed there and then to confront this callous man and make him apologise. That was to be my mission and I would not rest until it was accomplished.

As I left the plane and walked across the concourse at Manchester Airport on my way to the car park, I spotted a public figure, recognising him at once. David Alton was a prominent Liverpool Liberal MP. He stood, back against the far wall of the waiting area, a solitary figure in a long dark overcoat. He looked sad and dispirited. Emotion was etched on his face. I decided I would go over and speak to him. There was little need for dialogue for he seemed to know instinctively from my own demeanour why I had approached him. He, too, had seen the article. He, too, had felt equally as enraged and desolate as I had and had also determined to do something about it. Leaving him after our brief encounter, I knew he was patently a decent man, and I felt further reassured I was not alone in my feelings and hoped, in my own small way, I had similarly reassured him.

Driving home I reflected on my feelings. I was deeply and profoundly distressed by the article but I had also been disturbed by the apparent indifference shown by my fellow passengers who had read the same newspaper.

A week earlier on the Monday immediately following the tragedy, I had had to travel down to London with a property developer, a man from a southern based company. Somehow, that terrible morning, I had managed to overcome my wretched state of mind and drag myself to the airport to meet him. He had greeted me at the check-in gate, the usual meeting place. "Bit of a bad do at Sheffield with your lot", he had said, matter of fact, seemingly without emotion, almost as if he was telling me what he had eaten for breakfast.

I know some will counter and say perhaps he was trying not to be morbid or heavy. Whatever, his apparent flippancy was light years away from connecting with my emotions. I had nodded and grunted and immediately changed the subject. Inside, I was numb. There was no way I could have risked trivialising the immeasurable desolation I felt by talking about the tragedy with someone like him who, patently, was not experiencing the same despair.

In the capital that day, life had gone on unerringly. It was as if the momentous events only two days earlier had never occurred. I had survived my ordeal down there only by continually suppressing my feelings and emotions whenever they threatened to surface.

I related all this to the aftermath of the Heysel tragedy four years earlier. Liverpudlians, along with the rest of the world, had been stunned and bewildered as that horrific event had unfolded. They had felt horror and disbelief at what had taken place; sorrow and pity for the victims and their families; anger and rage at the mob of fellow Liverpool supporters for rushing the Italian fans. Feelings of intense guilt and shame pervaded us all, hanging like a pall over the city, since we knew our own kind were ultimately culpable, despite outrage at the authorities for their gross incompetence. Quickly, support had been mobilised throughout the city, money donated, letters written, sympathy expressed, as decent folk had tried to make amends to the distraught people of Turin. And yet, for all our rage and anger, all our guilt and shame, all our sorrow and sympathy, none of us back then could have understood what those people of Turin were really feeling; quite how devastated the people of that entire city must have been.

That night however, as I drove home from the airport, I was able to reflect that it was only the experience of Hillsborough and the traumatic effect it had wielded on the people of Liverpool, which had now permitted Liverpudlians to comprehend the enormity of the devastation experienced by the Italian people following Heysel. Until we, as a community, had been similarly stricken by tragedy – in a cruel intensifying of reaction, Liverpudlians now also had to contend with the trauma of allegations that our own kind at Hillsborough were responsible for the deaths of their fellow fans – we could not possibly have begun to imagine their feelings nor relate to the intensity of their desolation. In the same way, outsiders, whatever their viewpoint, could not possibly understand how ordinary Liverpudlians, let alone the bereaved, now felt in the wake of Hillsborough.

As I reached the end of the motorway and took the turn off for Knotty Ash, I felt I was beginning to come to terms with my own feelings. I would now be suitably composed to tackle this vile man and his vilifications. It would be scant consolation to the dead, the bereaved or the people of Liverpool but, at least, I would be doing my own little bit to put things right. My own form of retribution.

Eventually I impersonated a magazine publisher, thinking it might appeal to the journalist's vanity and entice him into answering my telephone call. I had previously tried over a dozen times to call him, without success. He was indignant at first, aloof even, as I revealed my true identity and purpose. I was nervous and apprehensive but nonetheless resolute and determined. At times during our conversation, he must have been perilously close to hanging up but didn't. Perhaps his vanity, his own conceited perception that he was right, prevented him.

My representation of the dialogue which ensued is not, of course, precise, since it was not recorded but it is as near to the gist as to make no difference at all.

"What was the basis for your assertion that the mourning and the processions around Anfield were contrived and not genuine, that it was stage-managed for media consumption?" I enquired.

"I could sense it from the television footage; the people were peering at the cameras; it all seemed so contrived." he responded.

I had started to relax slightly and explained to him that I had been to the ground on three separate occasions, the first of which, on the night of the disaster, had been spontaneous, as it was for most people who congregated there.

Arriving back in Liverpool from Hillsborough with my friends, I had been drawn to the ground as if by some subliminal compulsion for succour and comfort from the warmth and familiarity of the stadium. Hundreds of others, overnight perhaps thousands, had patently felt the same urge. We had simply stood silently by the gates at the Anfield

Road end of the ground, the Shankly Gates. Some had already placed flowers and scarves. I had done likewise with my own scarf. It was twenty-four years old; I was still wearing it from the ill-fated match only five or six hours earlier. All this had occurred without any prior knowledge, on my part, of anybody else going to the ground; of any pilgrimage. I am certain the same was the case with the others who were also there with me and those who continued to file to the ground through the rest of that night and the following morning. It was the instinctive reaction of the people of a city in mourning.

My next two visits had been with my family and other relatives, similarly moved and affected by the events, to pay their respects. By that time, the club felt obliged to provide some form of organisation to alleviate the confusion and congestion so they had opened the gates and organised the orderly queues and processions which, several days later, along with the carpet of flowers, had attracted television coverage. Each time we had visited, we had queued for as long as two or three hours, simply to express that we cared. We had not seen any cameras at all. The queues and processions had been continuous for a whole week. All day, every day. Ever respectful, ever reverent. As the week wore on and the crowds grew, any spontaneity had disappeared but that had not reflected any diminishing of the sincerity of the people's feelings. The people had gone for one reason and one reason only: to pay their respects and to show they cared.

"The references in your article to fans urinating on the dead and picking their pockets. Did you by any chance, get them from the Sun or Star tabloids?" I asked.

He admitted he had. He had little choice. Only the Sun and Star had presented those lies. I informed him, for he had been unaware of it, that the stories had been fabrications, allegedly by a police constable, just as the initial police story of Liverpool fans breaking down the stadium gates had similarly been the fabrication of a senior police officer. The urinating, more distressingly, had been a misinterpretation by newsdesks of the involuntary action of those whose life was being crushed out of them. He mumbled, but could find nothing to say. Perhaps the minutest semblance of humanity existed after all in his blinkered mind.

I continued, by now in full flow, but still fearing he may slam down the phone as I overwhelmed him with my truths. "With respect, have you lost your parents or anybody very close?".

He informed me he had not. His views on any type of profound grief were therefore not first hand. I explained my own circumstances with my own parents, pointing out the small degree of comfort which is derived simply from knowing someone cares; from the simple expressions of sympathy – not a lessening of the grief, but something which is appreciated nevertheless and stored warmly and safely in the memory for a time to come. Certainly not an intrusion. Hopefully, the bereaved of Hillsborough would in time be able to accept a small part of the warmth and caring which had poured from the hearts and souls of their fellow Liverpudlians.

I left my most telling question until last but I already knew its answer. He, by then, already knew that his arguments were flawed and that he had committed a terrible wrong and injustice.

"Have you visited the city since the tragedy?" I asked finally.

"No." He admitted that he hadn't.

"So you won't have experienced the very tangible sense of communal grief throughout the city. More pertinently, you won't be aware that most people in Liverpool know of at least one person who died or was injured or was at Leppings Lane, making the tragedy very immediate to most of us. You won't be aware that our feelings for the dead and bereaved are the genuine feelings of a community. That Liverpool is not a metropolis. It is not ten million virtual strangers not knowing or caring about each other. True, it has its faults, its warts, its scars and its lesions like anywhere else. But it also has a sense of identity and community. People do know and care about each other. Hurt one and you hurt the other."

The line was silent.

I finished, "You've got it all wrong, haven't you; hopelessly, utterly, absolutely wrong? What you have done is unforgivable."

The line went dead.

An apology from such a man would have been worthless.

Writing in his ivory tower, detached from the events in Sheffield and Liverpool, the man had neither cared about nor bothered to find out about the realities of the situation. Many others like him had done the same. They could neither identify with nor relate to the reaction of the people of Liverpool. Nor did they want to. It was not how they would have reacted and so, in their ignorance and bigotry, they had offended the dead and the living. They had derided them; condemned them; discredited them. They had filled their pages and, perhaps, appealed to their targeted audience. They had insulted the people of a city who cared, who dared to show warmth and feeling and compassion for others, most of whom would remain unaware that such things had ever been written, oblivious of what a large proportion of the population of the country were reading about them.

I understand the journalist concerned has since acquired a responsible position on a national newspaper.

More often than not, my efforts at telephone contact with the perpetrator of a deed I consider to be unjust prove unsuccessful. This leads to a double sense of frustration: the failure to instantly relieve the burden off my chest and the realisation that hours of toil lie ahead as I compose my written response. Apart from consuming valuable time, a written response provides neither instant therapy nor feedback and tends to alienate everyone around me, all of whom find it impossible to identify with my infuriating obsession or to sympathise with the stance I often find myself compelled to take.

Once in a while, my efforts at writing prove worthwhile. My aim is true and my written volley finds its target as in December 1993 when I wrote to Peter Robinson, Chief Executive of Liverpool Football Club:

Dear Mr Robinson

It may have been a perception bordering on the imaginative, but throughout the Shankly/Paisley eras it always seemed as if the players in red shirts were prepared to run through brick walls for the cause of Liverpool Football Club and the Kop.

When such honest toil and endeavour was fused with high skills and a passionate crowd who reciprocated the players' commitment, Liverpool FC became an irresistible force in world football.

No object was immovable, no prize unattainable. The bond between fan and club seemed unbreakable. Even during the unsuccessful periods the players' efforts were warmly appreciated by the fans.

Towards the end of Kenny Dalglish's management and especially since, any such passion and commitment has disappeared.

Spirit, effort and character appear alien to the players, who give the distinct impression of not being prepared to even climb over walls, let alone run through them.

Financial reward dominates our players' and manager's agenda. Dedication, consideration for the fans and professional pride are absent.

And so we watch the absolute professional absurdity of three players, Molby, Stewart and to a lesser extent, Barnes, carrying four or five stones of surplus fat between them onto the pitch, while earning obscene weekly salaries which equate to, or exceed, the yearly incomes of some fans.

These are by no means the only ones who appear to be less than fully fit, injuries apart.

Running off the ball and close support-play, which require maximum effort throughout the team, are conspicuously absent from our pattern of play week in, week out, with the odd exceptions.

Nobody in the team seems prepared to hurt or sweat honestly for the cause of the team and the fans. The fans' loyalty deserves more than the current players appear to be prepared to give.

This dearth of genuine feeling for the club in the face of the inflated rewards is virtually fraudulent, and the insincerity is choking Liverpool FC to death and is destroying the "unbeatable bond" created by the great man.

I implore you, Peter, do something about it now. Do everything within your powers to cure this disease before it is too late and things have slipped too far to recover.

Yours most sincerely

Alan Edge

I had knee-jerked and written in desperation following a midweek Coca Cola League Cup debacle against Wimbledon at Anfield in December 1993. The game, I believe, represented Liverpool's nadir as a team. All the team's faults and shortcomings, which over a two or three year period had gradually become evident, came together that night. The team, which for a long time had been but pale shadows of their predecessors were utterly unrecognisable as representatives of the club. We had all seen poor performances, even by the great sides. This, however, was different. It was utterly shameful; lacking in every single positive aspect of the game of football, which, over the years, Liverpool teams had come to stand for. The most damning absentees of all, that night, had been the honest effort and commitment always synonymous with the club. The fans had found that unforgivable.

It had been evident for some time that something was drastically wrong at the club. We had gradually become adrift from our time-served principles. Most fans had blamed Graeme Souness, the manager, whose reign had witnessed the seemingly inexorable decline in our standards. I tended to support this view but I was not completely sure, since there had been visible indications of deterioration towards the end of Kenny Dalglish's reign when the terrible effects of Hillsborough had so clearly taken their toll on the Liverpool legend.

What I was certain of, however, was that the disgraceful attitude of some of the Liverpool players was reaching an unacceptable level of apathy. If they had performed in a similar vein in the big, bad world outside, they would undoubtedly have been sacked on the spot. I was livid at the way they were increasingly turning in performances which were betraying the club, the supporters, the past players and managers who had made the club a famous, world-wide name, and most of all, themselves and their own families. I felt they were cheating the fans, taking the supporters' money and giving little back in return. That night against Wimbledon, I determined to do something and so I wrote to Peter Robinson, the only man at the club I felt had the authority and standing to bring any influence to bear on the shambles the club had become. From a subsequent telephone conversation Peter Robinson told me it was his intention to show the letter to Graeme Souness. Who knows if he did – it couldn't have been the only one he received on this topic.

Several weeks later, Graeme Souness was forced, inevitably, to resign his position as manager of Liverpool Football Club. I do not presume for one moment my letter had any bearing on his departure for the fans' frustrations were there for all to see. What my letter had done, was to capture the mood of many seasoned Liverpudlians, such as myself, who, whilst we were prepared, albeit reluctantly, to suffer the indignity and despair of watching an unsuccessful team, had, however, reached the end of our tether as far as turning up to watch players who had appeared to become indifferent to the significance of the Liver Bird on their chests.

I subsequently sent a copy of the letter to Tommy Smith's Letters column in the Liverpool Football Echo. Tommy published the letter and gave me a "Fair Tackle" which meant he agreed with my sentiments entirely. That was good enough for me for Tommy was always right, as far as I was concerned.

Looking back on it now it's amazing how pompous the tone of the letter sounds. I mean, who the hell do we Liverpool fans think we are? What divine right have we got to expect any more commitment from our players than anyone else's? The thing is, however, that is precisely how it is. We do expect and demand more and as an historical and hysterical cameo the letter does capture perfectly that high and mighty indignation we were all experiencing during the Souness years – the solitary period in thirty-odd years when we didn't actually get the goods delivered; we behaved like spoilt kids not getting their own way, which is exactly what we were. Mind you, what else are you supposed to do when you're being cheated by your own team.

In the autumn of 1994, I exploded, almost literally. Ian Wooldridge, a respected sportswriter for a major national daily gave publicity to the release of Brian Clough's autobiography highlighting a section of the book in which Clough blamed late, ticketless and disorderly Liverpool fans for killing their own people at Hillsborough. It was bad enough that the writer and his newspaper granted Clough uncritical publicity; what festered was the question posed in the writer's final paragraph: "Could it be that, stripped of the emotion of Hillsborough, Brian Clough's analysis might be absolutely right?" Such slanted insinuation was reprehensible. Soon, others were regurgitating similar bile. I commenced a personal mission to reject Clough's distortions and relay the truth of Hillsborough. In this instance, my countless efforts at so doing exhausted me, ultimately causing my family to stop me from carrying on in case I did actually explode.

What cut deeply about the whole Clough business was the sheer injustice of it all. Here was a tragedy so devastating to the bereaved and to the whole of Merseyside, which had been caused so clearly and unequivocally by the utter incompetence and bloody-minded indifference of the authorities and had been so demonstrably proven to have been so by indisputable visual and photographic evidence and eyewitness accounts. The official independent enquiry of Lord Justice Taylor had no doubts whatsoever of the authorities' culpability and the fans blamelessness having scrupulously examined the huge volume of evidence.

And yet here, in Clough, we had a person whom many reasoned observers consider to be nothing more than a complete buffoon, claiming that the actual facts of the matter counted for nought and that the convenient scapegoat of Liverpudlian "thuggery" was to blame. And the saddest, most despicable travesty of all was that the views of the man's misguided mind were allowed to hold sway in our media. We yet again had lost the battle for fairness because in the fight for truth the ordinary Joe Bloggs is impotent against media power.

In the saga of Hillsborough, of course, the ordinary people are the families of the victims. It is they who are denied a real platform. In the course of my own personal campaign, I was privileged to make the acquaintance of two of them – Phil and Hilda Hammond – who had lost their son Philip in the tragedy. Phil and Hilda are ordinary people – nice, friendly yet also extremely brave and resilient. The thing which struck me most was their restraint and dignity in spite of the loss they had suffered and the indignities and injustices they had endured at the hands of authority. Phil and Hilda's son had been declared officially dead at 3.15 pm yet they knew from witness evidence he was still alive at least thirty minutes after that time. They have come across many similar inconsistencies. They have spent hour after hour, day after day, week after week, poring through the evidence of Hillsborough. They attended every day of the Inquest and the Inquiry. They, after all, had lost their son so they had to know how he died, why he died, when he died. Their grief compelled them to do so. Through their research, they have learned precisely what caused the tragedy, who was to blame and who wasn't to blame. If anyone has the right or the knowledge to make accusations about the causes of Hillsborough, it is the likes of Phil and Hilda Hammond, not Brian Clough. Sadly, ordinary people don't often get the chance , no matter how justified, though in their case, maybe one day, God willing, they just might.

I, too, was an ordinary person armed only with telephone and biro. Nevertheless, I did manage numerous potshots and, amongst several minor successes, managed to establish a dialogue of sorts with Ian Wooldridge whose stance had so enraged me. Though inevitably our exchange of views ultimately petered out, he did at least publish a precis of a 4,000 word letter I sent him on the topic. Most encouraging was a revealing response from a sports journalist from the *Observer*, to whom I had sent a copy of the Liverpool City Council Preliminary Report on Hillsborough. His letter makes particularly disturbing reading and is, to me, a serious indictment of the media in this country.

Dear Alan

Thank you for the copy of Professor Scraton's report on the Hillsborough tragedy. I have placed it alongside the Taylor Report on my study shelves where it has already proved a valuable work of reference in refuting the views of a Sheffield reader blind to the complex causes of a tragedy that he sees as the sole work of Liverpool supporters.

As Scraton shows in identifying the impact of Middup and Patnick on the public perception of the causes, Hillsborough was another case of a lie being halfway round the world before truth could get its boots on. Maybe the true picture will emerge, as you believe, but I fear many more years may slip by before the present polarised factions accept facts and reason.

There was press distortion, no doubt about that. It emanated from impetuous ignorance, though, not wickedness; and from news desks and editorial conferences hundreds of miles from the action and not from the sports reporters on the spot and able to see most of what was happening. There can be no more ideal position for a newspaper than to have two experienced staff reporters and a phone in the heart of a disaster; this was so in the case of my own newspaper.

Myself and a colleague (who slipped the police cordon and penetrated the makeshift mortuary) kept constant contact with our news desk and copytakers, but, in three pages of coverage, only two sentences of ours were used.

Fleet Street offices, like the police, mistakenly saw the issue as hooliganism, not as a failure of safety in which the city of Sheffield did almost everything wrong, as revealed so clearly in their ambulance dispatcher having no address for Hillsborough or any idea of its whereabouts.

I don't know exactly what could be achieved by an investigative journalist for it's plain from the inquest verdicts that officialdom is loth to charge a few individuals, while arraigning all the guilty parties would require a dock the size of a penalty box.

Yours sincerely

Mike Langley

Of course, the bitter pill as far as Livepudlians are concerned is that the shameful media coverage of Hillsborough both at the time and frequently since is, arguably, the most repugnant of its type ever. It is particularly ironic that Mike Langley implies in his letter that the scale of the guilt prevents the guilty being brought to justice, especially as size restrictions have never prevented his colleagues in the media condemning Liverpudlians en masse. If anything, it is precisely because of the magnitude of the injustice surrounding the disaster that the guilty parties have to be brought to book and why the people of Merseyside actually voted with their 20 pences against the Sun Newspaper, one of the leading transgressors. In truth, Merseysiders would have been equally justified for similar actions against virtually every other tabloid and broadsheet, and, indeed, most TV and radio stations, except our own local media.

Sadly, with Hillsborough, all the damage has now been done. The lives have been lost, suffering endured, sides have been taken, the opinions formed and the real truth obscured by lies. To many, the convenient scape-goats have proved just too irresistible; the imagery and hearsay just too powerful to ignore. The boisterous mob of late, drunk and ticketless fans, hell-bent on entry whatever the price fits the bill a little too perfectly to be discarded. So what, if Lord Justice Taylor did say it wasn't the case? What does he know about such things? That's what fans do, especially the Liverpool fans. Look at Heysel. Look at Wolves in 1976 when they did break down the gates, or Wembley in 1986 when they were scaling the walls. It was bound to happen sooner or later. If it hadn't been Hillsborough, it would have been somewhere else. End of argument.

That, at once, is the beauty and the problem with life. Everyone is entitled to their opinion, whether informed or not. Anyone can orchestrate a convenient response to represent 'the other side of the coin'. Some, like Brian Clough and Ian Wooldridge have the added advantage of having a platform to do so. Regrettably, with Hillsborough the whole issue has become a breeding ground for a plethora of opinions and prejudices. My own for one, so passionately relayed in my letters of the time, whilst remaining in principle the same, have had to be modified after watching the official Police videos, which so clearly demonstrate the direct link between the Police opening of the gates and the final outcome of the tragedy.

Professor Scraton and his team's Final Report for Liverpool City Council – "No Last Rights" – and the Jimmy McGovern drama documentary "Hillsborough" brilliantly clear all the waters and relate the truth of Hillsborough . If there was any justice at all, they would also blow away for good all the misconceptions and prejudices. The thing is, though, "No Last Rights" and "Hillsborough" also run the risk of preaching only to the converted. What they will struggle to do is enter, let alone change, the closed minds of others who view Hillsborough as the fault of Liverpudlians. It is precisely for that reason why the truth must continue to be pushed. Why the efforts of Phil Scraton and Jimmy McGovern are more important than ever in procuring a realisation that Hillsborough does indeed constitute a grave miscarriage of justice. Wrongs need to be righted, myths dispelled and those responsible, both for the disaster and the subsequent cover ups, need to be made answerable. Anything less can never be good enough for it means that Phil and Hilda Hammond and the ninety or so other families like them would be denied justice. Only an all embracing, unequivocal absolution of guilt on behalf of the dead and their fellow fans, together with a clear identification of those culpable, will enable the families and survivors of the tragedy to complete a grieving process begun in 1989. It is their right and it is long overdue.

With Penance being the last word in punishment and atonement, it would be little short of remiss of me to conclude a passage on the subject without at least a passing reference to two phenomena, both of which in their own distinct ways (one incidentally nothing to do with football whatsoever but which, nonetheless, demands inclusion in any account relating to modern-day Liverpool) have inflicted more pain and suffering on Liverpudlians, and Evertonians for that matter, than almost anything else I can think of.

Apart from her occasional blue rinse, at times matching the colour of a Seventies Man City shirt, Margaret Thatcher's sole connection with football had been her abortive attempt to introduce an identity card scheme which was both naive and misguided and, in hindsight, speaks volumes about her. In contrast, her relationship with Liverpool was by no means so tenuous, being, regrettably, only all too real and tangible and the cause of infinite hardship and heartache on Merseyside. Indeed, it would probably not be exaggerating things too far to say that to many in Liverpool, the merest mention of Margaret Thatcher's name evokes emotions not that dissimilar to the loathing still found within some South American Indians for Cortez the Killer.

Thatcher had attempted to destroy Liverpool but not in the open way Adolf Hitler had tried, with bombing raids. Her way had been masked by veils, opaque to many, though not to us, of 'laissez faire', free competition, 'sink or swim' and 'lame ducks'. Ably assisted by her propaganda machine, her hidden agenda had been for us to become the flagship sacrificial lamb of her new found 'out with the old' plaything and, as if to order, a certain Mr Derek Hatton together with his motley crew, was destined to play right into her hands, transforming her despicable deeds into some sort of phoney ideological warfare in which the people of Merseyside were the losers on all counts.

Our own 'lame ducks' had been the original Liverpool homes of many major companies, who, when squeezed by her free market obsessions were forced to make inevitable economies which simply closed their archaic Merseyside plants, turfing around eighty thousand people onto a scrap heap from which many would never emerge. Not content with plunging the knife of dereliction into the backs of these people, she and her cronies proceeded to hold responsible for the desertion of these companies the very people whose lives her policies had wrecked, accusing and successfully tainting the majority of them as militant, strike prone, workshy, lazy, bolshie and unmanageable.

In contrast to Margaret Thatcher Manchester United, although many a bigoted Liverpudlian may tell you otherwise, did have something to do with football.

There had always been rivalry between Man Utd and both Merseyside clubs. After all, the outskirts of the cities are only 20 miles apart, not that much more distant than say, Newcastle and Sunderland. In the Sixties and early Seventies, the rivalry was what could be termed healthy. We were, in truth, probably envious of their glamour which was, to a great extent, the legacy of first, the legendary Busby Babes, then tragically Munich, and finally the magical names of Best, Law and Charlton, culminating in their European Cup success of 1968, when they became the first English club to lift that trophy. They, for their part, were probably slightly more than mildly irritated by the close geographical proximity of a team such as ours which presented a very real threat to their generally acknowledged position as the country's biggest club. In terms of gates and support, at the time, there was, probably in all fairness, very little in it. United did command a greater average gate than Liverpool but this was essentially due to their superior ground capacity. Against that, Liverpool could boast the uniqueness of the Kop. Liverpool's fan catchment at the time was mainly the Merseyside area, United's was nation-wide.

By the mid-Seventies, things had begun to change rather dramatically. Liverpool had started to become synonymous with success. A decade still further on and Liverpool had developed into by far the most successful side in the history of English football, and, more pointedly, second only to Real Madrid in terms of European success with six trophies won on the Continent. During the same period, Manchester United had won the FA Cup on several occasions but they had also been down to the Second Division and had hardly looked remotely like winning the First Division title nor achieving European success. The two Clubs' respective records between 1970 and 1990 provide sobering contrasts: Manchester United won three FA Cups; Liverpool meanwhile won three FA Cups, four League Cups, eleven Championships, two EUFA Cups and four European Cups. Need I say more.

The consequence of all this as far as United fans were concerned was that Liverpool went from being a mere irritant to the prime enemy; the target of all their bitter frustration and jealousy. Every one of the twenty-four major trophies we won represented a barbed arrow to their heart. It went deep; very deep. United's fanatical hordes hated us, as I knew only too well from my personal experience of working in Manchester for four years in the Eighties.

A factor which had a major bearing on the depth of their hatred was also, as it happened, the prime cause of our contempt for them. The people of the media, like fans everywhere, had feasted upon the Busby Babes. They had witnessed many of the cream of their own profession perish at Munich. They had seen United with Matt Busby and Jimmy Murphy at the helm rise from the ashes and build another great side which on a wave of public emotion had lifted the European Cup. They had savoured three of Britain's finest ever players, the pick of whom was, at the height of his powers, arguably (undoubtedly in my opinion) the greatest footballer ever seen – Pele, Puskas, De Stefano, Finney, Matthews, Beckenbauer, Dalglish, Cruyff, Maradona, Gullit, Weah, Vinnie Jones, all included.

Actually, I must pause here for a moment, and I know my mate Billy Hall, who's forgotten more than I know, will disagree – Best was the best. The first time I went to Old Trafford was 1965 and we lost 2-0. I remember the game for one thing alone – I learned all about shitting myself, for that's basically what you did every time Best got the ball – even when he was in his own penalty area. He must have been only about eighteen and looked younger and slighter than me – I was a skinny teenager – but the thing was, no-one could get near him to make a tackle and we had three of the best – Big Rowdy, Smithy and Gerry 'Crunch' Byrne – and every time they tried, they tackled thin air, for the dark Beatle-haircut, the flapping red shirt and the ball were spirited away by a magical talent.

So the game became like a ninety-minute long white knuckle ride. Your stomach was in a tight knot for the whole time, praying he wouldn't get the ball but the worst of it was, he was actually as good a tackler as our three heavies so he could always win it for himself. It seemed as if he actually had the ball for the entire game. Each time he would come gliding forward head down, zig-zagging and slicing his way past everyone, it seemed United would score and most times, they all but did. It was a nightmare.

Thankfully, though, he never got any better than he was that season – not that he got worse, just no better – so after that, you always knew what to expect and, as with the very scariest of horror films, you learned how to cope with it. You just used to shut your eyes at the most frightening bits – when he got the ball – and then keep peeking out to see if we had got it back and when we did, you could relax for a few seconds in the hope that the ball wouldn't go anywhere near him again and, if it did, you held your breath and when he got it, you closed your eyes again and peeked and so on all the time, wishing for it to end. And from where I used to stand that's what it was like with George Best.

And looking back, you realised you'd been watching God's greatest ever gift to the game. And if you ask me why he was the best and what one thing set him apart, I would say it was speed of reaction. We used to play with a lad called Willcox, who wasn't particularly that interested in playing but when you tried to get the ball off him, it wasn't there because he had always flicked it away first. He didn't have to feint or dummy or shimmy, he was just quicker to the ball; in fact, he made all of us look slow and though we weren't that fast, it would be the only time we did look that slow.

What I'm saying is the whole Best phenomenon was nothing more than Einstein's Relativity Theory – essentially, everyone else was miles slower than Bestie. His reactions were on Level Ten of Space Invaders when the best of the opposition's were on Level 5. No wonder he used to use a defender's leg for a wall pass. No wonder he never had any nerves before a game. The rest was merely a formality; the ball control, the balance, the timing, the dribbling, the passing, the shooting, the feints, the flicks, the tackles, the headers, the stamina, the speed, the courage. Oh, and I suppose it also helped a bit that he knew where the goal was and that the object of the exercise was for United to win, and that, from what we've all learned since, he was hung like Ron Harris.

Back to the rivalry. As a consequence of all this tragedy and glamour and Bestiality the media clung to the name of Manchester United like a mother suckling her infant. Inevitably, a great many of the media were Manchester United fans. The Club was accordingly thrust into the limelight for the slightest possible reason and the more this happened, the more all the hype and glamour attracted yet more fans and this, of course, meant even greater newspaper sales if the back pages were filled with United hype and so the whole thing became a self-feeding, self-perpetuating, hype-ridden monster which non-United fans, particularly us and more recently, post Cantona, Leeds fans, all hated.

The most ridiculous manifestation of all this absurd media attention was almost certainly in the Eighties with the return on one occasion from a lengthy, (but not unusually lengthy), injury of Bryan Robson, when it was impossible to read a newspaper or watch television without him giving an interview about his comeback or without having the highlights of his comeback games for the reserves thrust down your throat (though even all that was possibly surpassed with Cantona's return from suspension in the autumn of 1995). Around the same time, Liverpool (and Everton for that matter), were winning doubles and trebles and sweeping the board clean to the accompaniment of relatively token media acknowledgement.

These imbalances represented just the tip of the iceberg. The return of United to Manchester after an FA Cup success or defeat would be afforded an hour long television documentary on Granada. Liverpool's (or Everton's) return following inestimably greater successes would attract a two minute local news snippet the next evening. Meanwhile, the distorted coverage in the press continued to devote twice as many column inches to United's trials and tribulations as to Liverpool's triumphs and triple-ations.

In direct proportion to the unprecedented degree of their success and consistently outstanding quality of their football, the praise and acknowledgements bestowed on Liverpool during this period seemed meagre. Two prominent, respected writers, David Lacey and Brian Glanville, had, by the early Eighties only barely managed even by then to acknowledge the Reds' abilities as a "fine passing side". Persistent ignorance against any modicum of praise merited by a club which was terrorising Europe on England's behalf (what price that now?) was hard to believe, though in my opinion, partly seemed to stem from the relative infrequency with which the principal writers of such newspapers visited Anfield to witness the team at its best, which, as all Liverpudlians know, was not necessarily always in the major European games, often the only time most of these scribes chose to visit the ground. Of course, it could be that I haven't a clue how many times leading football writers attended Anfield or eulogised the Reds in print because I was too busy watching Liverpool sweep all before them to read anything other than the Liverpool Echo. But there you go.

The result of all this was double-edged. First, it gave United fans a completely distorted image of the greatness of their own club and made it far more unpalatable for them to accept Liverpool's continued success. Second, at the same time, it deeply enraged Liverpool's (and to an extent, Everton's) fans who could see the shambolic imbalance in media coverage of the respective teams but were powerless to do anything about it.

The ensuing bitterness festered. It all became enmeshed with the already intense natural rivalry which had existed for years between the respective fans and by the Eighties had degenerated into unhealthy, malevolent, two way rivalry which had its most nauseous manifestation in the loathsome Munich Runway song and later the song of Shankly's death.

The Nineties saw an escalation of the hatred on the Liverpool side, though thankfully the Liverpool fans' reaction to their own disaster saw an end to the contemptible Munich song. As the fortunes on the playing front of the two sides virtually interchanged, (though it is unlikely that even United can ever hope to come anywhere near to emulating Liverpool's matchless success story), it left Liverpudlians with the prospect of beating United at Anfield as the highlight of their early Nineties seasons of drudgery with the result that the ensuing atmosphere at the ground for the fixture became during that time the only one to generate anywhere near the same electric intensity as the great occasions of bygone days.

Regrettably, of course, the massive downside to these affairs – and I hold my hands up to this like any other Liverpudlian – is that most of the electricity was, and still is, powered by nothing more than sheer contempt for United which, given our unrivalled pedigree, is surely not the way it should be. There's got to be more to Liverpool fans than simply being United haters. And it's not just us who are so afflicted. Like most cases of longstanding and entrenched bitterness, it cuts both ways. A few years back for instance when United won their first double a book celebrating their glory was entitled 'Are You Watching Liverpool?' Now I ask you, the prime consideration of a United fanatic on winning a glorious double is to ask Liverpudlians whether they saw it. Pathetic isn't it? That's football for you though. The one thing better than winning a trophy is to win it at the expense of a close rival.

Okay, so let's not get too hypocritical about all this. After all, the original title for this book was 'You Lost the League on Merseyside' but the publisher's cat is a fanatical Man Utd fan so he wouldn't wear it. But so what? The tit-for-tat mentality has surely had its day and become almost tiresome. Personally, I feel it's high time for we Liverpudlians, at least, to look for a way to rise above it all; to bring a touch of class into the proceedings and put a stop to all the nonsense. Let's begin with the actual hate thing itself.

Okay, fair enough, so we all know where the contempt comes from; after all, we all feel it in varying degrees. Okay too, so we all know as well that not a single Liverpudlian could possibly ever like Manchester United the Club, or United individuals such as Gary Pallister, Ian Ure, John Fitzpatrick, Joe Jordan and Lou Mancari (for not signing for us and for his flukey 1977 Cup Final goal against us) and certainly not

Alex Ferguson and Peter Schmeichel, David McCreerey and Roy Keane; all of them, without any doubt, truly horrible manifestations of the very worst of the United kind which once roamed free around the Stretford End. Also, I'm pretty sure, too, everyone would agree that some of the media's blind prejudice for United would make even the most placid Kopite want to peel off his skin, and Paddy Crerand's too, for that matter.

Just for once, though, let us overlook the bad side and turn the entire thing on its head. Let us look at the other side of the United coin (or the Krugerand as it is more likely to be these days) for the more pleasant aspect, for there definitely is one, if you look hard enough. I mean, there's a little bit of good in everything, or so they say, so by definition the same must apply to United.

Take the United Sixties side as a case in point. Now, I find it difficult to believe that there exists any true Liverpudlian, even those wearing the most tinted Anfield specs, who could actually hold in their heart of hearts any real contempt for the likes of Bobby Charlton's shining dome, Nobby Stiles' toothless grin – so delightful and ripe for a nutmeg – or even those bandy legs – just as juicily nutmeggable – of old Paddy Crerand himself. And, while we're on the point, what about the likes of Bill Foulkes, Albert Scanlon, Shay Brennan, Albert Quixall, Tony Dunne, Harry Gregg, David Herd, Phil Chisnall and later on, Gordon Hill and Steve Coppell. I mean, give all of them their due, they were all true gentlemen and scholars; all likeable, normal guys, whom any Liverpudlian would be proud to call their own.

In fact, let's be perfectly frank here, when it really comes to the crunch, even where Man United are concerned, isn't it the case that we all invariably react positively where such credit is due. For instance, don't we all really sympathise over Munich and praise Sir Matt Busby while recognising the talents of Bobby Charlton, Denis Law, George Best and Duncan Edwards and the Busby Babes. Didn't we also, too, all have grudging admiration for the qualities of Giggsy, Andrei, Denny, Sparky, Brucey and now too the new batch of kids Nevvyone, Nevvytwo, Becky, Scholesy, Butty and Bacon Sarny – and even Eric Cantony if push came to shove? It's in our genes. It's our tradition for God's sake. We've got no say in it; our overstated sense of Liverpudlian fair play and lashings of innate Kopite schizophrenia see to that. We're stuck with it whether we like it or not.

Of course, paradoxically, in spite of all I say and all their redeeming qualities, we do all really hate the bastards. Daft, isn't it? But then, what else can we do? Just be ourselves, as our dear old mums would have said.

So we are and that's why we all end up as United haters. Maybe it's just that some things are already mapped out for you. All to do with destiny and fate. A bit like the Shankly thing, I suppose. And besides, when you think about it, it could be worse – I mean we could have all been born in Buckingham Palace for a kick off, in which case we'd no doubt have ended up actually supporting United and speaking the Queen's English, which just goes to show you doesn't it, you really do have to be grateful for the small Merseys in life, penance or no penance.

Epilogue

It is an inescapable fact that there is always someone worse off than yourself and, if it was the case that the fanaticism of Liverpudlians underwent dramatic upheavals in the Nineties, then on a broader front, fandom itself scarcely knew what hit it as we all hurtled remorselessly towards the Millennium, blown there by an irresistible hurricane of change. One thing was certain, being a fan would never again embrace those elusive arts of dodging the muggers behind the cages of the Anfield Boys Pen or taking a piss down a rolled up 'Echo' as you did the 'hokey-cokey' and sang to the tune of "Yellow Submarine" on a red and white Kop.

For all the relative successes and failures, for all the highs and lows, the underlying principles governing most fans and their fandom were broadly the same. They all shared, whatever their initiation, enthusiasm or experience, a similar spirit of devotion, duty and attachment to their beloved team and their fellow fans, promoting a sense of oneness which could fairly be termed a communion. No matter whether your love stemmed from the cradle or from early teens or even a middle-aged late conversion, the idea was you supported your team through thick and thin. Such commitment ensured that true fans of AC Milan would still support their team even if they were the Italian equivalent of Darlington and vice versa in respect of every single fan of Darlington (presumably, by definition, all fans of Darlington are true, since they would hardly be along for a glory trip). Though the packed terraces of the San Siro for a glamour game against Juventus might forever remain a far cry from the bleak rainswept terracing of the Feethams Stadium for a relegation tussle with Workington, the fans of either club were there for the same basic reason – to support their team.

This act of communion has been re-affirmed week in, week out from before the time Mr Bugler was a lad, at every ground wherever football is played. It is present in every tackle made, shot saved, goal scored and game won or lost, for it was not just the players who performed these acts. Scarcely did fans ever leave a ground without having strained every sinew and kicked every ball and rarely did the commitment of the players ever exceed that of the fans. After all, the fans would still be there long after all the players had retired to their big house in the country or, in the case of the Darlington lads, presumably to race whippets on the plains of Allendale.

Occasionally, in the course of their turbulent life as a fan, some supporters were fortunate enough to support a team which won a League Championship or a Cup or some other honour. Such success did not cause those fans to be any more or less committed or attached to their team than fans of non-successful clubs, nor indeed did it make the fandom of those starved of success any less valid or fulfilling. After all, supporting your team is as much about adversity and disappointment as it is about glory and success. Who is to say that a last minute equaliser for Darlington averting relegation to non-League football would not invoke a thrill in Darlington fans to equate with that amongst Milanese fans when AC Milan won a European Cup.

What success did bring about was a change in the experience of the fans concerned, enabling the lucky ones to reap some reward for their loyalty and allowing their sense of communion to manifest itself in an extreme fashion. Though such success may have oiled the wheels, it was no more vital to fandom than failure. Both were simply part and parcel of the fan experience and fans have thrived on both extremes since the first ball was kicked.

As the Nineties progressed, there was a major shift in all this. Two major new players emerged to challenge the old ethos of fandom. The problem with these new participants was they were only too aware of the high stakes involved and they were intent on sweeping away our traditions and changing for ever the complexion and composition of the game's bedrock – namely us. The money-men and media had got hold of fandom by the wallet and were determined to shake it around until their coffers were swelled, their fortunes realised and our faith had become unrecognisable to that practised by our fathers. 'Football is now big business', was to became one of the cliches of the Nineties and though as far as the fans were concerned it has always been so, the difference now was its magnitude and importance were being measured in terms of monetary profit and loss, not the strength of emotional ties. The fact is, money does talk and the market does dictate and fans of Darlington and, even, AC Milan will, I fear, never be the same again; the face of the game is altering dramatically and there will be no going back, not even for Stumpy and Frankie Amerigo on their time-travels back and forth to the Grafton Club on West Derby Road.

Clubs big and small had become increasingly alive to the mouthwatering commercial prospects offered by the comparative resurgence and newly found fashionability top flight football was experiencing. A vast new market for anything remotely football related had materialised virtually overnight. No matter how tenuous the football links might have been, the demand was there and, as if to illustrate this very point, record sales of an obscure Seventies Granada comedy series called 'The Dustbinmen' had been reported, due simply, it was felt, to its nostalgic evocation of the rather static goalscoring style of the Everton centre forward of the same era, Bob 'The Bin' Latchford. Such an obsessive degree of interest in the game – albeit, in this instance, from Evertonians desperate for anything to lift their spirits following the departure of Howard Kendall (he'll be back again soon lads like a bad penny, mark my words) – was unprecedented and, predictably, football's leading lights were determined to grab any of the considerable number of other similar opportunities which either presented themselves on a plate or could be engineered to fall invitingly into their ample laps.

Of course, the sale of football memorabilia, books, magazines and the like had existed for some appreciable time and, over the years, had evolved into an important element of the whole football scene. Intense emotional attachment could sometimes be forged with the most unlikely football-related objects and, putting it all into context, I suspect even those on the very fringes of soccer's male fraternity will be able to recall clutching their very first 'World Cup Willie' hot water bottle cosy with every bit as much fondness and relish as their first female breast. Certainly, regardless of what anyone else may think, I've got no problem whatsoever, with placing my own cosy a good way ahead of fondling the beautiful Irene Wilcox on South Road beach in my all-time treasured memories list. Mind you, both Irene and I were only just turned six at the time and the pair of us were heavily into buckets and spades and making sand-pies, so I daresay our liaison hardly ranks as what even Jackie Collins would call an erotic encounter.

Inevitably, innocence of the sort displayed by Irene and myself soon began to disappear at an alarming rate, both on and off the pitch – and on South Road beach too from what I've seen there recently. For the most popular clubs, sales of football merchandise came to represent, for the first time ever, a significant source of revenue. The marketing of replica club shirts, previously restricted in the main to the childrens' end of the market, and worn to play the game in the street or at the local park rather than as a fashion garment, mushroomed into a booming multi-million pound industry, with skintight handstitched adult beer belly jerseys its principal line. Club fashion and leisure wear followed, if not quite so spectacularly.

To cater for the burgeoning market – and the bellies – the cramped club shops were replaced by spacious souvenir supermarkets. Sponsorship and advertising deals, swish restaurants, executive boxes, corporate entertainment and conducted guided tours were suddenly in vogue, complementing perfectly the steady shift to the altogether more bourgeois environment which football had undergone since the enforced introduction of all-seater stadia. At some clubs, fans were even being offered free introductory memberships into the National Trust and the RSPB along with special offers on the very latest in waxed Barbour jackets.

No longer content to be merely football grounds housing thirty-odd professional footballers, a dozen or so apprentices, the manager, his coaching staff, a board of directors and the obligatory team of meat-pie nutritionists, all dedicated to providing a footballing and dietary focus for the local community, the clubs were striving to develop into thriving commercial organisations with radically extended horizons. Football was simply the principal line of business that they happened to be in. Money was becoming the name of the game.

Now, I know I tend to be a bit of a dinosaur when it comes to these things, but it does strike me that somewhere along the way we have lost the plot in all this. Sure, there has never been any harm in footballing or any other memorabilia, even on a grand scale. Nor commercial gain, either, for that matter. They are all hallmarks of a consumer society. All perfectly natural traits. Surely, though, there is a point at which all the non-stop milking, with which football is now saddled, must stop. What on earth has happened to the trusty old maxim, 'don't kick the arse out of it', I'd like to know. After all, following your football team is meant to be an affair of the heart, not an American Express Gold Card. I mean, for crying out loud, there's now even a state-of-the-art Planet Hollywood style football restaurant in the West End. I'm not talking about behind the goal at Chelsea, either. And from what I've heard about the place, there isn't so much as a lukewarm pie in sight, never mind in the oven. Now, does that smack of footy to you? Are we still talking here of the game we all know and love? You can bet your sweet Tony Adams, we're not.

And while we're on this tack, what about a visit to your club megastore to collect your £30 stand ticket, £40 club shirt, £50 club table lamp and £120 club duvet, not to mention a £10 bottle of club wine with which to wash down the non-existent pie. Christ, uncle Ebba and Jimmy O'Toole would have had a blue fit with it all. Or a red one come to that. Either that or else they'd have taken up dominoes and gone to watch Man City.

Some might argue that, to an extent, all the reorganisation and driving ambition had been an essential ingredient in the survival of many of the clubs within the ever more competitive and cut-throat world that professional football had found itself. The financial burden, a culmination of extortionate wage bills, inflated transfer fees and the crippling, if partly subsidised, cost of ground modernisation, as well as other recent money-sapping trends – rehabilitation programmes for those players with agent addiction problems being a particularly costly one – was unprecedented.

What it all meant was that revenue through the turnstiles alone, albeit boosted by the hiked up seating prices, was not enough. The clubs had virtually been forced to concentrate on the business side of their operations in order to make ends meet and retain the ability to compete at the highest level. The commercial processes had not stopped there, though, and, for certain clubs, it was not too long before the pursuit of profit became their corporate goal. The underlying traditions which underpinned the game were all but forgotten, swept aside in the rush for more loot.

It is undeniable that some of the tycoons behind this revolution were genuine lovers of the game and the clubs they were trying to buy or buy into. Others, in contrast, were merely genuine lovers of the game's new found dosh. While none of them could scarcely be termed new phenomena, the sheer scale of some of their operations meant that top flight football seemed in grave danger of selling its soul to the highest bidders. Meanwhile, never to be found wanting where effort off the pitch was involved, the players simply instructed their agents to cash in on the increasing financial lunacy to exact their own slice of flesh from the game's bloated carcass. Times may well have been hard elsewhere but certainly not as far as those in top flight football were concerned. Okay, so maybe they might have been missing out on such simple delights as standing at a bus stop in the wind and rain – so popular with Billy Liddell and his mates – but when you can afford to buy your very own double-decker with just a couple of weeks wages it's the sort of deprivation you scarcely notice.

In keeping with the prevailing monetary spirit, the latter half of the

Nineties appears destined to go down as the era when the market place for the 'soul selling' process flourished. Football did not so much come home during this time , as move – lock, stock and goalpost – to the City, with the flotation of football clubs on the Stock Market almost as commonplace an occurrence as a bland interview with Alan Shearer. Whilst to most of the clubs concerned, there might have been immediate tangible financial benefits arising from these flotations, it is, nevertheless, hard to view this trend of clubs going public as anything other than the desire of those controlling the purse strings to realise maximum earnings potential. Football clubs became simply a commercial brand to be exploited at will.

It is hardly surprising that many football lovers regarded such passing of their club's metaphorical ownership from the fans to faceless institutions with suspicion and cynicism. It was a situation difficult enough for an armchair aficionado to come to terms with, let alone the very diehards who had followed their clubs through thick and thin for countless eons. After all, skipping down the Daily Mirror's business page once a week is one thing, but a daily slog through the Financial Times is surely asking that little bit too much even of those fans with a firm grasp of really hard sums.

Just as unsurprising as the fans' disgust for what was happening to their game, was the fact that the club in the vanguard of this latest development, and the prime mover throughout all the financial musical chairs, was Manchester United. Indeed, the Red Devils had actually become a high profile public company with an extremely attractive investment portfolio, valued at mega-millions and, whilst way out of range of all the rest, it was they who were setting the Stock Market yardsticks for all the others to aspire to. The fact that they also became successful and fashionable around the same time just helped hike up the share price. On reflection, you do wonder, with some justification, quite how popular the whole trend would have become, had Man United not displayed such a powerful example of wanton commercialism for the rest to follow. Mind you, at least there is one aspect of the whole thing which has given most true fans a bit of a warm glow. I mean, if we are all a bit pissed off with all the greed business then just imagine how Michael Knighton, Man United's one time prospective buyer is feeling as he bites, despairingly, through his bedpost each night up in Carlisle, reflecting on what might have been.

Man United may well be the best example of a club pursuing the commercial trend. They are certainly not on their own, though, and all the leading clubs have now, without question, elevated money to star status. Nevertheless, some clubs have at least bucked one trend and have not so far clamoured to join the big sell-off.

In Liverpool's case, it seems this is because they feel that they owe an allegiance to the local community, with its inherent social and economic problems, and consider a public share issue might signify a betrayal of that local loyalty by shifting control of the club to outside the region. Such a stance is an admirable one which I know even Uncle Jack and Aunty Matilda for all their Blueness would have approved of. Sadly, it is only too rare. In fact, in the prevailing climate it is scarcely believable and yet, if true, its underlying principle should be welcomed by fans everywhere. It remains to be seen, though, whether future financial pressures, in particular the requirement to compete in the ever spiralling transfer market, will ultimately force Liverpool to revise their options and go public in order to maintain their lofty status and stay within financial sight of Man United.

One thing is certain, whatever transpires with Liverpool, Man United or the rest, the transformed attitudes to money, when viewed alongside the host of other changes which have taken place – most notably, I suppose, Jimmy Hill's momentous decision to expose the naked splendour of his famous chin at the 1992 FA Cup Final – make the game at the very top barely recognisable to what it was even as recently as six or seven years ago and it may not be a coincidence that all the transformations, though particularly the pre-occupation with money, have occurred at the same time as the advent of Satellite Television.

Sky has become the biggest football player of all. In terms of relative size, when compared to the enormity of Sky, even Jan Molby, at his grossest, would be merely a podgy little amoeba with boots on. Although, seemingly, at only an early stage of its development, it now effectively has control of the timetable for Premier League football in this country, dictating who plays when, if not, at this point, where and how, although that will undoubtedly come.

Currently – 'true' Blue, Andy Gray's gob excepted – we are still witnessing, relatively speaking, Sky's palatable face. Though many fans may resent the degree to which it has infiltrated the game, with its control of football and its ensuing partial disruption of the Saturday afternoon matchday, the fact is that its football menu is, inarguably, a highly desirable one to all those who can afford the monthly subscription.

Remember, fans have been deprived, apart from Cup Final day, the World Cup, the European Championships and action repeats of

Sylvester Stallone in 'Escape to Victory', of any real attempt at in-depth, comprehensive football coverage by BBC and ITV. So with several channels able to be devoted exclusively to sport – something which all the sporty types over on the main networks, not to mention Bob Wilson, can currently only have digital dreams about – the extensive coverage provided by Sky of the country's national game, together with its usually proficient though infuriatingly idiosyncratic presentation, is enough to fill a glaring gap in the football viewing market and satisfy the non-sexual cravings of most fanatics.

Heresy it may be, but it is worrying how easy it is to become used to the way Sky covers football; the funny 'cash register noises' every now and again; the camera angles cunningly positioned not to show empty stands on a wet mid-week evening match. Incidentally, I should mention that Satellite TV is hard at work on a way of satisfying the other type of base craving too, which is a rather worrying development for those pillars of society, such as the chairman of Birmingham City, who hold the view that sport and sex shouldn't mix.

It is not, however, Sky's current coverage about which we should be most concerned. Nor, for that matter should we worry that unduly about the rapidity of Andy Gray's hair loss, however alarming it may be to see dirty great clumps of it dropping onto Martin Tyler's lap each week before our very eyes. No, what is disturbing, maybe even sinister, especially for many of football's traditional fan base, is the implication of the possible future measure of control of the game Sky may ultimately find itself able to wield. That's where the rub lies.

Sky exists for two reasons – to attract new viewers and retain existing ones, or, on a higher plane, to make pots of money and dominate the world of broadcasting. Given an open market few can argue with such aims. There is a colossal downside though and we are not referring here just to Richard Key's apparent inability to grasp what is happening on the pitch, nor to his infuriating habit of asking questions of his studio guests to which most fans' pet goldfish know the answers. Whatever pretensions it may make to the contrary, Sky's love affair with football begins and ends with profit; big profit. This is quite at odds with, say, the BBC's indisputable passion for sport (dare I mention public duty or is that no longer politically correct) and even with ITV's rather less passionate love affair, typified by a 'we've forgotten how to cover sport' approach. We are talking ongoing cable and satellite rentals here, not viewing figures. Sky's interest in the game of football will last only as long as the game remains a moneyspinner.

With football so trendy and so popular; with the product so good and so exciting; with all the foreign imports literally lighting up the Sky in every single match; with the fact that for many major games you can't get a ticket to see the match 'live' anyway; Sky is out to corner the market. At present, there is a status quo which suits Sky, the big clubs and the star players down to the ground. All are like the cat which has licked the cream. The whole thing reeks of exploitation and indulgence, with most of the players attired either as top-drawer barristers or Twenties mafia hit-men; exceptions are Barry Venison who invariably opts for the Max Miller look and John Barnes who usually plumps for an even more flamboyant Coco the Clown style. Meanwhile, the massive money injections continue to paper over any cracks in the game's infrastructure. While things remain as they are, the money will continue to talk and Sky will dictate the way things are to be. It is at this interface, where further major shifts may occur in our viewing and spectating habits, and perhaps, even, in Barry Venison's suits.

The profit potential of pay-per-view in co-operation with the big clubs is unprecedented. Could anyone really have forecast not so many years ago that the time would come when clubs had their own TV Station? Fans all over the globe will find it hard to resist the attraction of being able to tune into the weekly match of their choice. Catering on such an individual level has an obvious appeal for any fan. There has to be a real threat, though, that the impending digital/pay-per-view/one-club channels revolution will lead us only to a world of virtual football where actually travelling to a stadium to see a game 'live' will become a novelty.

Possibly even more enticing will be the juicy extra tit-bits which are to be offered as part of the overall package. For instance, the prospect of watching the players live, relaxing in the intimacy of their own homes, simply counting their money or sharing a steamy jacuzzi and Havana cigar with their agent, will surely prove irresistible even to those with the welfare of the game close to their heart. After all, even football purists like to see how the other half live, never mind dyed-in-the-wool fanatics. Why else do Aunty Kay and Uncle Denny continue to tune in to Emmerdale Farm?

Of course, we can always rely on the government to introduce special legislation to protect the public interest. Nude jacuzzi scenes may have to be transmitted after the nine o'clock watershed, while any excessive gloating during the money counting sequences will surely need to be curtailed a tadge to avoid offending any over-sensitive stockbrokers or such like who might be tuned in. And let's not forget the depth of desire of the more affluent fan to pay to watch the game on television. This only goes so far. Many of them, like Sky itself, are newcomers to the game and, jacuzzis or not, they will certainly never allow themselves to be exploited in the past manner of the captive traditional fan who has no choice other than to support their team come what may.

Even when everything else is balanced out, the main issue still looms large. Enticing people to pay to watch from home whichever games they wish, will, over an extended period, almost certainly impinge on the numbers attending games, even though it currently seems to be the view that the fans' appetite for the game is so insatiable that this doesn't matter. Fans, like people generally, are becoming creatures of comfort – one only has to witness the vast ranks of uniformed chauffers sat in stretch limos outside Old Trafford on match days for confirmation of this – and nothing fits this comfort bill better than watching your favourite footy team week in, week out from the depths of your soft leather armchair.

In the longer term, the lure of the couch for the slouch may prove to be just that bit too convenient, outrivalling the thrill of being there. Supporting rituals are not unbreakable, while the coke-like addiction of sitting in your favourite armchair can be. The trick of ultimately ensuring sufficient numbers attend the games thereby crucially retaining that all-important big match atmosphere, while, at the same time, optimising the numbers tuning in at home, may turn out to be one that is difficult to pull off and it may well need a David Copperfield or a Uri Geller or, perhaps, even Paul Daniel's eldest son to achieve it. Better still, how about a scenario where a fan has to audition to attend a match live and is then paid for coming along and providing the 'right' atmosphere for the watching millions at home. Now there's a thought to make Shanks turn in his grave.

The problems may well be hypothetical and all in the future but big business always plans ahead. The grass never grows under its feet. Sky itself, for instance, owns vast fleets of high-powered lawn mowers and legions of super-efficient gardeners to ensure the trimness of its own turf. There is no way that Sky will ever be caught napping; long grass and weeds are simply not on its agenda. It is a pity football does not think the same way. The top flight's incestuous involvement with Sky means the implications of pay-per-view are also football's, too. On the face of it, they would appear to give football a superficially healthy sheen as far as future financial security is concerned. There is more to it than that, though. The rewards from pay-per-view are likely to go the way of only the very big boys with worldwide drawing power. Besides, before even contemplating such possible riches, football has some acute dilemmas of its own to address in the far more immediate future and, by that, I'm not just referring to the sorry plights of the Rochdales and Darlingtons of this world.

The top flight clubs are generally wealthy but their profit and loss accounts are distorted by transfer fees and gains and their balance sheets massaged by the valuing of players – sorry, assets – and by the 'brand value' of the club itself. The new commercial approach to running a football club has seen to this, aided by the game's revival. Increasingly, though, many top flight clubs are becoming dependant on the infusion of money from Sky. The dangers of this reliance are only too clear. Sky, if it chose to, can simply walk away; football can't. If football was to lose its fashionable status, thereby inducing Sky, at worst, to pull the plug, at best, to cut its money, then there is a real risk of major problems; possibly, for some clubs, even collapse. If the game can't be self reliant, it may cease to be a game at all.

It should be remembered that football has not always been so fashionable. Not so long ago you mentioned your love for the game at the peril of inducing a snooty pained expression on the faces of most of those in your company, maybe even biting ridicule – and that, believe it or not, would be in the middle of the Kop at half-time on match day. God knows what it must have been like at some hoity-toity dinner party – probably a good old-fashioned garrotting would ensue. Football, then, to say the least, was distinctly unfashionable; we were all 'Millwall' whether we liked it or not; nobody loved us. Indeed, the opposite was the case.

Now, in stark contrast, those same cocked noses are very much in the minority. The word 'football' is on everyone's lips – even those of Mick Jagger, whom, it has recently been discovered, is a closet Wombles fan. Suddenly, everybody loves it; everybody is a fan of some team or other, most of them, rather strangely, with distant ancestors in Stretford or Salford, something which is scarcely that evident from their accents.

Dependency on the whims and fancies of such fickleness is hardly desirable. Neither, too, is the idea of putting too many eggs in one basket. Yet that is precisely what is happening. Sky money is balancing the books at many clubs and, while it may be foolish to look a gift-horse, or even Mick Jagger, in the mouth, especially when they may have helped pull you out of a mire of debt, it may be even more so to rely on them too heavily for your future well-being.

If some of the clubs need to keep an eye on their health, then some of the game's traditional fans should carry an 'endangered species' tag, after the way their position has been so undermined in recent years. As all-seater stadia have been established, pushing up admission prices; as the game becomes ever more dependent on revenue from Sky; whilst the game fondly embraces rampant commercialism and hands out City and pop star rewards for some of its players – is it any surprise that it is inexorably moving ever further away from its traditional fan base. It is, certainly, no overnight split and the deep loyalties felt by fans are not the sort which fade away easily. Even so, there is, undoubtedly, an alienating process at work and it is hard not to pine for some sort of compromise. No matter how buoyant football may now be, it surely cannot afford to let such a vital part of its composition simply slip away. After all Ebba Murphys, like new pairs of shoes, do not grow on trees.

Regrettably in some areas of the game, it may be already too late to do anything at all, for it is not only outside the game and inside some boardrooms that the mercenary forces exist, which are causing the polarisation processes to occur. Those who look towards the bodies who run the game will find a cupboard also seemingly bare of any real concern for anything other than money.

In April 1996 we were playing Aston Villa in an FA Cup semi-final at Old Trafford. It was to become the first major semi-final I had missed through my own volition since the Sixties. Tens of thousands more Liverpool and Villa fans had also elected not to go. The stumbling block was the ticket prices – £38.00 in my case – which even die-hard fans knew was a blatant rip-off. The Football Association had patently decided they had a captive market which was there for the taking. Many Liverpool and Villa fans had thought otherwise and had displayed commendable discernment by voting with their backsides and staying at home. It was rightly regarded as a triumph for the ordinary fan, though, regrettably, one that is likely only to forestall the inevitable drift of the game away from the same ordinary fan.

No doubt the corporate entertainment business was good on that day at Old Trafford. No doubt no-one really noticed the loss of revenue from a few thousand fans failing to snap up the tickets like lemmings. No doubt too it was a crying shame that a major FA Cup semi-final was played to less than a capacity crowd. Equally no doubt that ordinary football fans could see through the blatant attempt at syphoning money from their pockets. And absolutely no shadow of a doubt that the people running the game didn't care even one jot about the fans who voted with their feet or the long term significance of such action.

In the game's aftermath, as if to order, the FA's spokesmen had tried to cover up their cynical approach, claiming the prices were in line with comparable fixtures in previous years. Their weasel words rang hollow. A game which should have been capable of filling Old Trafford twice over, was little more than half full. The FA's underlying message to the game's 'bread and butter' was loud and clear and it smacked only too ominously of that same contempt and those same soul destroying characteristics which were taking the game away from its traditional base.

Mind you, I daresay, you couldn't really expect a great deal else from an organisation whose sweet initials so encapsulate its prevailing attitudes to fans and whose chairman, at the time, was older than Gary Glitter when he made his first comeback tour.

Of course, what I have said up to this juncture is, by no means, the whole of the story, though, as a traditional fan myself, I make no apologies for its one-sidedness. There are some who reject, as little more than paranoia and envy, all the cynical charges I have voiced and who believe that the real origins of the wind of change, revolutionising the game, are to be found within the fans themselves; that the seeds of the traditional fan's alienation lay, ironically, in their own efforts to make their voices heard and to spread the word. It is a slender analogy. However, it certainly cannot be denied that things had been moving in that direction for some time.

Fanzines had heralded a new era of self-awareness in the mid-Eighties, though remaining essentially novelty value, underground and cultish. They had become another way of fans expressing their love for their club and just about every club had one (if not two). The big innovation had come when the fans had acquired Six-O-Six, their own phone-in radio programme on Radio Five on Saturday evenings immediately following Sports Report. Up to then, local radio stations had dabbled with phone-ins but this was different – this was nationwide.

At first, its presenter had been Danny Baker, a working class Cockney sparrow but later, the prominent Tory MP, David Mellor took over. Now however he may have been regarded, David Mellor was a leading public figure, albeit one with an unhealthy penchant for donning his club's strip.Patently cultured, intelligent and intellectual, he was, to put it crudely, an Arts buff and a writer. No ordinary football fan he. He was also, as became increasingly apparent with each show, a quite reasonably knowledgeable football fan, albeit not a fanatical one, originally of Chelsea then of Fulham, and then once again of Chelsea, which was all a bit suspect, but nonetheless, it seemed, he knew what he is talking about. Most significantly of all, he spoke posh. Very posh indeed. In fact, it's true to say David Mellor had a plum in his mouth the size of a size 5 'case' ball with the lace still in.

The passions, the agonies and the ecstasies of football fans were now actually being aired and heard. What's more, they were being articulated in a manner and an accent which had never before been associated with fandom, unless it was in the admonishing tones of someone who had the window of their Jag broken by hooligans in the Seventies.

Sir Alf Ramsey had tried in the Sixties, to popularise this most proper form of speech but his efforts in this direction had lost all credibility when it leaked out that he was originally from Dagenham, and many, in fact, feel it was this and not the Poland defeat in 1973 which had cost him his job as England Manager. With the Right Honourable David, however, it was different. He was the genuine article – a real toff. The wagon was on the roll. No longer were we fans confined to raucous, unintelligible slanging matches in the pubs, clubs and workplaces and on the streets and terraces. No longer were we restricted to the back pages or the back allies. Even the Prime Minister was a fan. Football fan culture was starting to reach places never before even dreamt of. This was fantasy football indeed.

Around the same time, in keeping with the way things were moving, the fans own Viewing Watchdog Organisation (VWO), aware of a persistent tendency amongst certain fans to imitate the foul language and expressions of their soccer heroes, had ordered a complete ban on the use by all supporters of the words "Bastard", "Shit", "Sparky", "Giggsy", "Razor", "Psycho", "gutted", "nutmegged", "hospital ball". "dummy', "early doors", "Toon army", "Gaffer" and "Gazza", along with the phrases "he's come inside the full back", "they've got behind us", "they've closed us down", "he's given us some width", "so, Brian, we've come off at half time", "the boys done good", "he's not got any change out of the full back", "he's sat in the hole", "a good big 'un always beats a good little 'un", "play it down the channels", and "piss off, you stupid blind bastard".

In a further even more radical development, the Organisation had gone on to stipulate that regional accents and dialects were to be banned from all grounds and that, in future, all football conversations were to attain the Garth Crook's standard of Queen's English which was clearly the most daunting prospect of all, for Garth was a pretty posh bloke.

To assist in the implementation of the changes, the fans' own official language advisory body had promptly published an official guide, which they had later released on compact disc. These comprehensive publications had proved most informative and illuminating, providing the supporters with, quite literally, thousands of examples of how it was intended for the new vernacular to be introduced into their everyday football conversation, which it was felt would help speed up the entire process of fan refinement.

And so, for example, a question such as "Eh, pal, 'ow did yer gerr'on this'avvy?" was to be rephrased, "Excuse me, sir, may I enquire how your chaps fared this fine afternoon?"; similarly, the statement "We woz robbed" was now to be "I must say, I rather feel that lot somehow pilfered a result against our chaps!"; the chants "you fat bastard" and "Sumo!" were to become "I say, it seems Old Molby has developed quite a paunch", and so on. Certain other stock phrases or questions such as, "He's on his second yellow card", "How long to go (ref) ?", "He's played a lot of injury time" and "Elton Welsby's a complete dickhead" were to remain, unmodified, a fond reminder of the old days.

All told, the publications contained two thousand three hundred and seventy five examples of revamped phrases or the like. This impressive array contrasted starkly with the number of phrases the average fan would actually utter during the course of a normal ninety-minute game, which was estimated by research findings commissioned by the reformers, to be as low as a mere twenty two, rising to twenty three if there was extra time in a cup-tie. Startlingly, however, it was found that during the high pitched drama of a penalty shoot-out, this figure would soar dramatically to a remarkable two thousand five hundred, in time with the pulse rate. This, although only a rare occurrence, nevertheless presented a major problem to the entire re-learning programme because the research had also revealed that, by comparison, the practical maximum re-learning capacity of the average fan barely reached a paltry ninety-two new phrases.

The research had also pinpointed dramatic regional variations in the re-learning capabilities. The highest, as might have been expected, with two hundred and fifty was Cambridge with Oxford not far behind, followed, surprisingly closely, by the Maine Road area of Manchester, the village of Babbacome in Devon, and the Black Country of Staffordshire. The lowest, with a total of only ten, was the Stretford region of Manchester.

In fact, one individual from the Stretford area, a strange, old, endearing, baggily dressed character with delusions of youth, who answered to the name of Antonio Willuson, had failed to register a single new phrase. The researchers had found that, in all the time he had been a football fan, he had only ever known one phrase and that had had nothing to do with football. Evidently, at every football match he attended, he would shout out to the rest of the crowd from his seat high up in the snow-capped nether regions of Manchester United's Old Trafford Stand, "I'm dead trendy me, aren't I?", to which all visiting fans and even his fellow supporters would unerringly reply, "Piss off, Antonio, you gobshite".

As it happened, all the research carried out was to prove invaluable to the reformers and their programme of change, for within a matter of days of the research team's findings being published, the Football Association had issued a statement to say that Penalty Shoot-outs were to be abolished forthwith.

This gesture by the Football Association had been utterly magnanimous and was very much in keeping with its own refreshing new approach and attitude to the fans and their organisations. They had realised the impossible task which had faced the supporters in attempting to learn two thousand five hundred new phrases and, despite the possibility of admonishment from EUFA and FIFA, had promptly and humanely done the honourable thing. It was, indeed, a new age dawning.

The Football Association had also been instrumental in the production of the guidance publications which had been issued for the fans, for providing the voices on the instruction compact disc were none other than its two most eminent luminaries, Sir Bert Milligram and the Reverend "Mother" Kelly, both, as ever, in the vanguard of any innovations being introduced into the game.

On disc, the lovable Sir Bert was to prove that the comic timing, always evident in his number-crunching role at the FA Cup draws, was no flash in the pan, as he wrung every drop of humour and whimsy from the lines he had been given. "Mother" Kelly, meanwhile, always a firm favourite with the fans and a genuinely admired and respected figure throughout the game, was a revelation, switching effortlessly from one regional dialect to another in a series of brilliant and hilarious mimicry. Those previously only familiar with his role as the Swedish Chef in The Muppet Show were amazed at his virtuoso display of versatility. The fans would be forever indebted to this far-sighted pair.

Never to be found wanting, where any sporting history was being made, and always with one eye on the main chance, especially with the lovable old philanthropist, Rupert Murdoch, waiting in the wings, the BBC had immediately been alerted to the new trend and moved extra quickly to rush release a new video, astutely combining a "Football Language for Fans by Numbers" feature with a special "Keep Fit for Slobbish Fans" routine.

The timing of the release had been perfect and it very soon proved to be a big hit with the fans – even the small minority who were under twenty stone in weight – and strangely also with middle aged women. This latter phenomenon, no doubt, owed less to the content of the video and more to the magnetism of its three star presenters, for providing the language commentary had been the sure-fire winning combination of the sexy old silver streaked lounge lizard himself, Des 'Come to Bed' Eyesman, the most popular Television Sports Presenter of all time, together with Mr Nouveau Nineties, Alain "Heart-throb" Handsome. Meantime, presenting the strenuous keep-fit routine, in a striking scoop-necked, luminous green one-piece leotard, in his own unmistakable whinnying tones, was none other than the old "Green God" himself, Trevor "Babbling" Brook, the former "Hammer", with the neatest haircut in living memory. The BBC had produced another winner.

Fans nation-wide enrolled for elocution classes and signed up for correspondence courses in their concerted efforts to keep pace with the cultural revolution sweeping the game. If they couldn't pass the Club Entrance exam (oral and written) then there was little chance of them ever being allowed into the stadium to watch a game.

Surprisingly, the most receptive area of the country proved to be the Midlands, particularly the heartland of Brum. The wonderful Brummie fans, widely held to be amongst the warmest and friendliest in the game, had taken to the new vernacular like Stan Bowles to a bookies. This, almost certainly, had a great deal to do with the absence of any worthwhile distractions on the pitch, evidenced by the fact that, for many years, most Brummie fans had been taking with them a book to read during the match to pass the time and compensate for the monotony of the play. Now, the new movement had provided them, not only with an alternative form of entertainment but also with the opportunity to learn something worthwhile and practical at the same time.

Delighted with the innovation, this had manifested itself in the alacrity of their grasp of the entire concept. Within a matter of months, their absorption and mastery of the new diction had become so complete and their newly acquired dialogue and conversation so sophis-ticated that, with the exception of the strongly contrasting quality of the meat and potato pies on offer, a seat in the stands at Molineux, St Andrews, Villa Park, the Hawthorns or Highfield Road, had become indistinguishable from one amongst the elevated and privileged clientele at the North Bank Club in London.

And, indeed, talking of which, the effects of the new culture had, by now, spread to the very heart of the capital itself. The most exclusive business clubs in The City were beginning to witness scenes of their stuff-shirted membership loosening their collars and ties, flinging to the floor their personal organisers, share indices and copies of the Financial Times, donning their Chelsea away kits and soccer togs and crowding around their radios at six minutes past six on a Saturday evening to tune into Six O Six, whilst frantically attempting to get through on their mobile phones to air their views with Sir David Mellor, one of their own.

For once, football fans were moving with the times, rather than miles behind them. In fact, we had become the times.

The big question on everyone's lips, of course, was where would it all end? And I must confess, I really don't know, and I'm not sure for that matter if anyone else does either. However, if I were a big businessman or Stan Bowles or Lou Macaroni, I'd put my faith and my money on Old Trafford; certainly not, the Feethams Stadium in Darlington, which I suppose, all in all, is kind of sad really, especially considering how most of us feel about Old Trafford, or if it so happens, you come from Darlington or some place like it.

Still, that's footy for you; you can't win all the time, though I suppose the Darlingtons of this world wouldn't mind doing so once in a while, just to make their own faith that bit easier. There again perhaps, they shouldn't worry too much about whichever way things turn out, for I've heard there are many learned people – some of them within the game itself – who say there's more to life than merely following your favourite football team. Much more. Of course, the only problem as far as footy fans are concerned is figuring out precisely what that is and I'd imagine, as with almost everything else, such a task is a damned sight easier said than done.

After all, it's not every day you're faced with the prospect of having to give up your religion.